T0330437

The Russian Press from Brezhnev to Yeltsin

Как это может быть глупо или неправда
ведь это напечатано.

— Пушкин

Книга посвящается К.В. Коняеву

STUDIES OF COMMUNISM IN TRANSITION

Series Editor: Ronald J. Hill
*Professor of Comparative Government
and Fellow of Trinity College,
Dublin, Ireland*

Studies of Communism in Transition is an important series which applies academic analysis and clarity of thought to the recent traumatic events in Eastern and Central Europe. As many of the preconceptions of the past half century are cast aside, newly independent and autonomous sovereign states are being forced to address long-term, organic problems which had been suppressed by, or appeased within, the communist system of rule.

The series is edited under the sponsorship of Lorton House, an independent charitable association which exists to promote the academic study of communism and related concepts.

The Russian Press From Brezhnev to Yeltsin

Behind the Paper Curtain

John Murray

Department of Russian
Trinity College
Dublin, Ireland

Edward Elgar

Published by
Edward Elgar Publishing Limited
Gower House
Croft Road
Aldershot
Hants GU11 3HR
England

Edward Elgar Publishing Company
Old Post Road
Brookfield
Vermont 05036
USA

British Library Cataloguing in Publication Data
Murray, John
    Russian Press from Brezhnev to Yeltsin:
    Behind the Paper Curtain. – (Studies of
    Communism in Transition)
    I. Title II. Series
    077

Library of Congress Cataloguing in Publication Data
Murray, John (John Damian)
        The Russian Press from Brezhnev to Yeltsin: behind the paper
    curtain / John Murray
        p.   cm. — (Studies of communism in transition)
    Includes bibliographical references and index.
        1. Press—Soviet Union—History. I. Title. II. Series.
    PN5274.M87   1994
    077—dc20   93–49830
                                                                    CIP

ISBN 1 85278 885 2

Electronic typesetting by Lorton Hall

Printed and bound in Great Britain by
Hartnolls Limited, Bodmin, Cornwall

Contents

Preface   *vii*

1. Historical Background   1

2. Before and After *Glasnost'*   39

3. News Fit to Print   87

4. Language of the Soviet Press   115

5. Westernization of Press Language   144

6. Soviet Journalists Speak   169

7. Russian Journalists Speak   214

   Appendix   260

   References   263

   Index   273

Preface

The present study began as a doctoral thesis, the groundwork for which was done in Moscow in 1987–88. Spending a year at Moscow State University was made possible thanks mainly to the encouragement and help I received from the head of the Russian Department at Trinity College, Dublin, Mrs Winifred Greenwood. My supervisor, the late Dr Chris Roberts, also of Trinity College, was also helpful, though probably a little disappointed that I decided in the end to focus on the political rather than exclusively linguistic aspect of the Russian press.

In writing this book I received help from many people. My parents were always extremely helpful. Apart from giving me much moral support, in one typical gesture of generosity my father, Jim Murray, bought me a computer on which to write the thesis and the book. My mother, Charlotte Murray, was also a constant source of encouragement in writing the book. Her assiduous scanning of all sorts of newspapers and magazines for information on Russia and the Soviet Union provided me with a very valuable archive which I used freely when writing the book.

My main helper in Moscow was Dr Konstantin Konyaev, without whose support, advice and practical assistance the whole project would probably never have got off the ground, and to whom the book is dedicated. I would also like to thank the Russian journalists who gave so generously of their time in allowing me to interview them.

Much of the research for the book was done while working as a journalist with the *Sunday Tribune*. I would like to thank my editor at the time, Vincent Browne, for taking the decision to send me to Moscow when purely financial considerations might have suggested taking the Moscow story from the newswires. Working as a journalist also gave me access to Russian politicians and journalists.

I am grateful to the series editor, my former teacher and now professional colleague, Professor Ron Hill, both for encouraging me to turn the thesis into a book and for recommending the plan for transformation to the publisher, Edward Elgar.

To all these and others who have shown interest and encouragement, I am very grateful. It goes without saying that the responsibility for everything written here is entirely my own.

J.M.
January 1994

1. Historical Background

From the revolution until Stalin's coming to power

By 1953, the year Stalin died, the distinctive features of the Soviet newspaper had been set firmly in place. Over a period of thirty-six years a series of journalistic norms had accumulated resulting in a unique blend of content and language that characterized the Soviet press until the arrival of Gorbachev and *glasnost'*.

The monopolization of the press by the bolsheviks began almost immediately after the 1917 revolution. As a result of legislative and other measures taken under Lenin's leadership, by 1929 there were no newspapers remaining in the country that dissented from the party line. Freedom of the press for Lenin meant freedom from the influence of 'priests and landlords' (Lenin, 1972, p.199), an interpretation that rationalized the closing down of opposition newspapers and even the arrest of journalists.[1]

The days and months after the revolution proved to be a critical period for the non-bolshevik press, comprising both the liberal and conservative 'bourgeois' press and the socialist but non-bolshevik press of the 'appeasers'.[2] Many of the fundamentals of the future role of the press in the Soviet Union were established during this turbulent period.

Three pieces of legislation sealed the fate of the non-bolshevik press, the most important of which was the Decree on the Press,[3]

1 For an account, including first-hand descriptions, of the arrest of non-bolshevik journalists and the closing down of non-bolshevik newspapers, see extracts in Mochalova, 1991a, p.13. See also Nemirovskii and Kharlamova (eds), 1983, p.85, passim, on arrests and closures.

2 *Soglashateli*.

3 Given the immediate and far-reaching impact of the Decree on the Press, as well as the opportunity it provides for an understanding of the bolshevik attitude to the press, it is worth reproducing in full. Though signed by Lenin, Lunacharskii is credited with drafting the decree (Pipes, 1990, p.521):

1

passed by the Soviet of People's Commissars on 27 October (9 November[4]) 1917, the government's first day in office, and published in *Pravda* on the following day. The thrust of the decree, signed by Lenin, was to outlaw newspapers inimical to the bolsheviks, and with the potential to subvert the revolutionary government. The provisions in the decree allowing the government to close down and ban certain

---

Decree on the Press

In this difficult and decisive hour of revolution and of the days immediately following it, the Provisional Revolutionary Committee has been obliged to take a series of measures against the counter-revolutionary press of various shades.

Straight away from all quarters there were cries that the new socialist powers had thereby destroyed the basic principle of its own programme, infringing upon press freedom.

The government of workers and peasants would remind people that in our society, hidden behind the liberal screen, there lies freedom for the owning classes to grasp into their hands the lion's share of the press, to unrestrictedly poison the minds of the masses, and to instil in them chaos.

Everyone knows that the bourgeois press is one of the most powerful weapons of the bourgeoisie. Especially at this critical moment, when the new government, that of the workers and the peasants, is only just consolidating its position, it would be unthinkable to leave this weapon intact in the hands of the enemy at a time when it is no less dangerous than the bullet or the machine-gun. This is why these temporary and emergency measures have been taken, in order to stop the flow of dirt and slander into which the yellow and green press would gladly drown the young victory of the people.

Once the new order has been firmly established, all administrative measures affecting the press will cease, full freedom will be established for [the press] within the limits of responsibility decided by a court, in accordance with the widest and most progressive law in this area.

Taking into account, however, that constraints on the press, even at the most critical moments, are permissible only within the limits of what is absolutely necessary, the Council of the People's Commissars [*Sovnarkom*] decrees:

General Provisions on the Press

1. The organs of the press liable for closure are: 1) those inciting open opposition to, or disobedience of, the workers' and peasants' government, 2) those sowing discord by means of a clearly slanderous distortion of the facts, 3) those inciting clearly criminal acts, i.e., acts of a criminally punishable character.

2. The banning of organs of the press, either temporary or permanent, can only be carried out by decree of the Council of the People's Commissars.

3. The present provisions are of a temporary character and will be rescinded by special decree once normal conditions have been achieved in society.

Chairman of the Council of the People's Commissars
Vladimir Ul'yanov (Lenin)

---

4   The new-style date (adopted after the Bolshevik revolution) is given in brackets.

newspapers were of a temporary nature, to be rescinded by special decree once 'normal conditions' had been achieved in the country. This emergency legislation, however, became the cornerstone of subsequent bolshevik policy towards the press. Its basic premise, 'those not for us are against us', was to govern the press policy of successive bolshevik regimes in varying degrees right up to the introduction of the new press law in August 1990.

The decree was followed on 8 November 1917 (21 November) by another which introduced a state monopoly on advertising, thus depriving privately-owned newspapers of an important source of income. Lenin believed that this legislative measure would both expose and break the dependence of bourgeois newspapers on capitalist monopolies and banks.[5] Even before the decree was issued, however, the bolsheviks had taken the direct route to silencing opposition voices, in the process depriving them of income, by seizing their printing presses and using them to print pro-bolshevik newspapers. The day before the Decree on the Press was issued, for example, Kronstadt sailors had seized the Moscow printing presses of the rightwing *Novoe vremya* (New Times), which were then for a time used to print *Soldatskaya pravda* (Soldier's Truth) and *Derevenskaya bednota* (Rural Poverty), both bolshevik newspapers (Nemirovskii and Kharlamova (eds), 1983, p.85).

As a result of requisitioning printing plants and newsprint the printrun of bolshevik newspapers increased. On the same day the Decree on the Press was issued, the bolsheviks seized the printing plants of *Rech'* (Speech), the main newspaper of the Constitutional Democratic (Kadet) party, and *Den'* (Day), an important menshevik newspaper. The printing facilities of both were also given over to the printing of *Soldatskaya pravda* and *Derevenskaya bednota* (ibid., pp.85–6). The seizures were overseen by specially appointed commissars of the press placed in charge of Red Army detachments whose primary job was to protect the printing presses for the bolshevik press and move against those newspapers which were openly opposed to the new revolutionary government.[6]

5 Nemirovskii and Kharlamova (eds), 1983, p.92.
6 See Nemirovskii and Kharlamova (eds), 1983, p.90 for a more detailed description of the actions taken against the opposition press and further history of the press commissars.

The press decree caused widespread outrage. A famous and stormy meeting of the central executive committee,[7] at which Lenin and Trotsky were invited to explain the constitutionality and propriety of the Decree on the Press and other bolshevik decrees, was held a few days before the issuing of the decree on the state advertising monopoly. At the meeting, Lenin clarified his views on the position of the non-bolshevik press under the new government (quoted in *Russkie vedomosti* (Russian News), 21 November 1917):[8]

> We, the bolsheviks, always said that when we came to power we would close down the bourgeois press. To tolerate the bourgeois press is tantamount to cease being socialist. In the revolution one cannot stand on one spot. One must move either forwards or backwards. Those who speak of the freedom of the press are moving backwards and stopping the train which is racing at full speed towards socialism. We have overthrown the yoke of the bourgeoisie, just as the first revolution overthrew the yoke of tsarism. And if after the first revolution we were right to close down the tsarist press, then we are right now to close down the bourgeois press. We promised to close down newspapers, and that is what we will do. Our actions are supported by a huge majority ...

In the months following this meeting, efforts made by the non-bolshevik socialist parties as well as by journalists and largely menshevik print-workers to have the bolshevik decree rescinded came to nothing. Protests against the loss of press freedom fell on deaf ears as the bolsheviks tightened their grip on the press by applying the decree more extensively, in particular its provision to close down certain newspapers. The new government also implemented the decree giving the state a monopoly on newspaper advertising.

In retrospect, all the efforts of the non-bolshevik press to preserve their right to publish were destined to fail when measured against the

7 In Russian: *VTsIK*, an acronym for the All-Russian Central Executive Committee (*Vserossiiskii Tsentral'ny Ispolnitel'ny Komitet*). This was one of the centres of new revolutionary power. The revolutionary 'government', the *Sovnarkom*, of which Lenin was chairman, was responsible to this committee, itself formed from the All-Russian Congress of Soviets and charged with legislative functions between meetings of the congress. The bolsheviks had an overwhelming majority on the executive committee of the congress.

8 Quoted in Mochalova, 1991b, p.227. See also Nemirovskii and Kharlamova (eds), 1983, pp.90–2 for a pre-*glasnost'* (or, Soviet) account of the same meeting which completely omits to mention Trotsky's very lengthy intervention in the debate. Pipes (1990, pp.522–3), referring to the same meeting, concentrates on the constitutional aspects of the Decree on the Press.

determination of Lenin, Trotsky and others to do away with the opposition press, or at least to reduce it to insignificance.

The liberal and conservative press at first was slow to take seriously the decree concerning the state monopoly on advertising, calling it a 'meaningless piece of paper'. Lenin, however, had taken a personal interest in the framing of the decree in order to ensure its effectiveness and newspapers ignoring it were soon shut down.[9] The commissar charged with enforcing the decree, A.E. Minkin, requested, and was given, special permission to take 'vigorous and revolutionary' measures to make sure the decree was obeyed.

This measure was followed by another decree issued on 19 December 1917 (1 January 1918) which established a Press Tribunal empowered to investigate crimes against the people carried out by the press. The tribunal lasted until May 1918, when its functions passed into the hands of the revolutionary tribunals. It was set up initially as a measure to further harass and stymie the more persistent of the non-bolshevik newspapers which, despite the cascade of legal and other measures taken against them, continued to appear sporadically under different names. The aim of the tribunal was to shut them down for good.[10]

During 1917–18 the revolutionary government closed 319 liberal and conservative newspapers (Nemirovskii and Kharlamova (eds), 1983, p.93), while in the course of 1918 approximately 3,200 publications ceased to exist. By March of 1919 the bolsheviks had gained control of the country's entire media apparatus (McNair, 1991, p.36).

Newspaper extracts during this and later periods provide a flavour of the mood of the times. On 28 June 1918, for instance, the government newspaper, *Izvestiya*, reported in the following manner the closing down of the opposition newspaper, *Nash golos* (Our Voice):

Considering that the continuing provocation of the said paper, especially dangerous at the present moment, is not permissible, the All-Russian Extraordinary

9 Nemirovskii and Kharlamova (eds), 1983, p.93.
10 The tribunals, set up throughout the country, consisted of three members, usually bolsheviks. They were given jurisdiction over 'all crimes committed against the people by means of the press', including 'all untrue or distorted statements about public life'. The tribunals had the power to close down offending publications and imprison those responsible for their publication (see Shapiro, 1977, p.173).

Commission,[11] in its struggle with the counter-revolution and speculation, has decreed that it be closed and legal action be brought against it.

The critical post-revolutionary period in the new republic coupled with the already existing militaristic rhetoric of revolutionary writings proved to be fertile ground for a progressive militarization of the language of the press. An early example of the type of bellicose rhetoric used by the bolshevik-controlled press against its enemies is found in the following extract from a front-page article written in *Izvestiya* (31 October 1917),[12] condemning the socialist, though non-bolshevik, press:

> Their newspapers began a rabid persecution of the new government and of the parties supporting it, especially the bolsheviks. So furious was their attack that the reactionary rags of the tsarist autocracy paled in comparison. Every word in these papers (*Delo Naroda, Volya Naroda, Rabochaya gazeta, Narodnoe Slovo, Soldatskii Krik*, etc.) has been written in the spittle of a rabid dog. There is no limit to the depths of low slander, coarse abuse and vile fabrication to which these people, embittered by their failure, will stoop against the workers, peasants, soldiers and sailors who have risen in defence of the people's rights.

The bolsheviks, however, were not the only ones to compare their enemies to tsarist reactionaries. In a more literary, though no less impassioned, language, the liberal press taunted the bolsheviks with reminders that the revolutionary legislation on the press was a reversion to tsarist ways. The Kadet newspaper *Novaya Rech'* (New Speech)[13] reported a speech by the critic and thinker Dmitry Merezhkovskii, made on 10 December 1917 at a Writers' Union meeting in defence of freedom of speech:

> Lenin is right: freedom of speech for him is more dangerous than the bomb,[14] the dagger or poison. Before freedom of speech, which is unarmed and defenceless, he himself, with all his millions of bayonets, is unarmed and defenceless. While it lives, he is dead. Either one or the other lives, but both together cannot

11 The *VChK*, pronounced *Vecheka*, an acronym from the first three words of the first Soviet secret police established in December 1917, the 'All-Russian Extraordinary Commission for Combating Counter-revolution and Sabotage (*Vserossiiskaya Chrezvychainaya Komissiya po bor'be s kontrrevolyutsiei i sabotazhem*)'.
12 Quoted in Mochalova, 1991b, p.223.
13 Quoted in Mochalova, 1991b, p.237.
14 See Lenin's Decree on the Press, where he said that the press in the hands of the enemy was 'no less dangerous ... than bombs or machine-guns'.

be. It was the same for Nicholas Romanov II; so it is now, for Nicholas Lenin II; so it is for all tyrants.

While the closing down of the non-bolshevik press was easily justified on ideological grounds, it was above all a crude measure taken by a desperate government with the aim of ensuring its continued existence. In this atmosphere the ideologically charged and abstract revolutionary language characteristic of the bolshevik press often gave way to more effective plain speaking. So, for example, the civil war period (April–May 1918 to November 1920) saw the aspirational Marxist language of headlines such as 'World Revolution' (*Izvestiya*, 23 January 1919) give way to *Izvestiya* headlines such as 'The Red Front' (7 April 1920), 'In Occupied Areas', 'In Liberated Areas' (23 January 1919), 'Details of the Capture of Yekaterinoslav' and 'White Guards Evacuate Zlatoust' (31 January 1919).

The drastic government measure involving the requisition of food from the peasants and the nationalization of the economy in the summer of 1918 resulted in a further militarization of the language in the press. This policy of placing the economy on a military footing, which came to be known as war communism, operated until spring 1921. Readers already familiar with the civil war rhetoric of struggles, fronts, armies and deserters, now came across the same sort of language applied to the economy. Typical headlines for the period in *Izvestiya* such as the 'Work of Food Army'[15] or 'Penalty for Labour Deserters' (7 April 1920) appeared alongside those containing the two words 'struggle' and 'front', both of which were to become icons of the Soviet press right up to the Gorbachev era. Thus, for instance, the following *Izvestiya* headlines: 'Struggle to Resurrect the Economy', 'Struggle with Collapse of Transport, 'Labour Front' (7 April 1920),[16] 'Food Front' (6 January 1921), 'Victory on Labour Front' (11 January 1921) and 'Literary Front' (13 January 1921).

15 See *Izvestiya*, 28 June 1918: '[Headline] Creation of Food Army. [Article] To all who have begun to organize or have already organized food divisions, I request you immediately to send to Moscow for the means to buy uniforms, arms and provisions. Comrades, do not delay a minute. Armed force is necessary in the struggle against the *kulaks* for bread; the sooner you send food provisions for the divisions the better for us. Make haste!'.

16 See *Izvestiya*, 11 January 1921, for the compound neologism '*trudofront*' (= *trudovoi front*), or 'Labour Front'.

War communism had left in its wake an alienated and often terror-ized peasantry, as well as a devastated countryside and collapsed economy (Nove, 1975, p.86). In December 1920 Lenin secured a central committee resolution criticizing Trotsky, the mastermind behind war communism, for supporting a policy that had led to a 'degeneration of centralism' and to 'militarized forms of work'. In March 1921 Lenin presented the 10th party congress with a formula for replacing requisitions in agriculture, the so-called *prodrazverstka*, with the *prodnalog*, a tax in kind, but considerably less than the *pro-drazverstka*. After the peasants paid the *prodnalog*, they were free to dispose of their surplus produce as they saw fit. An *Izvestiya* editorial, headline *'Prodnalog'*, explained the effect of the new tax (20 March 1921):

> Thus the peasant, who now enjoys more freedom to dispose of his surplus pro-duce as he wishes, becomes, in his relationship to the State, a free contractor, exchanging his surplus produce for manufactured goods. This circumstance on the one hand removes the ground from under the speculator, on the other it draws the peasant closer to the urban proletariat. ... Thus Soviet power ... is going half-way to meet the needs of the very poor and middle peasantry and, freeing them from taxation, is providing them with the possibility to use their excess produce in order to increase productivity and generally improve their own economic well-being. ... The moment has arrived when we can allow ourselves the possibility of bringing over the country to methods of peaceful construction. Only by a strict observance of this method can it become the link in the creation of a close relationship between the proletariat and the peasantry and, at the same time, boost the development of our agriculture.

Thus, while retaining the 'commanding heights' of major industries, transport, banking and foreign trade, this initiative, known as the New Economic Policy (NEP), permitted light industry, retail trade and agriculture to enter the arena of private enterprise, simultaneously preparing the ground for a period of reconciliation between the town and country.

Official recognition that war communism had almost paralysed the economy meant that journalists and leader writers could now write relatively frankly about the economic tasks facing the country. A trend was beginning to emerge in the Soviet press whereby an official admission of a problem could bring about a descent from the heights of revolutionary rhetoric to more mundane language. Because the language of acknowledging problems was not aspirational in reference, it contained fewer figurative turns of phrase. An *Izvestiya* writer referred to the 'catastrophic state of our industry and our food crisis' (10 March 1921), while other articles spoke openly of 'our mistakes and tasks in economic construction' (10 March 1921). One *Izvestiya* article warned: 'We must come to our senses. We have four urgent tasks: bread, fuel, transport and the reconstruction of heavy industry and the mining industry' (10 March 1921). The same tone of urgency was felt in an editorial on the necessity to resuscitate the livestock industry: 'Without the horse and cattle in the countryside there will be no bread. ... What are our prospects for 1921? Everything depends on the grain harvest' (20 March 1921).

While the introduction of NEP at the 10th party congress had the effect of temporarily bringing the language of economics down to earth, Lenin's success at the same congress in prohibiting factions within the party[17] led to a further homogenization of both the content and language of the press. It now became more and more difficult for the already tightly-controlled press to devote space to the discussion of contentious issues within the party, to say nothing of providing coverage of non-party views. This further curtailment of freedom was justified on the grounds that public dissension within the party might threaten the integrity of a state still not strong enough to withstand criticism. The strength and unity of the party was for Lenin infinitely more important than the bourgeois concept of the journalistic licence to criticize. It was believed that only a monolithic party could resurrect the economy and prevent the country from being overrun by foreign enemies. It is from this period that slogans concerning party unity and unanimity, a hallmark of the Soviet press, became common.

A graphic example of how the press had become the voice of the government came a day before Lenin's opening speech to the congress, when the sailors of Kronstadt rebelled. The press weighed in behind the government's savage condemnation of the rebels. No attempt was made to give an objective account of what had moved the sailors to rebel. In a vituperative editorial headlined 'The Last Warning',

17 See *Izvestiya*, 9 March 1921: 'V.I. Lenin points out that in the heated discussion on trade unions we permit ourselves more freedom of discussion than is possible for a party surrounded by an entire world of enemies. But there is no doubt that the party will come out of this stronger and more fortified.'

Izvestiya demanded the 'severe penalty of the revolution for the traitors and spies!' (8 January 1921). In another front-page 'thunderer' on the same event (20 January 1921), the newspaper's editor[18] castigated the rebels in language presaging that found in press coverage of the show trials of the 1930s:

> Kronstadt, which from being the hearth of the revolution almost turned into a nest of betrayal, has fallen, and the red banner is again unfurled on its firmaments. The Soviet Republic has crushed the serpent of a counter-revolution in embryo and has again proved the total futility and hopelessness of uprisings plotted against the power of the workers and peasants.

The second half of 1921 was marked by the devastating famine along the Volga. The tragedy dominated the newspapers. There was no attempt to hush up the extent or gravity of the calamity, though its causes were not examined. Thus began the suppression of full reporting of catastrophes, natural or otherwise. The rationale behind this policy was not complicated: since the country's very existence was in the balance, there could be no justification for printing news that might reflect unfavourably on the actions of the authorities and thus promote a potential counter-revolutionary force. Nevertheless, in comparison with the total absence of coverage on catastrophes which became the norm under Stalin and lasted right up to the mid-1980s, the press coverage of the famine makes uncharacteristic reading for a Soviet newspaper (*Izvestiya*, 25 December 1921):[19]

> At that time [21 June 1921] it was thought we had up to ten million starving people. But with every two weeks these figures increased and now we have 22 million starving people and that is only the officially recognized figure. Undoubtedly, to these must be added about another five million. This figure threatens to destroy the entire State mechanism.

Throughout the worst months of the famine a daily rubric entitled 'Fight against Hunger' occupied the entire right-hand side of *Izvestiya*'s front page. The rubric included long lists of donations received by the newspaper in aid of the famine (1 September 1921):

18   Yuri Mikhailovich Steklov, editor of *Izvestiya* 1917–25.
19   From a speech made by Mikhail Kalinin, President of the Republic, at the ninth all-Russian congress of soviets.

On 31 August the newspaper received [the following sums] for the relief of the starving: 161) 597 roubles from Z.P. Poluentov, 162) 109,000 roubles from a collection made by the young people of the Danilovsk *mir*. ... 165) 468,900 roubles from the Bryansk medical centre, N°.3, the takings from a show. ... Donations are accepted daily, except holidays, from 12 pm to 8 pm.

Because of the dire situation, aid from abroad was accepted ('At Petrograd trade port the arrival is awaited from hour to hour of the American ship with its cargo of food for the population of the starving *gubernii*' (*Izvestiya*, 1 September 1921)). However, caution and 'revolutionary vigilance' (*revolyutsionnaya bditel'nost'*) were the watchwords in regard to the activities of some of the famine-relief groups set up within the country (*Izvestiya*, 31 September 1921):[20]

Comrade Kamenev concluded his report [at a full session of the Moscow city council] with a short resumé of the 'activities' of the recently abolished All-Russian Committee for the Relief of the Starving, which, under the guise of being a relief-agency, was in fact a centre for political groupings and an organ for political struggle.

It was during this period also that, as a result of the temporary economic liberalization brought about by the introduction of NEP, the press opened its pages to advertisements from small, privately-owned businesses.[21] In *Izvestiya*, for example, a front-page announcement

20 *Izvestiya* also used its columns to scotch rumours put about by Whites who wished to exploit the famine for their own counter-revolutionary ends, as shown in the following 'White Guard Dreamers' piece (7 August 1921): 'As was to be expected in connection with the harvest failure along the Volga, Russian White newspapers have become full of the most absurd and fantastic reports of "fierce revolts by the hungry" throughout the country, of havoc reigning in the Moscow railway stations, of the spread of cholera and like nonsense.'

21 The following advertisements, for example, appeared in the same 28 November 1921 issue:

Large selection of imported perfumes, knitwear and everything for
gents' and ladies' toilette.
ELEGANT
Kuznetskii Bridge
_____

First class restaurants
Breakfasts, lunches, dinners, cold snacks, tea, cocoa, beer and minerals.
Common Consumer Society
EPO
Products of highest quality at prices 25 to 50% lower than
private enterprise ones.

(28 November 1921) read:

> Advertisements are accepted from State institutions, cooperatives, industrial and trade enterprises and also from individuals. Advertisements are accepted daily. Telephone 2-52-53.

Soon the last page of *Izvestiya* was given over entirely to advertisements. One special edition of ten pages of July 1922, coinciding with the high point of NEP, gave over five and a half pages to small and large advertisements. The latter half of 1922 was also the period when Lenin's influence began to wane seriously due to his illness, while that of his eventual successor, Stalin, was beginning to assert itself.

Stalin

Elaborating on the groundwork carried out under Lenin, Stalin succeeded in muzzling free speech completely without, moreover, having recourse to additional empowering legislation. Essentially, he differed from Lenin only in the degree of ruthlessness with which he manipulated the press. Both demanded, and received, an obedient and uncritical press. Unlike Lenin, Stalin used the press to build up his own public image to godlike proportions. Lenin, on the other hand, might be said to have used the press to bolster the image of the Soviet state.

Stalin continued and deepened the process of party monopolization of the media set in motion by Lenin. The possibility that, for example, *Izvestiya*, the main organ of the soviets, might develop an independent voice from that of *Pravda*, the main party newspaper, became more and more remote as the functions and powers of the soviets themselves diminished to such an extent that by the early 1930s their role in the running of the country had become negligible. There was even less room for differences of opinion within the party. Following the general line put forward by Lenin at the 10th party congress in 1921, Stalin said at the 13th party conference in January 1924 that the party should become 'a monolithic organization, hewed from the one stone'. For Stalin, the soviets, the trade unions, the *Komsomol*, women's organizations, and all other public groupings in the country should be mere catspaws of the party.

By 1929[22] publishing material in the press that Stalin might find undesirable had become an exercise fraught with danger. The concentration of power in a centralized apparatus presided over by Stalin minimized to zero the residual amount of differentiation between newspapers that had been permitted under Lenin.[23]

An important feature of the press in the Stalin era which had its roots in the policy directions set by Lenin was the suppression of news which might reflect badly on the country's leadership. As the immediate threat of counter-revolution from external forces receded, so the suppression of bad news on the grounds that it would provide succour to the Whites was becoming more and more an excuse rather than a credible justification for maintaining a compliant and toothless press. There was no discussion on the possible repeal of the draconian Decree on the Press.

So, for example, the pandemonium that reigned in the countryside during the campaign to collectivize agriculture begun in December 1929, when peasants burnt their crops and slaughtered livestock as a mark of protest, went unreported, as did the massive deportations of those branded kulaks.[24]

This failure to report was in general accordance with Lenin's belief that the function of a socialist press[25] was to render active assistance to the leadership in its attempts to 'sell' a government or party initiative to the people in whose long-term interests it was in any case being implemented.

As Stalin proceeded with the twin initiatives of collectivizing agriculture and embarking on a policy of large-scale national industrial-

22 See Tucker, 1987, p.110: '... around 1929 when Stalin finally achieved ascendancy in the Soviet political leadership.' See, also, Goryaeva, 1990, pp.116–17, who writes that by 1928 the press had become the servant of the party, supporting all its initiatives.

23 See Goryaeva, ibid., who writes that Lenin allowed the existence of fellow travellers as well as non-bolshevik cultural groups and associations, some of which had their own publications.

24 See, also, Hosking, 1992, p.161: 'In effect the label "kulak" was now applied to anyone suspected of resisting the grain deliveries or of being unwilling to join the collectives.'

25 See, for example, Zasurskii (ed.), 1987, p.10: 'When V.I. Lenin named the press as the centre and basis of political organization (see Lenin, V.I., Complete collected works, vol.44, p.79), he was in fact emphasizing the role of the journalistic apparatus in supporting and developing specific aspects of each link in the political system in the most appropriate manner.'

ization, the relative liberalization of the economy, which the country had experienced under NEP, disappeared. The accompanying five-year plans, the first of which was launched in October 1928, set quantitative plans for both agriculture and industry to be filled by a certain date. This brought forth in the press a language of colossal figures and statistics, a feature that was to persist in the Soviet press until the Gorbachev era. Newspapers now regularly carried reports of a certain quantity of a certain product having been produced by or before a certain target date. Such reports were in time to become ritualized but meaningless boasts. In response to Stalin's own request, the first five-year plan was completed in four years (Selyunin, 1988, p.176). The press had no alternative but to take the main role in creating an atmosphere of 'hurrah-industry' (*ura-promyshlennost'*) (Gostyushin, 1989[26]), in which no sensible editor would publish statistics that did not match the results[27] expected by the country's leader (quoted in Nove, 1975, p.47):

> It is clear that the workers' living standards are rising all the time. Anyone who denies this is an enemy of Soviet power.

The Stakhanovite movement, named after the legendary Alexei Stakhanov who in 1935 had mined 102 tonnes of coal in one shift instead of the required seven, was one expression of the campaign to overfulfil normative production quotas. Pressure to overfulfil sometimes resulted in managers arranging the workings of their plants so that they would produce at least one Stakhanovite hero-worker, often at the expense of the smooth running of the rest of the plant (Traynor, 1988). By trumpeting the achievements of hero-workers the press was doing no more than fulfilling its function as enthusiastic supporter of government efforts to create a competitive atmosphere in both industry and agriculture that would lead to increased productivity. Typical of

26 See also these examples from *Izvestiya* of typical headlines glorifying life in the Soviet Union under Stalin: 'A Shining Peak' (on the subject of Russian culture), 'Indissoluble Bonds of Brotherhood' (on relations between Armenians and other Soviet nationalities), 'Life is Joyous, like the Georgian Sun' (all from 13 January 1937); 'To the Peaks of Soviet Democracy' (16 January 1937); 'The Remarkable Work of the Stakhanovites' (17 January 1937); 'To New Heights in Soviet Science' (27 February 1937).
27 The figures given for completion of plan targets, such as those provided on completion in four and a half years of the first five-year plan in 1932, are, according to Nove (1975, pp.46–7), suspect, considering that the targets set were unattainable.

the servile attitude of the press to official initiatives to improve productivity is the following extract expressing implicit support for the 'socialist competition' (*sotssorevnovanie*) campaign (*Izvestiya*, 4 January 1937):

The struggle for world records in the smelting of steel has found a very lively response throughout the entire country. On a broad front and with renewed strength, socialist competition has developed in all branches of the economy and especially in the area of heavy industry.

The unpublished and unpublishable reality, however, was quite different. In 1929 Stalin promised a bright future for the Soviet Union (Selyunin, 1988, p.177):

'In some three years' time [the Soviet Union] will become one of the most wealthy bread-producing countries in the world, if not the most wealthy.' In three years, as is known, a terrible famine took place taking millions of lives. Only in 1950 did the grain harvest finally surpass the level attained during NEP.

The failure of the press to report on both the widespread hostility to collectivization, as well as on the state's response to that resistance, marked the beginning of the period when the press decisively ceased to be a chronicler of events and became instead a purveyor of unrealistically positive portrayals of Soviet life. A sign of the times was the compliance of the press in attempting to hide the existence of the devastating famine that gripped Ukraine between 1932–34. The causes of the famine were at least in part a result of, and peasant reaction to, the state's grain-procurement policy that accompanied the campaign to collectivize agriculture.[28] According to one Soviet historian writing in the *glasnost'* era, 'on Stalin's instructions nothing could be written about the famine which had spread through a population of 25–30 million people' (Volkogonov, 1991, p.171). Compared to the partial coverage of the 1921–22 famine, the absolute veto on covering the calamity in Ukraine is one example among many others of Stalin interpreting with more rigour a precedent set by Lenin. Again, the ban could be explained in several ways: a famine fourteen years after the revolution might have denigrated the image of the Soviet government

28 In 1987 and 1988 the weekly magazine *Ogonyok* suggested that this famine had been artificially created.

at home and abroad and in the long run damage the interests of both Soviet citizens and world socialism. At another level it seems likely that journalists understood that bad news which might be construed as criticism of the regime's policy initiatives was not welcome on the pages of the press. For the Soviet journalist, the dictum had become 'bad news is no news'. It goes without saying that one finds no examples in the press to illustrate what it never acknowledged as having happened.

As Stalin tightened his grip on the country's press, so the newspaper columns became more and more the leader's personal weapon to be wielded at will in his power struggles against all those whom he saw as rivals and enemies. Those who crossed Stalin were likely to be verbally assaulted in the newspapers in the most abusive fashion permitted. Though extremely strong and offensive, the language used in name-calling remained just about within the boundaries of propriety. Typical of political oaths found in the Stalinist press were 'Trotskyite degenerates!' (*trotskistskie vyrodki*) 'depraved right-ultraleftists!' (*pravolevatskie urody*), 'bedraggled conciliators!' (*primirentsy zadrapannye*) and 'compromisers!' (*soglashateli*) (Ginzburg, 1988, p.38).[29]

The frequency with which such language appeared coincided with the growing atmosphere of fear and terror among the population. With the murder of Kirov in 1934, a wave of mass repression began, culminating in the show-trials of 1937–38. The press participated in creating the atmosphere of terror (ibid., p.36):

> The long newspaper columns which appeared [in 1934] with indictments concerning Kirov's murder made one shudder, but as yet one did not doubt their veracity. Former Leningrad *Komsomol* leaders? Nikolaev? Rumyantsev? Kotolynov? All this was fantastic, incredible. But it had been printed in *Pravda*, therefore no doubts could arise as to its authenticity.

Seventy per cent of the party central committee elected at its 17th

---

29 See also Amlinskii (1988) who describes the 'stylistic model' as 'revelatory–insulting (*razoblachitel'no-oskorbitel'no*), though in some way recalling the language not of politicians, but plain bad language: "swine" (*svolochi*), "blackguards" (*merzavtsy*), "scum" (*podonki*), "dregs" (*pogan'*), "rabble, waste" (*otreb'e*), "mix between a pig and a fox" (*pomes' svin'i i lisy*) ... this was the type of language produced at plenary sessions, meetings, courts of law; this is what was written in newspaper articles and in the editorials of the national newspapers'.

congress held in 1934, at which the defeat of the enemies of socialism within the Soviet Union was celebrated, were executed during the following five years. Of ordinary delegates, only 59 of the original 1966 reappeared as delegates to the next congress in 1939. It is in the newspaper coverage of the trials of the most prominent among Stalin's perceived enemies that the worst excesses of personal vilification are found. The 1937–38 show trials of leading party figures, for example, were covered extensively by an obedient press which wholeheartedly supported the equally obedient judiciary. One Soviet commentator has noted the role of the press in shaping public opinion for the trial of Nikolai Bukharin (Temushkin, 1988, p.17):

> One cannot leave unstated the methods by which public opinion was prepared for the trial. The day the trial began, 2 March, the national newspapers published editorials listing the 'crimes' of the 'right-Trotskyite bloc', as well as containing the call for the physical annihilation of the 'gang of bloody dogs' (this last comes from the lexicon of Vyshinskii). The following day three quarters of the space in the newspapers were given over to calls of the type 'One indictment is enough to justify executing the vermin!'. Letters were published from workers, collective-farm workers, prominent academics and army people which contained no less decisive suggestions.

While the language itself was initially very shocking the frequency with which it was used soon reduced it to the status of cliché,[30] though,

30 The following examples, taken from *Izvestiya* over a period of eight days in January 1937, give some impression of the repetitive force of the articles on enemies of the people:
21 January 1937:
Headline: *Accursed Traitors to the Motherland*, sub-headline: *Today the trial of the counter-revolutionary Trotskyite–Zinovievite band of murderers – Zinoviev, Kamenev, Smirnov, Mrachkovskii and others – has shown that apart from this grouping of maniacal enemies of the people who have been apprehended red-handed, there exists another centre for the Trotskyites where they carry out their villainous counter-revolutionary activity.*
24 January 1937:
Headline to editorial: *Traitors to the Motherland, Lackeys of Fascism, Base Restorers of Capitalism,* sub-headline: *The trial of the Trotskyite Centre. Indictment of Pyatakov, Yu.L., Radek, K.B., Sokol'nikov* [in all 17 names] ... *charged with betrayal of the motherland, espionage, sabotage, wrecking and the preparation of terrorist acts, i.e., crimes specified in paragraphs 58–1–a, 58–8, 58–9 and 58–11 of the Criminal Code of the Russian Soviet Socialist Federal Republic. The trial of the anti-Soviet Trotskyite centre. Cross-examination of the defendant Pyatakov.*
25 January 1937:
Headlines: *Allies and accomplices of the Fascist Aggressors; Base Traitors to the*

for all that, none the less ominous for those at whom it was directed (Ginzburg, 1988, pp.63–5). No newspaper raised a whisper in defence of the accused, no questions were asked as to the truth of the charges nor to the means by which confessions and recantations were obtained. The entire press joined in a chorus of condemnation such that, shortly before her own arrest in 1937, Yevgeniya Ginzburg was able to remark that all newspapers had become almost indistinguishable (Ginzburg, 1988, p.42):[31]

> Later on we were brought a pile of newspapers. But it was no longer possible to distinguish which of them was *Literaturnaya gazeta* (Literary Gazette), and which, say, *Sovetskoe iskusstvo* (Soviet Art). They all yelled and screamed in the same way about enemies, plots and executions.

Motherland; Despicable Arch-Traitor; Base Deeds of the Trotskyite Traitors, sub-headline: *The workers, collective-farm workers and the intelligentsia – all the Russian people – demand that the vile band of base Trotskyite traitors to the motherland, the fascist agents, the spies, wreckers, murderers and saboteurs be wiped from the face of the earth.*
26 January 1937:
Headlines: *Trotskyite Monsters; Suppressors of the People; Enemies of the People; Traitors to the Motherland; Hirelings of Fascism – to be Wiped from the Face of the Earth!* Headline: *My Request to the Supreme Court*, article: *It is difficult for me, a common collective-farm worker, to find suitable words to express all I have gone through sitting in the court. One thing I will say: never in my thoughts nor in my dreams did I think that the earth was capable of producing such villains. All their scheming and plotting has shocked me so much that I am ready to shout out: 'Death to you accursed cut-throats.' I can hardly hold myself back.*
27 January 1937:
Headline: *Trotskyite Marauders – Scouts for the Intervention.*
28 January 1937:
Headline: *The Trotskyite Vermin to be Crushed! The Formidable and Potent Voice of Millions; Execute the Traitors to the Motherland! Crush the Vermin! Destroy the Traitors!*
31 This impression is confirmed and elaborated upon by Adzhubei (1988, 7, p.106): 'Thus in some newspaper issues which appeared between 1937–1938 out of 10 pages only the odd piece of real information appeared. The remainder was devoted to articles exposing enemies of the people. They were written not so much in a dry manner, rather as if the subject matter concerned not people, but inanimate objects. There were articles published on the exposure and arrest of groups, bands and secret counter-revolutionary organizations. There were calls for vigilance. People were not only encouraged but ordered to seek out enemies everywhere – in village cooperatives, in the *Komsomol* and in party and Soviet organizations; among the military, writers, engineers, agronomists and *kolkhoz* workers. In hundreds of details there were descriptions of the enemy's disguise, of the absolute necessity not to trust anyone, to suspect all. Denunciations were rewarded and praised.'

The vilification on the pages of the press of 'enemies of the people' found its obverse in the virtual deification of Stalin carried out by the same journalists. Articles on the leader were a source of hyperbole that matched the ritualized rhetoric of denunciation. Throughout the thirties and thereafter readers became accustomed to seeing Stalin less and less as a person, and more and more as a cult figure, 'all-knowing' and 'all-wise' (Bestuzhev-Lada, 1988, p.14). Examples of extravagant praise being heaped upon the leader are plentiful. Adulatory letters printed regularly in the press addressed him as 'the great leader of peoples', 'the father and teacher' and 'the inspiration and organizer of our victories'. One letter from Leningrad railway workers addressed Stalin as 'the great train driver of the locomotive of the revolution' (*Izvestiya*, 10 January 1937).

Imparting to Stalin during his own lifetime attributes usually associated with deceased heroes helped in the construction of what Khrushchev referred to as the 'cult of personality'. Towns,[32] districts, railway stations, factories, parks, newspapers, ships and palaces of culture began to be named after Stalin as early as 1925 (Volkogonov, 1991, pp.159–60).[33] The naming of something after Stalin was considered a newsworthy event, and duly reported in the press (for example, *Izvestiya*, 3 January 1937, reported 'Today the Stalin Museum of Defence was opened in Tsaritsyn'), thus giving Stalin, in contemporary media jargon, a high public profile and positive media exposure. The cult of Stalin would not have reached the grotesque dimensions it did without the enthusiastic cooperation of the press in

32 Saint Petersburg was renamed 'Leningrad' after Lenin's death in 1924.
33 As early as 1929, on his 50th birthday, already half of a jubilee issue of *Pravda* was devoted to Stalin. Volkogonov writes: 'There was Kaganovich's piece entitled "Stalin and the Party", Ordzhonikidze on "The Rock-Hard Bolshevik", Kuibyshev's "Stalin and the Industrialization of the Country", Mikoyan punning on "The Steel Soldier of the Bolshevik Party" and so on.' Goryaeva (1990, p.119) writes that the campaign to glorify Stalin had by the mid-thirties reached a stage where the leader was obligatorily mentioned as the source of all achievement 'whether it concerned the building of a factory or the bringing in of a harvest, a newly-published book or a long-distance swimmer, the feat of a polar expedition or the opening of a school museum'. All negative phenomena in society, she adds, were said to be the result of 'isolated deficiencies' (*chastnye nedorabotki*) and 'inevitable historical barriers' (*zakonomernye istoricheskie bar'ery*) which would shortly be overcome. Khrushchev condemned these 'memorials to the living' in his famous 'secret speech' at the 20th party congress in 1956 (Whitney, 1963, p.255).

giving space to such blatant 'advertorialism', or publicity masquerading as news.

This type of news was commonplace in the press from the 1930s right up to Stalin's death in 1953.[34] Adzhubei, who worked for *Komsomol'skaya pravda* during the Stalin period, revealed the lengths to which newspapers were forced to go in order to avoid in any way undermining the leader's media image (Adzhubei, 1988, 7, p.83):

> In *Komsomol'skaya pravda* [after Stalin's death] we abolished the post of a special employee whose duty it was to scrutinize with a magnifying glass all photographs of the leader to ensure that no undesirable combinations appeared in the typographic signs. If one did appear, the negative was sent back to be redeveloped. There was no shortage of readers who supplied the newspaper (and not only the newspaper) with cuttings of photographs which had appeared in the press with the places marked on them where they had 'uncovered' a zionist cross or a fascist swastika.

Even before publication, however, photographs of Stalin were subject to alteration (Medvedev, 1980, p.74)[35]:

> It is not difficult to imagine what Bukharin [as editor of *Izvestiya*] thought of the confidential instructions issued to the main organs of the Soviet press with regard to the publication of photographs of Stalin. The retouchers were to increase the size of his forehead by one or two centimetres; a high forehead had long been considered a sign of intelligence and this was a cause of envy in the low-browed Stalin.

---

34 See, for example, Chegodaeva, 1989, and her description of how the entire media machine was rolled into action to join in the nationwide celebrations of Stalin's 70th birthday in 1949.

35 Thus Yevgeniya Ginzburg's reaction on seeing Stalin in the flesh is not surprising (Ginzburg, 1988, p.40): 'That summer [1937] Gorky died and at his funeral I saw Stalin for the first and last time. I was walking in the ranks of the Union of Writers and therefore was able to discern him at close quarters. ... But I tell no lie when I say that it was without any adoration that I watched his face, which struck me because of its ugliness and dissimilarity to the regal features which gazed benignly from the millions of portraits.' Similarly, Milovan Djilas, the Yugoslav communist, expressed shock on seeing Stalin for the first time in person (Djilas, 1963, pp.51–2): 'This was not that majestic Stalin of the photographs or the newsreels – with the stiff, deliberate gait and posture. ... I was also surprised at something else: he was of very small stature and ungainly build. His torso was short and narrow, while his legs and arms were too long. ... He had quite a large paunch. ... His teeth were black and irregular, turned inward. Not even his moustache was thick or firm.'

Criticism in the press carried large risks, in spite of the not infrequent appearance of headlines of the type: 'Self-criticism is a Sharp Weapon against Bureaucracy'. Konstantin Simonov, the author and former editor of *Literaturnaya gazeta* during Stalin's period of office, recalled a telling incident concerning the leader's real attitude to criticism (quoted in Adzhubei, 1988, 6, p.104):

> Stalin, while afraid of critical views being hidden, considered it useful to know what people were thinking. Thus, in 1947 he recommended that *Literaturnaya gazeta* become more critical but 'the sharper tone of the paper pleased comrade Stalin for a while, but then began to irritate him. I think the editor Simonov would have found himself in deep trouble had not Stalin died before he had time to sort out the whole paper of which Konstantin Simonov was editor.[36]

While publishing articles critical of society was a hazardous business, to criticize Stalin himself was simply unthinkable. Adzhubei (ibid., 7, pp.82–3) recalled, for example, how Stalin's words were regarded as sacrosanct by editors:

> The editor of *Komsomol'skaya pravda* after Stalin's death often removed from a story a quotation from Stalin if he thought it superfluous. At the beginning of the fifties even to contemplate this would have been impossible: an off-print of a page with the underlined quotation could end up in somebody's file.

Stalin 'systematically eliminated the very notion of non-subversive argument' (Nove, 1975, p.59). The regimented views appearing in the press of the thirties constituted the party line, and none other. A consequence of the absolute monopolization of the truth in all areas of the news was a general absence of ambiguity or uncertainty that lent to the Stalinist press an inflexible and categorical tone that was,

36 Simonov's fears would almost certainly have been realized. Adzhubei recalls that in 1938, for example, the editor and practically the entire editorial staff of *Komsomol'skaya pravda* were arrested (Adzhubei, 1988, 6, p.116). He also records a chilling footnote to another episode of Stalin's 'sorting out' of an entire editorial staff (ibid., 7, p.91): 'Witnesses have described to me the occasion in 1949 when he [Stalin] all of a sudden decided to replace the entire editorial staff of *Pravda*, basing his decision on the grounds that the paper was inflating the personality cult of Stalin. Pacing up and down the room, he began to name the members of the new editorial staff. As he proceeded, those present stood transfixed: he was recommending for the top jobs in the paper people who had long since ceased to be. They had all been destroyed with his agreement. Nobody interrupted the leader. Suslov, who was appointed editor, fixed up everything.'

moreover, to remain a hallmark of the Soviet newspaper until the Gorbachev reforms. Black and white coverage, typified by newspaper denunciations of 'enemies of the people' and paeons addressed to Stalin himself, was a feature that spread to all areas of news. As an extension and expression of the party, the editorial line of all newspapers would whenever necessary change to conform to whatever might be the official view of the moment, a policy that sometimes meant abruptly lurching from one editorial position to another diametrically opposed. An example of one such *volte face* was the sudden censoring of all anti-Nazi views following the conclusion in August 1939 of the non-aggression pact between the Soviet Union and Hitler's Germany. This was in complete contrast to the anti-fascist line that had hitherto been taken. In the same way the post-war split between Stalin and Tito in January 1948 meant that the Yugoslav leader, who had rejected Stalin's attempts to control Yugoslav police and other state organs, suddenly became a pariah in the Soviet press. The man whom *Pravda* had credited as late as 29 November 1947 with the 'truly inspiring transformation of Yugoslavia into a progressive state'[37] suddenly become a 'fascist monster' (Nove, 1975, p.102).

The war temporarily turned the attention of Stalin, and therefore the press, away from mass repression. As well as reporting the course of the war (for example, from *Izvestiya*, 6 April 1943: 'German Air-Raid in Rostov Region', 'German Air-Raid in Leningrad Region'), newspapers worked to raise the morale and patriotic spirit of the people, as illustrated by these examples of annual May-day slogans that appeared in the press during the war (*Izvestiya*, 25 April 1943):

> Long live the first of May, the inspection day for the fighting forces of the workers! Workers of all countries, unite in the struggle against the German-fascist aggressors! Under the flag of Lenin, under the leadership of Stalin — forward to the rout of the German occupiers and to their expulsion from the borders of our Motherland!

The end of the war, however, saw a return to Stalinist pre-war normality. The last wave of repression began in earnest in 1948 and lasted till Stalin's death in 1953.

Stalin succeeded in creating an atmosphere of fear among journal-

37   See Werth, 1971, pp.398–9.

ists which meant that no investigative journalism was carried out, no criticism of the government took place, no causes were taken up independently by the press, no innovative political commentary was permitted, and no opinions contrary to those held by the leadership were covered. Thus the false picture portrayed in the newspapers was of a country without economic problems and where everyone was happy. Stalin completed the construction, begun by Lenin, of a media machine which was totally obedient and so self-regulating that the censorship agency, *Glavlit*, was largely redundant. Most of these characteristics remained more or less intact until the coming to power of Mikhail Gorbachev.

Khrushchev
The death of Stalin was a dramatic event for the country. Millions genuinely mourned the loss of the great teacher, leader and generalissimo while others, more aware of the dictator's hand in enormous crimes, felt a sense of relief (see, for example, Yevtushenko, 1963, p.93). For the reader of the newspaper the most obvious change was the cessation of articles glorifying Stalin literally within days of his death (Roxburgh, 1987, p.40). Nevertheless any feeling of relaxation among newspaper readers and journalists was tempered by a sense of uncertainty over the question of his succession. So weakened had the role of the press in society become that there was no question of it backing any prospective candidate, less still of different newspapers supporting rival candidates. The matter of succession was an entirely internal party decision.

Neither could the press cover the feverish party manoeuvring that followed Stalin's death. Almost four months went by after his death before the press indirectly reported the removal from office of Stalin's last chief of the secret police, Beria, though no article appeared mentioning him by name. Instead, it was the omission of his name on a list of leading party members attending a performance at the Bolshoi Theatre published in *Pravda* (28 June 1953) that signalled to close readers of the press an ominous change in his status (Nove 1975, p.123).[38] He was eventually executed (McCauley, 1991, p.36), accused

---

38 Beria was arrested on 26 June 1953. His arrest was publicly announced on 10 July 1953, while his conviction by the supreme court was announced on 24 July 1953 (Andrew and Gordievsky, 1990, p.351).

of being an 'agent of world imperialism', a trumped-up charge on which millions had suffered during his time as head of the secret police. Those in charge were still using the idiom of the Stalin epoch to punish opponents, while the press continued to report obediently and uncritically all news, no matter how fantastic it sounded, so long as it came from high sources.

By 1955 the first secretary of the party, Nikita Khrushchev, had achieved a sort of supremacy over his rivals, though the press did not report on the continuing power struggle and jockeying for positions within the party hierarchy. Since the mid-1920s it had become impossible to inform either the Soviet population at large or the hostile outside world that the party was not completely united. Silence and 'revolutionary caution' were still the watchwords. The public was forced to piece together what might have happened in the leadership struggle from reports of its outcome. Thus in February 1955, when the press reported the 'resignation' of Malenkov, appointed prime minister after Stalin's death, the news came in the form of an announcement of a *fait accompli* with no journalistic speculative analysis of the reasons for his resignation. Instead, the press published the official explanation, said to be 'administrative inexperience' which had led to past 'agricultural failings'. More importantly, the language in which Malenkov's removal from office had been reported was not of the blood-curdling variety of the Stalin era. The message to the public was that power shifts in the Kremlin could now be non-sanguinary (see Nove, 1975, p.206).[39] Nevertheless the press coverage of the whole affair had been far from truthful. It had completely omitted to report the position of Malenkov in the Kremlin power structure, while falsely reporting that the resignation had come about as a result of a decision of the Supreme Soviet, when in fact it had been taken by the party central committee.

Khrushchev embarked upon a course of reform for which the 1956 20th party congress became the platform. The famous 'secret speech' which he delivered on 24 February at the congress was a symbol of the intermediary state which prevailed in the country between the period following the death of Stalin and the inauguration of Khrushchev's de-Stalinizing reforms. On the one hand the speech was the opening salvo

39 After his removal, Malenkov remained a member of the party presidium and was appointed director of a power station in Siberia.

of an active campaign aimed at the de-Stalinization of the country. On
the other hand its delivery behind closed doors only to those attending
the congress and, later, to members of party cells around the country,[40]
was a manoeuvre, consistent with the practice which had evolved at
the 10th party congress in 1921 under Lenin's leadership and
consolidated under Stalin, of disseminating information according to
the exigencies of the party. Leaked to the Western press, it soon
became well known throughout the world while remaining 'closed' to
the Soviet general public until the spring of 1989 (Volkogonov, 1991,
p.579). Deciding against publication in the press of the 'secret speech',
Khrushchev permitted the newpapers to print the text of a party
resolution on 'Overcoming the Personality Cult and its Consequences'
published in July 1956, more than four months after the February
congress. The newspaper report praised the speech in demagogic
fashion for its frankness (3 July 1956):

> The brave and merciless self-criticism regarding the question of the personality
> cult was the first glowing evidence of the strength and solidity of our party and
> of the Soviet socialist system.

The resolution talked of the party's 'merciless self-criticism',[41] as a
reflection of its strength. It also made a pre-emptive strike against the
capitalist world, which, as always, could be expected to make much of
any admission of weakness by the communists:

> One can say with certainty that not one of the ruling parties in the capitalist
> countries would ever risk taking such a step. On the contrary, they would try to
> hush things up, to hide unpleasant facts from the people.

The speech caused deep shock not only in the Soviet Union but also
in the Eastern bloc where its impact led to rebellions against Soviet
influence in Poland and Hungary in September and October of the
same year. Though the impetus for change had come from the Soviet

---

40 Some non-party members also heard the speech (Hosking, 1992, p.336).
41 Without, however, the 'horrible facts and ghastly exposures that had filled
 Khrushchev's secret report to the Congress' (Aksyutin, 1989, p.17). In fact the speech
 was itself a very selective condemnation of certain of the crimes committed under
 Stalin. The purges of the thirties and forties, the results of collectivization and the
 suffering of countless ordinary people during Stalin's dictatorship were not condemned.

Union, its leaders reacted with panic to its effects. As Moscow unhappily accepted the defeat by Gomulka in Poland of the Stalinist wing of the party, it did all in its power to prevent the revolutionary spirit from spreading throughout the rest of the Eastern bloc, and especially to the Soviet Union itself. As a result, the subsequent, and much more serious, Hungarian challenge to Soviet influence, which resulted in a widespread rebellion and a Soviet military intervention, was totally misrepresented in the Soviet press. The first reaction of the press was to ignore events completely in the hope that the uprising would be crushed before the Soviet public could learn about it. When this became impossible, it printed completely untrue and misleading reports of events.[42]

While the position of the press as the tool of politicians did not change under Khrushchev, and indeed survived into the Brezhnev era, the change of personnel at the top had its reflection in the press. One important change in the newspaper world was the appointment in 1959 of Khrushchev's 35-year-old son-in-law, Alexei Adzhubei, to the post of editor of *Izvestiya*. Part of Adzhubei's brief was to break the monolith which the press had become under Stalin, in his own words 'to separate the spheres of influence of *Pravda* and *Izvestiya*, not only according to their formal position (the paper of the party and the paper of the soviets), but in essence' (Adzhubei, 1988, 7, p.104).

Adzhubei made many changes to give the paper a new 'look' that, in the end, distinguished it from *Pravda* more in appearance than in essence. Headlines became larger, articles shorter and photographs more frequent.[43] The language also changed slightly with more first-

---

42 For a thorough analysis of the distorted Soviet coverage of the Polish and Hungarian revolts, see Leonhard, 1962, pp.222–8.

43 Adzhubei was probably attempting to move away from the newspaper format to which he had grown accustomed while working for *Komsomol'skaya pravda* (ibid., 6, p.104): '[*Komsomol'skaya pravda*] was dry because of the abundance of official news and protocol news. There might be two or three small photographs over four pages, though more often than not there would be none at all (there was a strict limit on 'ornamentation'). There were long unbroken columns of news, small headlines, no light stories and a minimum of illustrations and caricatures. Each centimetre of space was given over to news.' As editor of *Izvestiya* Adzhubei also abolished the practice at *Komsomol'skaya pravda*, and elsewhere, of obeying the official news wire-service, *TASS*, as it 'categorically tapped out' where each communiqué or story was to appear in the newspaper: 'top right-hand corner of second column', 'bottom left-hand corner of third column' (Adzhubei, 1988, 6, p.104). A by-product of the *Izvestiya*'s 'reconstruction' was a boom in circulation figures. Adzhubei's five years in the post

person reportage pieces and an attempt to move away from official language to a more literary style. Greater coverage was given to foreign news. Only very occasionally, however, did *Izvestiya* take serious issue with *Pravda*, and then on economic and non-political issues. Only on rare occasions was it possible for extremely oblique criticism of the first secretary himself to appear in the press. A leading party member, whose speech would automatically be printed in the press, might, for instance, imply something less than absolute approval for, or even omit to mention, one of Khrushchev's pet projects. The admission on the pages of the press of even this very indirect criticism was a sign that, though still the most important figure in the leadership, Khrushchev was not another Stalin and consequently 'could not afford to suppress or ignore the opinions and the powers of his superior colleagues' (Hyland and Shryock, 1970, p.13).[44] There was, in fact, no explicit questioning of any top politician on the politics of the day (Churchward, 1975, pp.112–13) unless in the form of a 'set-piece', such as the Malenkov affair. There was, none the less, a general widening of critical ambit of the press under Khrushchev. Whereas under Stalin the only criticism allowed had been very low level, of the type 'In parts of Siberia shoes on sale are not of high quality' (quoted in Nove, 1975, p.141), it now became possible to criticize details of government policy and bureaucracy at all levels.

While Khrushchev might encourage the press to write more critically, his own background as a politician brought up in the Stalin era, as well as a decidedly authoritarian streak to his character, militated against his liberal instincts. He demanded, and received, energetic support from the press for his own political and economic campaigns. Newspapers dutifully reported speeches of party officials who, instead of uttering encomiums to Stalin, now roundly and enthusiastically condemned what had almost overnight become known as the 'cult of personality'. Khrushchev himself as party first secretary tirelessly travelled the country giving many speeches, all covered by the press, which supported uncritically his initiatives in government administration and agriculture, including most notoriously the unsuccessful

---

yielded a quadrupling of the readership.
44 See also Conquest, 1965, p.96: 'Silence or tepid approbation is about as far as participants [in political quarrels] can go under long-established rules.'

attempt to promote the widespread cultivation of maize in unsuitable climatic conditions. Just as the Stakhanovite movement had generated hero-workers in the press at any cost, so the desire to comply with the expectations of campaigns launched by Khrushchev meant that the figures and statistics which were obtained and paraded in the press were often at variance with common economic sense.

As tens of thousands returned from the camps, the atmosphere in the country became more relaxed. For the country's intelligentsia, encouraged to show themselves again, the period was to become known as 'The Thaw', the title of a novel by the writer and former *Izvestiya* journalist, Ilya Ehrenburg. The high point in the cultural thaw came in 1962 with the publication in *Pravda* of Yevgeny Yevtushenko's poem *Stalin's Heirs* (21 October) and of Alexander Solzhenitsyn's *One Day in the Life of Ivan Denisovich* in the November issue of *Novy mir*. There followed a reaction from the conservative wing of the party, though by May of 1963 the campaign against the 'creative intelligentsia' had petered out. Once Khrushchev had been ousted, however, these opponents of liberalization once again came to the fore.

While the *gulag* theme was allowed on to the press, the final word on whether a sensitive piece should be published lay with the party and not in the hands of an editor, even though it was the party itself that fired and appointed editors (Conquest, 1965, p.101). Adzhubei recalled how he had been in doubt over whether to publish a story on a soldier who had been unjustly persecuted under Stalin. He telephoned the highly-placed Suslov,[45] party presidium member and former editor of *Pravda*, who told him to 'Print it' (Adzhubei, 1988, 7, p.107), though it goes without saying that Suslov might just as easily have withheld permission to publish.[46]

The practice of not reporting disasters and calamities continued unchanged under Khrushchev. This form of censorship, begun under Lenin and continued under Stalin, had by now become a device used by public bodies to cover up their own shortcomings in dealing with crises (ibid., 6, p.115):[47]

---

45   Suslov was the main figure involved in the ousting of Khrushchev in 1964.
46   Fazil Iskander's story, '*Kozlatura*', captures well the atmosphere in a provincial newspaper of the time.
47   Adzhubei's account of a particular case of news suppression is illustrative of the situa-

It seems both ridiculous and sad to recall that we were not always successful in 'squeezing' on to the paper even a short notice about a fire or a flood, much less about more serious incidents. According to the newspapers we had no airplane crashes, our ships never sank, there were never any explosions in our mines, cars never ran over pedestrians, avalanches never fell on mountain towns and towns were never threatened by flooding.

The often folksy tone of Khrushchev's official speeches,[48] unlike the cautious officialese[49] of the frightened politician or journalist in the Stalin era, had the general effect of modifying the stylistic register of political discourse to bring it closer to the language of ordinary people.[50] Though the first secretary was later accused by Suslov of

---

tion in general. The ministry for transport announced that two people had died as a result of a railway accident. An *Izvestiya* reporter was dispatched to the scene to cover the story. The report, however, could not be printed without the ministry's permission. Adzhubei telephoned a functionary at the ministry to request permission to publish and received the following response: 'There's no point in printing it! Those who know about it know about it. Those who don't don't. If you write that two people died, then everyone will think there were a lot more casualties.' Adzhubei continues, 'The well-placed dolt was aware that many people deciphered what they read in the papers in their own way. If we wrote that a film was rubbish there would be queues outside the cinema to see it, and vice versa' (Adzhubei, 1988, 6, p.115).

48 For example from a Khrushchev speech published in *Izvestiya*, delivered on 15 March 1963: 'In agriculture, unfortunately, you come across other facts. You ask someone: do you understand agriculture, and he tells you: what do you mean do I understand, I've eaten potatoes. You see, once he's eaten potatoes, that means he thinks he's an expert in agriculture. [animation in auditorium].'

49 Just as Khrushchev's manner of speech was reflected in that of party and government officials accustomed to taking their lead from 'the top', so too might the speech of officials under Stalin have been to some extent modelled on his limited command of Russian. According to Trotsky (1968, pp.47–8): 'The boy [Stalin] studied Russian speech only in school, where again the majority of pupils were Georgians. The spirit of the Russian language, its free nature, its inherent rhythm, Joseph never acquired. Moreover he was called upon to study this foreign language, which was to take the place of his native tongue, in the stilted atmosphere of a theological school. He imbibed the turns of Russian speech together with the formulae of churchly scholasticism. He learned the speech itself, not as a natural and inseparable spiritual organ for the expression of his own feelings and thoughts, but as an artificial and external instrument for transmitting a foreign and hated mysticism. In later life he was even less able to intimate with or to assimilate the language, to use it precisely or to ennoble it, because he habitually used words to camouflage thought and feeling rather than to express them. Consequently, Russian always remained for him not only a language half-foreign and makeshift, but, far worse for his consciousness, conventional and strained.'

50 However, Khrushchev's language also reflected his Stalinist political training. Alongside the folksy speeches were messages to the public transmitted by means of slogans: 'The Present Generation of Soviet People shall Live under Communism!'; 'We shall

building his own 'personality cult', Khrushchev's public image was more that of a rumbustious and gregarious party *apparatchik* who liked his own way than a demigod in the Stalin mode.

Towards the end of his days in office, the government paper *Izvestiya*, and its editor, Adzhubei, had become so closely linked that the newspaper was not printed on the day when Khrushchev was ousted for fear it might come out against the new leadership.[51] Adzhubei was immediately sacked and a new editor put in place by the newly constituted leadership.[52]

The successful ousting of Khrushchev showed the strength of those who thought that Khrushchev's experiments in reform had gone far enough and, in the words of one of Khrushchev's speech-writers, wished for a return to the 'command-and-administrative system of the Stalin years' (Burlatskii, 1989b, p.34).[53] The tolerance at the top that permitted occasional periods of liberalism for the intelligentsia was never underpinned by any law so that Khrushchev's 'thaw' froze over as soon as the new conservative leadership took over. In other words, *Izvestiya* could be considered more liberal than *Pravda* so long as a leadership permitted it to print 'liberal' stories. Thus the press continued to bear the particular imprint of the political complexion of the day.

Overtake and Outstrip the USA in per capita Production of Meat, Milk and Butter!'

51   It was no accident that neither Adzhubei nor Satyukov, the editor of *Pravda*, were at their posts on the fateful day. Conservative hackles had been raised at the inordinate influence which Adzhubei exerted over Khrushchev. Undoubtedly, the non-press-related activities of Adzhubei and Satyukov, who both formed an almost permanent part of Khrushchev's entourage abroad, were deemed inappropriate by the plotters (see Tatu, 1969, p.407). Adzhubei's visit to West Germany as Khrushchev's personal representative may have precipitated both his and his father-in-law's downfall. Khrushchev himself is reported to have been dismayed that Adzhubei had 'put his foot in it' (*naboltal lishnego*) in telling the West Germans that, when Khrushchev saw how well-behaved the West Germans were, 'not a stone of the Berlin Wall would remain' (Sergei Khrushchev, 1991, p.136).

52   Adzhubei recalls one high party official's anger at *Izvestiya*, the government daily, getting out of hand: 'At the central committee plenary session dealing with the removal of Nikita Sergeevich [Khrushchev] from office [Mikhail Suslov] favoured me with a few words. "Just imagine", said Suslov, "I open *Izvestiya* in the morning and I don't know what's going to be printed in it"' (Adzhubei, 1988, 7, p.102). Adzhubei was also removed from the party central committee.

53   Elsewhere Burlatskii wrote: 'Now, on the basis of the experience of *glasnost'*, we can see with particular clarity how little was done to inform the people about the past, about real problems, about practical problems ...' (Burlatskii, 1989a, p.239).

The Brezhnev period reversed the trends barely set in motion by Khrushchev. The small gains made by the press under Khrushchev were, however, not wasted. The next phase in the liberalization of the press, initiated by Gorbachev, began where it had ended under Khrushchev and culminated in its liberation from the party, though not before the autumnal days of the Brezhnev leadership.

Brezhnev

If the Khrushchev era could be characterized as one of noise, then the hallmark of the period under Brezhnev was silence. Khrushchev's lively personality and style, which had set the tone during his period in office, were now replaced by Brezhnev's much more sombre, somewhat faceless persona. Just as Khrushchev's own colourful discourse had prompted journalists, ever sensitive to the direction the wind was blowing, to write in a more informal way, so the anonymous speech of Brezhnev[54] brought about a re-emergence of a more clichéd and stylistically cautious manner of writing. In some ways the Brezhnev epoch was a return to ways of thinking typical of the postwar Stalinist era. The language of the press accordingly reverted to a style reminiscent of the Stalin era. For the reader of the newspapers it is hardly an exaggeration to say that a consequence of the new leadership was the 'near universal indifference' (Tucker, 1987, p.133) to what was written in the press.

Brezhnev did not make any institutional or even important ideological changes to the functioning of the press, most of whose key Stalinist features had remained unchanged under Khrushchev. The

---

54 See Burlatskii, 1991, p.222: 'The style of Brezhnev's speeches sharply differed from Khrushchev's. Khrushchev usually gave a draft to his speech writers, which clearly set out what he thought and wanted, even if the literary style was chaotic. He carefully watched to see how scrupulously we had fulfilled his instructions and passed such expressions and jokes as "give it to them hot" and "we have one quarrel with the Americans on the question of land, who will bury whom", and so on.

'Brezhnev never dictated anything and did not formulate his own thoughts. The most one could expect of him were instructions to speak with greater warmth about women, youth, workers and so on. He did not like to read his speeches beforehand and preferred to hear them out loud. Usually he would gather the whole group of speech writers and one of them would read, while the others made comments and suggested corrections. His decisions were simple: he would listen carefully to everybody and go for the majority opinion; and of someone who was particularly stubborn in his objections, he would recommend that we meet him halfway and correct it.'

policy of not reporting major accidents or natural catastrophes, for example, was one area which the 'hare-brained' Khrushchev had left intact and which was carried over unchanged into the Brezhnev canon. Similarly, the press continued to present to the newspaper-reading public the façade of a monolithic, absolutely united party. An ominous harbinger, though one not unexpected given Khrushchev's own policies towards the press, was the failure of newspapers to show anything other than their normal aspect on 10 October 1964, the day Khrushchev was deposed.

Because of Khrushchev's insistence on not breaking with the tradition of keeping internal party conflict out of the papers, he had, by default, been responsible for his own ignorance of the imminence of the plot to unseat him.[55] He had thus deprived himself of the time to organize any resistance. Only seven months earlier, on the occasion of his 70th birthday, Khrushchev had been the object of extravagant praise, all dutifully published in the newspapers. To Western Kremlin-watchers, and probably most Soviet citizens outside the plotters themselves, nothing particularly unusual appeared in the press to suggest an impending coup. 'The façade was so smooth. How could anyone believe that the inside of the structure had fallen into such disrepair' (Tatu, 1969, p.386).

The role of the press in the 'structure' was, however, still functioning normally. Six days after the coup took place, Khrushchev had become a non-person. The newspapers played along with the lie printed in the official communiqué of 16 October, which stated that Khrushchev had resigned 'because of advancing age and continued deterioration of health' (*Pravda*, 16 October 1964).

The day after the newspaper communiqué, however, *Pravda* printed an editorial which made it clear to careful readers that the leader had in fact been removed. The whole event came to be known as the 'October Plenum', a euphemism typifying the style of the new leadership. When some criticism of Khrushchev did appear in the press the following year, while some referred to him as 'comrade Khrushchev', others simply as 'Khrushchev', Brezhnev, typically, managed to avoid uttering his name at all (Tatu, 1969, p.422).

55   An elaborate plot had been hatched to oust Khrushchev and replace him with Brezhnev, who was intended as a stop-gap (Burlatskii, 1989b, pp.36–7).

The custom of using bland words to stand for taboo subjects was not innovative, as Khrushchev's own euphemistic 'Cult of Personality' had shown. In the same way, the 1980–82 Polish crisis came to be known in the press as the 'Polish events'[56] (*pol'skie sobytiya*). To have called the crisis 'the Polish Revolution' would have been tantamount to admitting that a Soviet-style socialist system could collapse into chaos. For the Brezhnev leadership, whose main task was to re-establish order and stability after the Khrushchevian chaos, such an admission was inconceivable.

The unwillingness of the new collective leadership to air in public any embarrassing issues, especially where the past was concerned, was matched by a policy of smoothing over any differences within the party in economic matters. The Brezhnev leadership soon set about dismantling Khrushchev's administrative reorganizations, which they described as 'voluntarist' schemes and considered fraught with a potential both to destabilize the system and divide the party. Gradually the organizational innovations were undone and the centralized economic ministries, which had been dissolved, re-established.

Khrushchev's energetic attempts to reform the administrative structure and to make agriculture work within the collective system had antagonized the conservative wing of the party, thus committing the cardinal sin of dividing the party. After his fall, Brezhnev worked to neutralize conflicting points of view over economic and institutional reforms that persisted within the party. Internal party controversy was to be avoided at all costs.

Given Brezhnev's near obsession with stability, it was not surprising that the press was discouraged from airing different points of view. One of the few occasions when *Pravda* and *Izvestiya* disagreed relatively openly during the Brezhnev era took place soon after Khrushchev's removal and concerned the role of the party in Soviet life. *Izvestiya* took the side of the (pro-Kosygin) 'reformists', calling for flexible management structures based on the operation of the market and the laws of profit (*Izvestiya*, 21 May 1965, quoted in Tatu, 1969, pp.451–2), while *Pravda* supported the active role of the party within industry.

---

56 At the height of the Hungarian uprising in 1956, the daily back-page *Pravda* reports carried the innocuous headline 'The Situation in Hungary'.

The real argument, however, went much deeper: if the profit element were to enter industry, then the party would no longer be needed to provide ideological stimulation for the workers. No more would one read of hero-workers, shock brigades, productivity plans achieved before the deadline, and so on. The retention of the party apparatus within the factory meant a re-endorsement of the Stalinist philosophy of 'command supplemented by enthusiasm' (ibid., p.453). It transpired that the issue was never resolved satisfactorily. The resulting stalemate none the less meant that all through Brezhnev's period in office the press continued to report on essentially fictitious competitions between factories and enterprises. At a deeper level the entire affair was symptomatic of the policy of the new leadership to avoid friction, especially within the party apparatus.

As Brezhnev consolidated his power, innovative thinking was stymied for fear it might bestir the calm. The neutralizing of differences of opinion soon began to assume the status of policy. Gorbachev's term for Brezhnev's eighteen-year stint, the 'period of stagnation', is in large part appropriate. Accordingly, the sporadic permissiveness enjoyed by the 'creative intelligentsia', including journalists, under Khrushchev, was laid to rest as the Brezhnev leadership established itself. There was no need to change or amend the Constitution in order to put a stop to the publication in newspapers or books of what was now regarded as material damaging to the unity of the party and, consequently, the stability of the country. It was sufficient merely to change government policy regarding the degree to which the absence of any law guaranteeing the freedom of the media could be exploited.

Those who believed that a liberal attitude might still exist at the top were soon disabused. In a series of articles in *Pravda* entitled 'The party and the intelligentsia', Rumyantsev, the recently appointed editor, took a stand for free experimentation and 'the free multilateral development of the personality of each member of society' (*Pravda*, 22 February 1965, quoted in Tatu, 1969, p.468). Rumyantsev praised diversity in the arts, science and literature, and condemned the Stalinist and Khrushchevian approaches to the intelligentsia which, he said, both demanded obedience and differed only in degree of enforcement, not in essence (Levada and Sheinis, 1988, p.8). *Izvestiya*, under its newly-appointed editor, Stepakov,[57] riposted by publishing a violent article attacking young artists 'in search of sensationalism' who produced 'an ideological hotchpotch of items from the Vanity Fair of an alien bourgeois culture' (*Izvestiya*, 3 March 1965, quoted in Tatu, 1969, p.469). The tit-for-tat argument went on, though, significantly, neither openly criticized the other's position. Rumyantsev was soon removed from his post, an indication of the direction in which cultural policy was moving.

The arrest in September of the same year of the writers Sinyavskii and Daniel', who had published abroad under pseudonyms what was deemed anti-Soviet literature, provided confirmation that there was indeed a crackdown on the creative intelligentsia. Levada and Sheinis describe the period leading up to the trial, which was to take place in 1966, and the role of the press in prejudging the verdict, a Soviet instance of 'trial by media' (Levada and Sheinis, 1988, p.8):

> The trial of the arrested was preceded by a newspaper campaign in which the accused (not yet found guilty) were denounced as traitors. What their fictional characters said was ascribed to them. The satire in their works (quite mild by today's standards) was said to be in breach of an article in the criminal law. Reactions from [newspaper] readers unacquainted with the authors' works were printed which poured scorn on the authors themselves. The court sentenced Sinyavskii to seven, Daniel' to five years' incarceration in 'colonies of harsh regime'.

One of the major themes of the 23rd party congress, held the same year as the trial, was how writers had abused the freedom accorded to them under Khrushchev. Brezhnev spoke in a belittling manner of 'artistic hacks' who 'chose as their speciality the denigration of our system and the slandering of our heroic people'. *Novy mir* and *Yunost'*, both liberal journals seen as symbolic of the Khrushchevian cultural 'thaw', were branded 'cynical bearers of barren and *petit bourgeois* licentiousness'. Under the pretext of 'a struggle against the consequences of the personality cult' and 'appearing to be advocates of historical truth and authenticity', these publications were said to be 'flaunting themselves in front of the mirror of history [and] running down [the country]'. They were accused of 'generalizing from isolated

---

57 The appointment of Stepakov to the post of editor of *Izvestiya* was an attempt to reverse the perceived damage done to the newspaper by Adzhubei.

facts' and 'scouring the political life of the country in search of elements of so-called 'Stalinism''. As the Brezhnev leadership grew more secure, writers critical of the past were driven underground and began to appear in *samizdat* (ibid., p.9):

> The wave of *samizdat* grew more powerful. Reminiscences, historical research, works of literature, restricted access photocopies from journals and magazines, everything that had not managed to make its way into the press during the period of mild relaxation of the censorship system, went into *samizdat*. A. Akhmatova's 'Requiem', E. Ginzburg's 'Into the Whirlwind' (*Krutoi marshrut*), 'Discussion in Biology' by Zhores Medvedev and 'Let History Judge' by Roy Medvedev.

As well as pursuing a policy of 'de-Khrushchevization', Brezhnev set about partially rehabilitating Stalin[58] by means of placing vetoes on large areas relating to the unattractive sides of the dictator's career, while puffing up other selected areas in the hope of restoring some of his lost prestige. In particular, the media began to focus on Stalin's role in the war, 'the only moment of his biography which could be morally winning in society's eyes', while hushing up everything else (Burtin, 1987, p.196). The press stopped printing anti-Stalin stories, references to the Stalin-inspired purges appeared less and less, accusations against individual Stalinists were no longer published and there were no more spectacular rehabilitations, except of those discredited under Khrushchev. An article in *Pravda* of 26 February 1966, praising Brezhnev's description of the 'cultural commissar' Zhdanov as an 'outstanding patriot and political leader' (quoted in Tatu, 1969, pp.485–6), was evidence that the reassessment of the Stalin period was being sponsored from the top. Excessive criticism of the Stalin period had, in the view of Brezhnev and his supporters, damaged the party's public credibility. Also, many *apparatchiki* of the 1960s felt threatened by Khrushchev's de-Stalinization programme, having themselves come from the Stalinist system (ibid., p.475).

58 Medvedev summarizes the atmosphere of 'moderate Stalinism' under Brezhnev (1988, p.8): 'But was it really so bad in our country under Brezhnev? Were not the seventies the calmest decade in the history of the USSR? Yes, but this was the calm of stagnation, when problems were not solved, but set aside while the storm clouds continued to gather. The Soviet Union had moved away from the horrors of the Stalinist terror. On a smaller scale, however, unlawful repressions were also carried out during Brezhnev's time, thus preserving in society an atmosphere of "moderate" fear, supported by continuous efforts aimed at the rehabilitation of Stalin.'

The high point of the campaign to muzzle any criticism of the Stalin era had come earlier in the year on 30 January 1966 with an article in *Pravda* describing Khrushchev's expression to denote the Stalin era, 'the period of the cult of personality', as 'erroneous' and 'non-Marxist', effectively prohibiting its further use. Again, Tatu suggests that the order must have come from very high sources since the expression disappeared from public speech, and the press, overnight (ibid., p.484).

The first sign that the party wanted to build a personality cult around Brezhnev came when an article appeared magnifying his role in the war. In language which was to become one of the characteristics of the period, the new leader was referred to as 'the soul of the army'. Although a political officer, he was 'often to be seen amidst the valiant parachutists' (ibid., p.512). The ousting of Khrushchev had been hailed as a return to 'Leninist principles', while Brezhnev's own actions were often characterized as 'Leninist'. However, the campaign to build up Brezhnev into a popular hero never succeeded (Levada and Sheinis, 1988, p.9):

> Naturally, the attempt to create the illusion of unbroken succession of power and authority ('from Ilyich to Ilyich')[59] had no more chance of succeeding than the exaltation of the literary and military talents of a colourless leader.

By spring 1966 Brezhnev felt strong enough to bestow upon himself the high-sounding title 'general secretary', the first person to hold the title since Stalin. This was acknowledged as a return to 'Leninist principles', since Stalin had become general secretary[60] of the party during Lenin's lifetime. (Khrushchev had dropped the title 'general secretary' and was known as 'first secretary'.) Brezhnev's restoration of Stalinist nomenclature was an oblique favourable reassessment of the only previous bearer of the title. It also betrayed Brezhnev's love of grand titles.[61] The press carried out its role in exaggerating the merits of Brezhnev, though its efforts to glorify the general secretary in the collective psyche of the people failed. The Stalinist methods to build a

59 That is, (Vladimir) Ilyich (Lenin) to (Leonid) Ilyich (Brezhnev).
60 Brezhnev may have preferred the more exalted and military-sounding foreign borrowing *general'ny* rather than its unexotic, native doublet *obshchy*.
61 Towards the end of his life Brezhnev had been awarded more medals and orders than Stalin and Khrushchev put together (Medvedev, 1988, p.8).

personality cult might still be used, but they no longer worked (Medvedev, 1988, p.9):

> For almost fifteen years all our propaganda had made extraordinary efforts to
> create a Brezhnev cult – 'the great fighter for peace', 'the great Leninist', 'the
> great theoretician', etc. However the entire costly propagandistic machine was
> working in vain. The cult of Brezhnev in the end failed to enter either the
> conscious or the subconscious mind of the Soviet people, whose attitude to him
> was one of indifference, becoming in the final years of his life one of barely
> concealed disdain.

2. Before and After *Glasnost*'

State control of the press

Since 1917 the Soviet press had occupied a position in society different from that of its Western European or Northern American-style counterparts. The fundamental difference was that in the Soviet Union, although various newspapers were 'organs' of, normally, party or state bodies and were in fact owned by them,[1] all the print media were effectively and comprehensively controlled by the Communist Party of the Soviet Union (CPSU).[2] Under *glasnost*', especially in the period from 1987 to 1990, this control drifted away from the party. After the August 1991 *coup d'état* and the subsequent suspension of the party's activities by a Russian presidential decree, the CPSU lost even the nominal control over its own publications that it once enjoyed over the entire print media. Under the post-Soviet Yeltsin government, the formal independence of Russian newspapers from the dictates of politicians is threatened by economic hardship which leaves some newspapers vulnerable to manipulation by the new authorities.

In the Soviet period, the function of the press was to serve the party and the government by educating the public to support the policies of these two bodies (Hill and Frank, 1986, p.136). It is therefore not surprising that, even five years after the introduction of *glasnost*', much of the press was still administered, albeit less and less authoritatively, by a network of party and state bodies.

Party control over the national[3] press was exercised by a clutch of departments attached to the permanent secretariat of the CPSU central committee. Before the 1988 reorganization of the secretariat (*Irish Times*, 3 October 1988; *Guardian Weekly*, week ending 9 October

---

1 See Hill and Frank, 1986, p.155 on the party press, and p.126 on the *Komsomol* or 'Young Communist League' press.
2 According to *Pravda*'s London correspondent in 1992, with the paper since 1987 and previously with the government news agency, *TASS*, the 'whole press, not only *Pravda*, was in effect party press that followed party rules and orders' (Lutyi, 1992).
3 Referred to in Russian as 'central' (*tsentral'ny*).

1988), the secretary of the ideology department was the most important figure in determining general media policy, as well as being usually the second most important figure in the party's politburo after the general secretary. Other party bodies contributing to the formation of newspaper policy included the department of culture, the letters' department, the international department, the information department and the department of propaganda. All Soviet republics had their own department of propaganda analogous to and in close contact with the national department (Mickiewicz, 1984, pp.654–5).

The institutional cohesion achieved by the hierarchical national–republican structure was reinforced by the party *nomenklatura* system which ensured that the right people were appointed to important jobs in the media. At national, republican, regional and local level only those whose political background merited inclusion on party *nomenklatura* lists were eligible to fill the posts that appeared on the other party lists of important and influential jobs.

As a consequence of the *nomenklatura* system, according to one study of who ran the Soviet media, 'a minority have had actual experience working for a long time in the individual media they now control'. The same study found that there was a 50 per cent probability that those in charge of the media, including the press, would have attended special party higher education schools. It also concluded that many would have held positions in the party youth organization, the *Komsomol*, reflecting the importance attached to the newspaper's role in educating the country's youth and 'guiding them away from the counter-culture' (Mickiewicz, 1985, pp.40–41). As for the journalists themselves, over 80 per cent were party members (Afanas'ev, 1977, p.4; Hill and Frank, 1986, p.133).

So, for example, the entire editorial board of the main government newspaper, *Izvestiya*, was included in the list of political and administrative positions which the party central committee had responsibility for filling. The appointees figured in the list of approved and reliable people suitable for such positions. All newspaper editors as well as the directors of the two national news agencies, *TASS* and *Novosti*, were selected in the same way.

Each newspaper was as important as the party committee that appointed its editorial staff. Thus *Pravda*, *Izvestiya* and the national, all-Union publications were the most important and authoritative not only because they represented national state or party organizations and had a larger circulation than lower-ranking publications, but also because their editorial staff had been selected from the *nomenklatura* lists of the party central committee, the highest party committee in the country. The editors of *Pravda* and *Izvestiya* were also traditionally members of the party central committee.

At the lowest level of the newspaper hierarchy stood the wall-newspaper of the factory or institution (*stengazeta*). Mirroring the procedure of more important newspapers, the appropriate party committee, in this case the factory or other institution's primary party organization (PPO), in conjunction with the trade union committee, decided who was to become editor of the newspaper. The appointee was usually among 'the most active, politically mature and authoritative comrades', and likely to be a *Komsomol* or party member. Indeed, so institutionalized had the link between the party and the *stengazeta* become that the post of editor was sometimes considered one of the long-term duties allocated to a member of the PPO by the local party committee bureau, secretary or party meeting (Hill and Frank, 1986, p.135).

This power to make appointments to senior positions in the press at all levels was the most effective way of controlling what was written in the newspapers. It was more important for the day-to-day running of a newspaper than the more general control exercised by the ideology or other party bodies, or by the largely redundant censors. As in the rest of the world, the editor made decisions on what was to appear in a particular newspaper. An editor appointed with the blessing of the party made for a compliant 'politically correct' though usually unadventurous newspaper.[4] Editors of the major national papers were not usually journalists by profession.[5]

But this was not always the case. Because the appointment of editors to national newspapers was in the gift of the party, it was not surprising that the innovating party leader, Nikita Khrushchev,

---

4 See Mickiewicz, 1984, passim, for a study of who can be selected for the top posts in the Soviet media world. See also Hill, 1985, p.95, on similar selection criteria for deputies to the councils (soviets). See Hill and Frank, 1986, pp.88—9 on the *nomenklatura* system in general.
5 See below, Shcherbachenko, p.257.

appointed the relatively liberal Aleksei Adzhubei as editor of *Izvestiya*. Nor indeed was there anything extraordinary in the appointment of journalist Ivan Laptev[6] to the same post under the radical Gorbachev[7] leadership.

The appointment of a 'liberal' to a national newspaper did not in practice mean that republican or regional party bodies followed suit. Because of the hierarchical structure of the Soviet newspaper world and the consequent superiority of the national newspapers over the rest, what was innovative and liberal for *Pravda* or *Izvestiya* became an inflexible orthodoxy for newspapers occupying a lower position in the hierarchy.

Under Gorbachev, the Soviet press monolith began to break up. Because of the split in the leadership between those for and against *glasnost'*, different messages began to emerge from different elements from within the party. Thus, instead of fostering conformity of views, the party in effect was instrumental in polarizing the press into so-called 'left' and 'right' groupings. The 'left' group, headed by Gorbachev, began cautiously to sow the seeds of havoc in the becalmed world of the press inherited from the Brezhnev era. The securing of the appointment in 1986 of Yegor Yakovlev to the editorship of *Moskovskie novosti* (Cohen and vanden Heuval, 1989, p.206, Remnick, 1992, p.73)[8], until then an unimportant and very lightweight tourist giveaway, was on the surface an insignificant bringing in from

6 Elected chairman, 4 April 1990, of one of the two chambers of the Soviet congress of people's deputies (O'Clery, 1990).
7 Karpenko, in a personal communication (Karpenko, 1987), was pleased with the appointment of Ivan Laptev to the post of editor of *Izvestiya* and compared him favourably to the last editor under Brezhnev who was not even a journalist by profession. However, see below in this chapter, p.67, n.57, on the row in *Izvestiya* following the appointment of Laptev's successor, Yefimov, according to what had become by 1990 the increasingly unacceptable *nomenklatura* system.
8 That Yakovlev was a Gorbachev *protégé* is confirmed by Vitaly Tret'yakov, former deputy editor of *Moscow News*, from 1990 editor of *Nezavisimaya gazeta*: 'Without realizing it, Yegor was turning *Moscow News* into *Pravda*. Just as *Pravda* was the tribune of the old powers, he wanted *Moscow News* to be the tribune of the new power, the left-of-center position in the Politburo. When I became Yegor's deputy, I began to see how many visitors and calls there were from the Central Committee, and it was obvious that the paper was not operating independently. ... And then there was Gorbachev: we could not criticize him directly' (quoted in Remnick, 1992, pp.74–5). Yakovlev finally broke with Gorbachev in January 1991 after the activities of the Soviet army in Lithuania.

the cold of a quasi-casualty under Brezhnev of the Khrushchevian 'thaw'. In a short time, however, Yakovlev's weekly became the scourge of those opposing Gorbachev's idea on how the country should be reformed. It was clear to the newspaper's targets that Yakovlev was working to a pro-Gorbachev agenda.

Though all editorial policy was determined ultimately by the party under the Brezhnev regime and in the early stages of *glasnost'*, not all newspapers printed the same news, nor was all news presented in the same manner. Despite the impression of sameness created by the frequent obligation imposed on all important newspapers to publish simultaneously and *in extenso*, for example, important speeches of politburo members (see *Irish Times*, 18 July 1988), each newspaper had its own particular 'face', formed by its style of news presentation as well as the type of news to which it might give prominence.

The somewhat austere and formal mode of presentation in *Pravda*, for example, was commonly perceived as unattractive. This, however, was not always a result of bad writing by journalists. As the organ of the party central committee, *Pravda* was obliged to print large amounts of official party news composed in an anonymous and largely colourless style that had become *de rigueur* since the days of Stalin. This unattractive language, sometimes called *dubovy* (coarse, wooden, from *dub*, 'oak'),[9] permeated the entire newspaper.

Izvestiya, on the other hand, though only only rarely differing substantially in editorial policy from *Pravda*, had always tended to present its news in a more attractive manner, printing shorter articles written in a less hide-bound style. It approximated more to the Western understanding of how serious journalism ought to be written. Being the official government paper, *Izvestiya*, too, was obliged to give prominent and extensive coverage to the official 'news' of the country's Supreme Soviet.

Trud, the newspaper of the official trade unions (*profsoyuzy*), with a much larger circulation than both *Pravda* and *Izvestiya*,[10] was the Soviet Union's and, indeed, Europe's largest-selling daily. Its mass appeal rested not on particular coverage of industrial issues but on its

9 Yevgeny Langfank of *Moskovskie novosti*'s editorial board characterized *Pravda* in derogatory terms as *partiiny ofitsioz* (semi-official party organ) (*Moskovskie novosti*, 1988).
10 See Appendix below pp.260–62 for circulation figures.

generally 'pop' style and subject matter. In the words of one of its former journalists, *Trud* catered for the 'working class'.[11] It carried light stories about UFOs, folk medicine and the rediscovery of Atlantis (Walker, 1987). According to one former Soviet newspaper editor *'Trud* doesn't write about serious subjects. It has short articles, and lots of bits and pieces on this and that' (Alexander Baranov,[12] quoted in Steele, 1989). At the other end of the scale came *Literaturnaya gazeta*, a small-circulation newspaper catering for the Soviet intelligentsia (Murray, 1988a, p.28, and Roxburgh, 1987, p.93).

So, as in the West, different newspapers attracted groups of readers classified according to a combination of factors such as social and educational background, economic status, and so on. In addition, party members would subscribe to at least one party publication, usually *Pravda*.[13]

A readership survey carried out before *perestroika* (Mickiewicz, 1985, p.59) showed that 64 per cent of *Literaturnaya gazeta* readers had some university or other form of third-level education. The same survey found that 25 per cent of *Trud* readers had some higher education, a surprisingly high figure considering its low-brow status (see below, Shcherbachenko, p.243).[14] The Mickiewicz survey (1985, p.46) confirmed that *Izvestiya*, 47 per cent of whose readers had 'some college education', was, and remains, the 'thinking person's' paper, or, in the words of a senior *Izvestiya* journalist (Karpenko, 1987), the newspaper of the *'sredny intelligent'* (average member of the intelligentsia). Of *Pravda* readers, 39 per cent had some third-level education, placing it somewhere in between *Trud* and *Izvestiya*.

The coming to power of Mikhail Gorbachev and his support for more openness in the media was the first real challenge to the old

---

11 See below, Shcherbachenko, pp.243–4, for a fuller description of *Trud*. Shcher-bachenko added after the interview that *Trud* was directed at a very particular readership, giving the examples of the miners of the Kuzbass and Donbass and textile workers.

12 Former editor of the *Sotsialisticheskaya industriya*.

13 Karpenko (1987) said that *Pravda*'s circulation figures were boosted because of pressure on party members to subscribe.

14 The unexpectedly high percentage of *Trud* readers with a tertiary education, more than twice the national average, is consistent with the correlation found by Mickiewicz between the practice of newspaper reading and educational levels. A survey of female farm workers, among the poorest-educated group in the country, found that only one-third of the respondents said they read newspapers (Mickiewicz, 1985, p.59).

system that had come from the party itself since the days of Stalin. Khrushchev's flirtation with liberalism, though important for the time, amounted to superficial tinkering with the party's media control mechanisms. As was plain from the practically seamless transition to the obedient Brezhnev media, Khrushchev's liberalism had not changed the position of the press as little more than a reflection of the political complexion of the day.

As the first fruits of Gorbachev's *glasnost'* policy appeared in the press, dissonant voices from the top ranks of the party began to be heard. The public expression of internal disagreement in an organization whose byword had since the 1920s been internal unity[15] was a sign that Gorbachev's liberal media policy was going to be more than superficial.

Yegor Ligachev, the ideology secretary, in time emerged as the most influential opponent of *glasnost'*. Given the traditionally key role of the party ideology secretary in determining media policy, Ligachev's increasingly open hostility to *glasnost'* was in itself a minor revolution. Things had certainly changed from the Brezhnev days when the post was occupied by the sinister figure of Mikhail Suslov, the second most important individual in the party after the general secretary (Mickiewicz, 1984, p.642). Under Gorbachev the flowering of *glasnost'* in the media took place despite Ligachev, who remained ideology secretary until the October 1988 party reforms when Vadim Medvedev[16] became head of a newly-formed ideology

15 Selishchev named some of the common phrases often used in the press of the 1920s (and, as it transpired, long after) to describe party unity: *tverdoe, stabil'noe, zheleznoe, tverdokamennoe edinstvo* (firm, stable, iron, stony-hard unity), *monolitnaya partiya* (monolithic party).

16 Medvedev's appointment to this new position, which took place simultaneously with his promotion to full, voting membership of the politburo, was viewed initially by Moscow-based Western correspondents as one which would enhance the position of *glasnost'* (see, for example, Keller, 1988 and O'Clery, 1988a). However, later assessments of the balance of power within the party politburo placed Medvedev, along with Vladimir Kryuchkov, KGB chairman, somewhere in between the conservative camp, led by Ligachev, and the more pro-reform, Gorbachev camp (Cornwell, 1990a). Boris Yeltsin gave an insider's view of Medvedev, whose chief virtues, he said, were 'obedience and a total lack of new ideas'. Yeltsin continued (Yeltsin, 1990, p.124): 'As has become obvious, however, in today's stirring times these qualities are not enough to cope with that job. Nowadays, in the era of *glasnost'* and *perestroika*, even to defend the status quo of the party bureaucracy and the command system of running the economy, a different, more flexible and subtle mind is needed. When I was still first secre-

commission. In the period up to the 1988 reforms it was mainly Gorbachev himself who actively encouraged what he understood as *glasnost'* in the press. He showed what both opponents and sometimes supporters saw as an excessive interest in the press by arranging frequent meetings with its leading representatives[17] and was supported throughout by his party propaganda secretary and politburo colleague, Alexander Yakovlev,[18] widely perceived by the press as a liberal opposed to the conservative Ligachev. The editor of the country's main foreign affairs weekly magazine *Novoe vremya* (published in English as *New Times*) described the early days of *glasnost'* as a time of wait-and-see (see below, Pumpyanskii, p.205). Most editors who wanted to publish daring stories in the spirit of *glasnost'* refrained from doing so until they were certain that the Gorbachev–Yakovlev alliance was strong enough to prevent the aggressive anti-*glasnost'* rhetoric of Ligachev and his followers from becoming a reality that might result in straying editors being fired or worse.

Despite the increasing regularity with which *Moscow News* and *Ogonyok* in particular published challenging and mould-breaking stories, the old certainties and hierarchies were far from being a thing of the past. In 1987 *Pravda* was still recognized as being the most authoritative newspaper in the country and the one from which other newspapers took their lead (*S"ezd*, 1987, p.23)[19] or, as a senior *Izvestiya* journalist put it (see below, Karpenko, p.175):

---

tary of the Sverdlovsk provincial committee of the party, I remember Medvedev came to speak at Sverdlovsk and after half an hour, without even having finished his speech, he was obliged to leave the rostrum in disgrace. Even in those days his clichés, his grossly sententious remarks and his stale vocabulary that reeked of hack journalism were unbearable.' Shestakov of *TASS* also knew Medvedev before he became the chief ideologue and expressed a similar low opinion of his qualities as ideologue (see below, Shestakov, p.186).

17 See, for instance, Gorbachev's meeting (*Vstrecha*, 1987) with prominent members of the 'creative' unions (of cinema workers, the press and writers).

18 Known among the Moscow foreign press corps as 'Mr Glasnost' because of his supposed major contribution to the creation of the policy of *glasnost'*, Yakovlev was appointed head of a commission on international affairs in the October 1988 re-organization of the central committee.

19 According to political commentator A. Belyaev, bemoaning *Pravda*'s superior position in the hierarchy of the Soviet newspaper world, 'it can hardly be called contemporary when a mere article written by a *Pravda* journalist signals the end of debate on a matter'.

The general understanding among newspapers is that *Pravda* is, if you like, above everybody else. Nobody can criticize *Pravda*.

Ligachev's anti-*glasnost'* rhetoric was seized upon by senior party members opposed to reform and soon percolated down from the centre to the periphery of the country. One provincial journalist writing in the union of journalists' monthly magazine, *Zhurnalist*, complained that 'no sooner does *glasnost'* begin to manifest itself when all of a sudden, as if from beneath the earth or from the heavens, we get the appearance of influential persecutors of criticism' (D'yachenko, 1987, p.9). One such 'persecutor', referred to as 'not a minister but in rank not lower than a minister', faithfully imparted the Ligachev message to a meeting in Voronezh (ibid., p.8):

> Our newspapers are going to pieces, they have begun to publish so much critical material that the moment has come when it is necessary to talk about the good things which are becoming more and more common.

Becoming ever more vocal in his opposition to *glasnost'*, Ligachev became the standard-bearer for those in the party opposed to the direction in which *perestroika* was moving. In 1989 Ligachev, still a powerful figure, spoke out against 'excesses of *glasnost''*, warning that *perestroika* should be about 'creation, not negation'[20] (reported by *Irish Times*, 22 July 1989). The spectacle of Western politicians railing in public against the excesses and negativity of the press is commonplace and often seen as a sign of press independence from the legislature and executive. The appearance of a similar phenomenon in the Soviet Union showed that a section of the fourth estate was gaining some independence from the party, the country's effective executive and legislature.

Another sign that augured well for the Soviet press was the persistent public squabbling over its behaviour among prominent members of the party. This resulted in Soviet society, including the press, for the first time since the 1920s seeing a party divided and therefore fallible.

20 Ligachev was consistent in his appraisal of *glasnost'* and *perestroika*. On 23 March 1987, he told a group of radio journalists that 'we are for an honest and open look back, but we are decisively against falsification of our glorious past, against portrayals of our history as a chain of constant mistakes and disappointments. *Perestroika* is construction, and not negation.' (*Navstrechu 70-iyu letiyu*, 1987).

For a press still very much shackled to that party, it allowed the 'freedom' to choose between either the Gorbachev or the Ligachev party faction. It was thus as a result of internal party divisions that the Soviet press for the first time since Stalin began to represent more than one point of view.

Glasnost' allowed the press to publish what for the Soviet reading public at the time amounted to sensationalist scoops, be they concerned with the fate of politicians or writers who perished under Stalin or with contemporary revelations about the existence of prostitution and drug-addiction in the Soviet Union. The public appetite for sensation further sharpened the emerging distinction and antagonism between pro-*glasnost'* newspapers, whose circulation figures grew according to the degree to which they satisfied this appetite, and their anti-*glasnost'* counterparts, whose print-run fell sharply.

Circulation

The early *glasnost'* period saw the circulation of publications that embraced *glasnost'* (and printed good stories) increase in proportion to the intensity of the embrace. The weekly magazine *Ogonyok*, which stood at the vanguard of *glasnost'* in the early period, experienced nothing short of a meteoric rise in circulation.[21] The government daily *Izvestiya*, which was cautiously leaning in favour of the pro-*glasnost'* faction, experienced a correspondingly modest though significant rise in circulation.[22] Several other current affairs and literary publications also increased their print-run to cope with the greater demand from readers eager to read as much as they could about previously taboo subjects. During 1987, for example, the print-run of *Novy mir* had doubled, that of *Druzhba narodov* had increased fivefold while *Literaturnaya gazeta* had gained 700,000 new subscribers (*Vstrecha*, 1988, p.3). Such, indeed, was the hunger for news and information that it was not unusual at this period for one household to subscribe to several daily newspapers as well as weekly and monthly publications.

The existence until 1990 of government-imposed price controls on

21 The circulation figures for *Ogonyok* were: 1987: 561,415 (subscribers); the beginning of 1988: 1,313,349; 1989: 3,082,811; the beginning of 1990: 4,454,573 (*Ogonyok*, 1990). See also below, Korotich, p.182. For comparative figures relating to other publications in various years, see Appendix A.
22 See Appendix, pp.260–62. See also below, Karpenko, pp.172–3.

newsprint meant that subscribing to many publications was still affordable. The fall-off in circulation following the lifting of price controls was due however not only to the rise in the cover price of newspapers and magazines, but also to a fall-off in the public's appetite for news. Thus the party through its support of government price controls on the cost of newsprint, and therefore newspapers, had unwittingly been instrumental in satisfying the public hunger for the press when it was at its keenest. Since the press played a large part in the ultimate destruction of the party, it could be said that the party in this way enabled its own demise.

While the pro-*glasnost'* press saw their circulation rise, that of the conservative press fell. *Pravda*'s resistance to change in either direction led to a drop in its circulation which was catastrophic when set against the gains made by the pro-*glasnost'* press.[23] It is important to distinguish between publications such as *Pravda*, whose attitude to *glasnost'* was one of passive resistance, and those such as the albeit much smaller *Voenno-istoricheskii zhurnal* (Military–historical magazine), whose violently anti-Gorbachev and *perestroika* stance was as much a manifestation of *glasnost'* as that of 'progressive' publications such as *Ogonyok* or *Moskovskie novosti*. The rise in circulation of *Voenno-istoricheskii zhurnal* under its radical editor, General Viktor Filatov, was just as spectacular, if on a smaller scale, as that of his sworn enemies in the pro-Gorbachev camp.[24]

No longer strong enough to silence journalists or editors who published stories reflecting poorly on the now divided party, those opposed to *glasnost'*, perhaps with the tacit permission from the pro-*glasnost'* faction, worried that the whole business was getting out of hand, succeeded at least partially in limiting the damage caused by the more insolent publications. This was done by artificially reducing the state allocation of newsprint, and thus the print-run, of politically suspect publications. The size of a newspaper's allocation of newsprint

23 See Murray, 1989 and Yeltsin, 1990, p.94: 'At that time it had already become obvious that subscriptions to *Pravda* were falling off, despite the fact that every member of the Communist Party was obliged to take out a subscription to *Pravda*.' See also Roxburgh, 1987, p.93: '*Pravda* is virtually obligatory reading for Party members, and almost all subscribe to it rather than relying on finding it at kiosks.'

24 See below, Filatov, p.209. When Filatov became editor of the magazine in 1988 it had a circulation of 27,000. At the time of the interview (25 October 1990), it had 327,000 subscribers, according to Filatov.

at state prices was determined by *Goskompechat'*, formerly *Goskomizdat*, the state committee for publishing (Ivanov, 1988, p.253), which worked under the influence of the central committee secretary for propaganda (Mickiewicz, 1985, p.39). The economic consequences for a newspaper deprived of its state allocation of newsprint were grave. In 1990 newsprint bought within the official price quota system cost 200 roubles a tonne, while outside the official procurement system, according to one estimate, the same amount cost 8,000 roubles, or 40 times more than the state price (Simpson, 1991, p.21).

Thus the extremely popular weekly, *Moskovskie novosti*, could only afford to print a small number of copies for sale to non-subscribers, as well as being restricted to a limited print-run for the newspaper's Russian edition available for subscription within the Soviet Union. According to Yevgeny Langfank, a senior journalist at the paper, circulation had been limited because some members of the party central committee did not trust *Moskovskie novosti* (Murray 1988b, p.29). There was no doubt that more people would have bought the paper at the time if more had been on sale at newsstands. This was demonstrated by the quick sale of their extra print-run in November 1988.[25]

As the liberal press gained more and more independence from the party, including its pro-reform faction, the party role as press watchdog and ideological mentor reduced. By 1990 its ideological function, except possibly for party publications, had become a dead letter (Pumpyanskii below, pp.204–5). *Pravda*, for example, had by this time lost its pre-eminent position in the Soviet newspaper world. Opinions expressed in the party's main newspaper could now be challenged. This was no longer the 1930s, when a critical article in *Pravda* could mean 'several shootings', or the 1970s, when it meant 'several heart attacks' (Soloveichik, 1990, p.7). Nevertheless most key posts in the

---

25 The circulation figures of other newspapers would also have changed rapidly at this time if the number of copies available for retail sale at *Soyuzpechat'* shops (the state retail outlets for the press) had been determined by popular demand (see below, Grigoryants, pp.169–70). The Soviet tradition of selling newspapers mainly through subscription and thereby excluding casual purchase, while appropriate enough during the stable Brezhnev era, was certainly not suited to this period when sensations might appear unpredictably in any number of newspapers.

national media were still held by *nomenklatura* appointees not in favour of the liberal interpretation of press *glasnost'*. Even as late as 1990, the country's two national news agencies *TASS*[26] and *Novosti*[27] were still said by an employee and former employee, respectively, to be barred from criticizing their 'masters' (see below, Shestakov, p.187 and Zakharov, p.194). The director of *TASS* up to late 1990, Leonid Kravchenko,[28] according to one of his subordinates, was a member of the conservative, pro-Ligachev camp (see below, Shestakov, p.186). Though ownership of newspapers by official bodies was becoming less and less viable as these bodies began to fall under the ever-widening basilisk stare of *glasnost'*, it was still impossible at the end of 1990 even for the increasingly liberal government daily *Izvestiya* to be 'sharply critical of the central authorities' (see Zakharov, below, p.194).

Even after the introduction in August 1990 of a press law permitting the existence of independent, privately owned, publications, newspapers refrained from cutting their ties with official bodies for sound economic reasons. Newspapers that were registered with official bodies were still entitled to a greater allocation of state-subsidized paper from the state publishing committee. This meant that independent newspapers had to buy newsprint at the much more expensive non-subsidized price. This was an indirect method employed by the party–state apparatus to stymie *glasnost'*.

Thus in October 1990, two months before the newspaper *Nezavisimaya gazeta* began circulation, its deputy editor explained that his newspaper would have access to a certain amount of newsprint at the subsidized state price because it had been founded by an official body,

26 There is evidence that *TASS* foreign correspondents were appointed by the KGB, a state committee whose chairperson was normally a member of the party politburo (Dzhirkvelov, 1987, p.179): 'In the mid-70s, when I worked at *TASS*, I used to meet the General Director, Leonid Zamyatin, daily. I was present one day when he agreed by telephone to allow the *TASS* correspondent in Dublin, Yuri Ustimenko, to be replaced by a KGB officer, because the situation in Northern Ireland was of such interest to the KGB.'

27 The *Novosti* press agency changed its name from *Agenstvo pechati Novosti* (APN) (*Novosti* press agency) to *Informatsionnoe agenstvo Novosti* (IAN) (Information agency *Novosti*) in 27 July 1990 under a presidential decree, whereby the agency came under the control of Gorbachev's presidential council.

28 For an unflattering assessment of Kravchenko's career in the media, especially in his next job as head of the state broadcasting agency, *Gosteleradio*, see Petrovskaya, 1991.

the Moscow city council (see below, Zakharov, p.201).

A journalist from the largest selling Moscow daily, the sensational-ist and, for conservatives, politically suspect *Moskovskii komsomolets*, told this writer a month later (November 1990) that the journalists at the newspaper had decided in favour of maintaining a formal link with the Moscow city *Komsomol* organization to ensure that the paper would continue to be published in the party-owned presses of *Moskovskaya pravda*, and because the link with the *Komsomol* organi-zation gave the paper a better chance of receiving more newsprint at the state price.

Speaking in February 1991 the deputy minister for information of Boris Yeltsin's Russian government, Mikhail Fedotov, said that the price of newsprint sold to periodicals by the state depended on the political face of the newspaper, though his examples suggested that this arbitrary implementation of the law was more blatant in the provinces than outside Moscow, Leningrad and other large cities (Fedotov, 1991):

> There is an active economic blockade on the independent press. The ministry of communications places a huge burden on the mass media. When newspapers are published that are obedient to the local authorities, then the prices for paper and printing facilities are fairly 'loyal', but when it's a question of newspapers failing to pursue *the* political line, then the prices are raised accordingly. This is the situation in which the Lipetsk newspaper *Vybor* [Choice] finds itself. And it is by no means unique. Practically all similar newspapers have the same problems. The newspaper *Grazhdanskii mir* [Civic world], sold in the Northern Caucasus area, mainly in the Krasnodar' and Stavropol' areas, is in danger of closing down altogether. The local authorities have declared categorically that they will not allow them to be published on their territory. In the Oryol area the newspaper *Golos demokrata* [Voice of the democrat] only with immense dif-culty managed to register, but now they simply won't allow the paper inside the printing works.

Restricting access to printing presses was yet another method used by conservatives to keep the liberal press in line. Because the party owned about 90 per cent of the printing facilities in the country, most newspapers relied on the good will of the party to allow them to use their facilities. In the case of *Moskovskii komsomolets*, as we have seen, the threat was enough to convince the staff to retain the '*komsomolets*' in the newspaper's title. Another journalist from

Nezavisimaya gazeta, Andrei Poleshchuk, was worried that it would prove 'easy' to close down the newspaper because it was printed in a plant owned by *Izvestiya* (Womack, 1991), which, though liberal in tendency, was still the 'mouthpiece' of the conservative and party-dominated all-Union Supreme Soviet (see below, Zakharov, p.194).

Yet another 'damage limitation exercise' on the more outspoken publications was the reported refusal of the state-owned retail and distribution organization, *Soyuzpechat'*, either to accept subscriptions to independent newspapers or sell them at its kiosks (Tolz, 1990, p.6).

In accordance with the introduction of economic reform, state-imposed price controls on newsprint lessened during the course of 1991 while producers began to demand much higher prices for their product for their own economic reasons. The increase in the cost of newsprint throughout 1991 led to a rise in the cost of the cover price of newspapers, which, in tandem with a growing feeling among the public of *glasnost'* saturation, led to a fall-off in sales even among the pro-*glasnost'* newspapers. *Izvestiya*, for example, cost three copecks in 1990, and twelve in 1991, while *Trud* cost three copecks in 1990 and eight in 1991.

So, from the enactment in August 1990 of the press law until the August 1991 coup attempt the press enjoyed a sense of freedom, unparalleled since the 1917 revolution, tempered by the indirect attempts of the conservative establishment to prevent the dissemination of what it believed to be subversive views.

The situation after the August 1991 coup and into the Yeltsin era was one of increased economic hardship for the mass circulation newspapers. Periodical publications with circulations in millions, irrespective of political orientation, suffered the most because of the triple expense of buying newsprint and paying for printing and distribution. Mass circulation city newspapers, such as *Moskovskii komsomolets*, employed paper-boys to sell their newspapers on the streets, thus saving money on postal distribution costs. Mass circulation national newspapers, though, had to pay the postal service for delivery around the country and so incurred greater costs. The income raised from advertising did not compensate the newspapers for production, printing and distribution costs. In 1992–93 Russian newspapers found themselves in the unusual position where an increase in circulation meant economic problems. Two journalists[29] estimated that the optimum circulation for a newspaper was around 150,000. Higher sales would incur costs higher than the profits made from increased sales.

After the failure of the August 1991 coup and the suspension by Boris Yeltsin of the communist party, the ownership of that organization's publishing houses passed into the hands of the new Russian government. While the lifting of the state's monopoly on publishing removed the possibility of the new authorities to directly control what could and could not be printed, the overall increase in paper (the country's paper factories were still state-owned[30]), publishing and distribution costs brought many newspapers to the brink of bankruptcy.

Circulation figures for the main mass circulation newspapers plummeted during 1992 (see Appendix, pp.260–62). The whole subscription system ran into difficulty as inflation began to render subscriptions paid months in advance of the subscription period a fraction of their worth by even the beginning of that period. Newspapers that had to rely on the state postal service (ministry of communications) and the retail and distribution system (*Rospechat'*) were faced with enormous increases in costs.[31]

As costs spiralled, the country's main newspapers had the added difficulty of trying to survive in a marketplace without the prop of official subsidies which came as a result of being organs of state and party bodies of which most had rushed to divest themselves in the

29 See below, Shcherbachenko, p.245, and Ostal'skii, pp.219–19.
30 According to Boris Yeltsin's information minister at the time, Mikhail Poltoranin, Russia's three main paper and pulp combines, in Kondopoga, Balakhna and Solikamsk, were deliberately holding down output in order to keep prices high. A Yeltsin decree of February 1992 ordering the paper producers to sell 70 per cent of their produce at a fixed rate, was, according to Poltoranin, an 'administrative and economic' measure to 'prevent the diktat of the monopolists' (*Trud*, 1992).
31 McKay (1992, p.14), for example, reported the plight of *Komsomol'skaya pravda*, which began advertising and accepting subscriptions for 1992 in June 1991. Their price was based on a newsprint price of 1,500 roubles per tonne. By the end of 1991, however, the cost of newsprint had risen to 2,000 roubles rising in the course of January 1992 to 5,000 roubles. By February, the 40 copeck price charged for the paper at the newsstands was not covering production and distribution costs, which were raised by 500 per cent by the communications ministry in January 1992. According to the paper's deputy editor, Yadviga Yuferova, the 360 million roubles gained in subscription fees would finance *Komsomol'skaya pravda* until mid-April.

aftermath of the failed August 1991 coup (see Tolz, 1992, pp.4–5). Attempts to offset production and state distribution costs by selling advertising space and hawking newspapers on the streets did not resolve the crisis. Finally, in February 1992 the Yeltsin government responded to appeals to bail out the press. As well as offering loans to several newspapers, the president issued a decree obliging the paper factories to sell 70 per cent of their produce at a fixed rate. The decree also promised subsidies for the state retail distribution agency so that it might lower its charges to newspapers.

The offer of state loans to newspapers was seen by some as a means of exerting a political hold over the press (Brown, 1992, p.46), though Yeltsin's information minister, Mikhail Poltoranin, told a *Trud* journalist there would be 'no kind of pressure on the publications or any infringement of their freedom and independence' (*Trud*, 14 January 1992). Newspapers began to point to the comparatively generous loans to the government's own newspaper, *Rossiiskaya gazeta* (for example, Lutyi, 1992). The accusations from the liberal press that the government was trying to buy its compliance by offering loans were not entirely convincing since the government could have chosen not to offer any assistance, as indeed the then deputy minister for economic affairs, Yegor Gaidar, proposed (McKay, 1992, p.14).

Even with government loans, 1992 proved a very difficult year for the press. It took a government grant of 21 billion roubles to prevent the closure of the once mighty *Pravda*, which had ceased publication for three weeks in early March 1992. It resumed publication three times a week. That *Pravda* remained an anti-government newspaper further weakened the argument that the government aid was a subtle form of political blackmail, though the loans were distributed 'unequally ... and in an arbitrary way' (Wishnevsky, 1993, p.87). *Pravda*'s cash injection, however, did not secure its future. In September 1992 the paper was saved from bankruptcy when, in one of the most bizarre events in the post-Soviet media world, it was bought at the eleventh hour by a Greek Cypriot millionaire, Yannis Yannikos.[32] The paper's London correspondent reported that he had

---

32 *ITAR–TASS* reported that some Russian journalists believed that *Pravda* had been bought by the Greek Communist Party with money it had received from the CPSU (reported in Wishnevsky, 1993, p.87).

tried to ease the newspaper's financial pain by targeting potential advertisers 'with some limited success'. He continued (Lutyi, 1992):

> ...our man in Ashkhabad, in the republic of Turkmenistan, organized a small company, Pravda–Asia, and is trying to sell beautiful hand-woven carpets to the West. The head-office in Moscow is organising a cruise along the Volga for Western businessmen who could meet their Russian counterparts in the region.

By the end of 1992 most major Russian newspapers received government subsidies (except *Kommersant*) while still operating at a per-issue loss.

While both the executive and the legislature did attempt without particular success to gain some control over the post-Soviet media by means of imposing indirect political censorship (see below, pp.57–73 on censorship), it would be mistaken to suggest the existence of a concerted state campaign as the main cause of the dire economic situation of the new Russian press. Instead, the dismantling of the 'command' economy has seen the paper, chemical, printing, transport and distribution industries all set increased charges for their services. It was inevitable that the product at the end of this chain, the newspaper, should cost the consumer more. That newspaper editors should demand and then receive subsidies, and then complain that the subsidies were a form of government blackmail, shows that they still believed they should be supported by the state, as in the Soviet period, but ought not to be expected to show any loyalty to the state as the price for financial support. In other words, newspaper editors wanted the best of both worlds. When the official newspaper of the Russian legislature, *Rossiiskaya gazeta*, received a disproportionately large subsidy, the independent newspapers complained. The official argument against the political blackmail theory, that the government was helping newspapers such as *Sovetskaya Rossiya* and *Pravda*, which took a violently anti-Yeltsin line, seemed to fall on deaf ears. The relatively even-handed treatment of newspapers by the government, compared to the blatant attempts of its presidential and legislative components to gain control over national television, may have been a consequence of the decline in their importance compared to the broadcast media.[33] Even under Brezhnev the authorities were more liberal with the less influential media.[34]

Censorship

On 1 August 1990, the main body responsible for censoring the press, *Glavlit*, was formally abolished in accordance with a law on the press which became active on that date.[35] *Glavlit* was replaced by the short-lived 'Main Administration for the Protection of State Secrets in the Mass Media'[36] (*GUOT*), closed down in July 1991 following protests that it contravened the Law on the Press that had abolished its predecessor. Until 1 August 1990 all publications[37] legally had to be submitted for prior vetting to *Glavlit*. Following the 1990 press law, *Glavlit*'s main activity, preliminary censorship, became illegal.

The function of the censorship agency was to prevent the publication of forbidden material. Under the Brezhnev government the list of topics about which journalists could not write was very extensive.[38] As *glasnost'* threw more and more light on the previously hidden corners of Soviet life, the 'list' shortened, for, as we shall see, the real purpose of the censorship agency was more to protect the interests of the political establishment than to keep state secrets.[39]

The 'Main Administration for the Preservation of State Secrets in

33 According to a survey carried out by the *Zhurnalist* magazine, and quoted in Tolz (1992, p.6), television was the main source of information for 85 per cent of citizens of Russia, followed by radio, including Western radio broadcasts and in third place, newspapers.

34 Ilya Suslov, formerly a journalist with *Literaturnaya gazeta* (1989, pp.145–6), reported one instance which suggested that material considered too sensitive to be broadcast on television might find its way on to the printed page.

35 See below, pp.73–8, on the Law on the Press.

36 Called *GUOT* in Russian (*Glavnoe upravlenie po okhrane gosudarstvennykh tain*).

37 With the exception, according to Golovskoy (1985, p.25), of newspapers, journals and books published for export by the *Russkii yazyk* publishing house.

38 The list actually existed in a book known as the 'Talmud' or 'compendium' (Golovskoy, 1985, p.5; Kaiser, 1976, pp.224–5). A former member of the top editorial staff of the magazine *Znanie–sila*, Leonid Vladimirov (1989, p.17), referred to the 'Talmud' as the 'List of materials not for publication in the open press' (*Perechen' svedenii, nepodlezhashchikh opublikovaniyu v otkrytoi pechati*). The list which he saw in 1966 contained 'over 400 pages in rather small type'.

39 See Medvedev 1975, p.172: 'Preliminary censorship protects the *apparat* from criticism.'

58   *The Russian Press from Brezhnev to Yeltsin*

the Press', the official title for the government censorship agency, was known colloquially as *Glavlit*, an abbreviated acronym of 'Main Literary and Artistic Administration',[40] the name of the original censorship agency set up in 1922 by Lenin and Trotsky. Following organizational changes in the 1950s and 1960s, *Glavlit* emerged as the agency with overall control of a network of bodies responsible for censorship in the press, the theatre, cinema, radio and television, and of affairs concerning the military, the atomic industry and the space programme (Golovskoy, 1985, p.8). *Glavlit* had an elaborate internal structure[41] as well as a plethora of territorially subordinate divisions ranging from the republican level *Glavlit* to the municipal or regional branch. Officially, *Glavlit* was subordinate to the USSR Council of Ministers, though it worked closely with the main party propaganda and state security bodies, as well as practically any official organization that might come under the media spotlight.[42]

An interview in 1988 with the head of *Glavlit*, Vladimir Boldyrev,[43] provided a unique glimpse from the inside of the organization during what turned out to be its dying days (Parkhomovskii, 1988). The job of *Glavlit*, as Boldyrev saw it, was to prevent the press from

40 *Glavnoe upravlenie po okhrane gosudarstvennykh tajn v pechati*. In 1992 *Moskovskie novosti* (1992) published extracts from the *Glavlit* archive, including the orders to remove from circulation all works and references to Alexander Solzhenitsyn and Viktor Nekrasov.
41 According to Golovskoy (1985, p.9), it employed about 70,000 censors throughout the country.
42 According to Golovskoy (1985, p.9): 'Glavlit is subordinate both to the Secretary of Propaganda and the Department of Propaganda of the Central Committee of the Communist Party of the CPSU. It also has close ties with the KGB, and one of its deputy chiefs must be a KGB general. The Ministry of Internal Affairs (MVD), the Ministry of Foreign Affairs, the Central Committee of the Comsomol (CC VLKSM), the Ministry of Defence, and the Ministry of Education are also consulted.'
43 Boldyrev declared himself proud to have given 'the first interview by the head of *Glavlit* in the entire history of its existence'. Boldyrev was appointed in June 1986 by Gorbachev and, according to one report, 'ordered...to start implementing the new policy of glasnost' (Karacs, 1990). He replaced P. Romanov, who had been the director of the organization since 1966. Julia Wishnevsky (1990, p.7) noted an ironical sequel to the *Izvestiya* interview: '...Boldyrev claimed that most previously forbidden books had been removed from the closed shelves of Soviet libraries, and that the public had been given free access to these books. An attempt by *Knizhnoe obozrenie* to disprove Boldyrev's statement was censored.'

undermining or liquidating the socialist system of the USSR, from spreading war propaganda, from preaching racial or national exclusiveness, enmity or violence based on nationality or religion...from damaging the interests of [national] security, defence and public order, from publishing material incompatible with the requirements of public morality and the protection of health.

Under this loose definition, *Glavlit* had two main formal functions. The first, narrow function was to prevent the publication of the more obvious state secrets, such as the location of troops or weapons.[44] The second, broader function was 'ideological' and could be used to suppress the publication of almost any story.[45] Unlike a state secret, ideological error was often intangible, unpredictable and dependent ultimately on the politicial complexion of the government of the day.[46]

In another section of the same interview, Boldyrev revealed that 'state secrets' before *glasnost'* included industrial and transport accidents, facts and statistics on crime and illness and ecological problems. While *Glavlit* certainly did ensure that secrets such as these were never revealed on the pages of the press, reporting accidents, for example, could be stopped as a result of a telephone consultation with a ministry official, concerned about negative coverage (see above, p.29, n. 47).

Under Brezhnev the censors of the press operated a system of preliminary censorship, which meant that copy had to be vetted and passed by *Glavlit* before it could be published. Boldyrev argued the case for preliminary censorship in his interview, calling it a more efficient and less 'painful' method of safeguarding state secrets than 'subsequent' censorship, which, he said, was 'essentially punitive' and 'totally inapplicable' to newspapers, television and radio broadcasts. He decidedly did not favour confiscating, destroying or altering publications that had already been typeset and were ready for printing.

---

44 Alexander Yakovlev, the 'father of *glasnost'* said that 'censorship in the past and today is concerned only with the protection of military and state secrets'. He added, however, that powerful political figures had the power to frighten newspapers into not publishing anything too critical or outspoken (quoted in Cohen and vanden Heuval, 1989, p.45).

45 Conor O'Clery reported an interesting way around the censorship employed by one Western correspondent before *glasnost'*: 'Journalists had to work hard to find chinks in the Kremlin wall. One who succeeded was Harrison Salisbury, of the *New York Times*, who in post-war Moscow discovered a lot by bombarding the censor with speculative stories. Those which were "correct" got through' (O'Clery, 1991).

46 See below, Zakharov, pp.196–8, for one description of how censorship worked at the *Novosti* news agency.

According to one source, senior editorial staff were kept abreast of changes in the list of proscribed topics at meetings with the censor held 'two or three times a year' (see below, Zakharov, pp.196–7). Because journalists were forewarned in this way, in practice *Glavlit* served as but the last link in a chain of other informal but just as effective preliminary censors, starting with the journalist who wrote a story. In the same way as a journalist in the West would avoid writing anything potentially libellous, so the Soviet journalist would learn by experience to avoid writing about things that would never see the light of day.[47] After passing the perusal of the self-censor, the article would be vetted by the section editor (if the paper was large enough to have section editors) and then by the general news editor. Only then was the article passed on to the *Glavlit* representative, who, again, if the publication or news agency was large enough (see below, Shestakov p.190), worked from an office in the same building as the newspaper. The preliminary 'vetting' by the section and news editor was not, however, expressly carried out to check whether the author had stepped beyond the legal limits. It was primarily a journalistic, sub-editorial exercise that allowed for editorial or stylistic changes before typesetting. Naturally, the usually more experienced editorial staff would keep one eye open for anything trespassing the boundaries. As a result, by the time the final, edited copy reached the desk of the censor, there was little chance of it containing anything which fell into the category of forbidden topics, unless something new had been added to the list of proscribed topics.

One radio journalist, Leshchinskii, described the first, internal stage of censorship (*S"ezd*, 1987, p.23):

> When I sit down to write a story, I have in my head a 'censor' who says: my superiors won't authorize this, the editor will throw it out. Only with great difficulty can one fight this in oneself.

As Leshchinskii implied, journalists had become used to writing in a certain way before *glasnost'* changed the rules. Such was the structure of the press before *glasnost'* that there could be no question of an

---

47   The function of the self-censor in both cases is similar, though for the Soviet journalist, the list of proscribed topics was very extensive.

individual reporter writing in any other way, much less defying the censors. However, the tameness and docility of much of the press under Brezhnev was not entirely due to the heavy hand of the censor. History had turned the Soviet press into an obedient tool of the party, so much so that the face of the press presented to the public had become a reflection of the party. During the conservative and unadventurous Brezhnev era, editors were reluctant to encourage writing on subjects that were not safe. Neither would they rush to support writing on safe subjects in original ways. The rule of thumb was: if it has not been done before, then it was not to be done. Changes in the Soviet press came about only when authorized by the party at national level, as under Khrushchev and Gorbachev, or when pushed through with vigour by a brave editor, as happened occasionally under Brezhnev.

Mikhail Nenashev was one such editor under Brezhnev. According to a former colleague (see below, Shcherbachenko, pp.242–3), Nenashev, not a journalist by profession, made *Sovetskaya Rossiya* the most radical and innovative Soviet newspaper of the late 1970s by dint of courageous opposition to party pressures. Stylistic changes, such as introducing the paper's special correspondents to the readers, were among the most important innovations introduced under Nenashev and his deputy editor Chikin. That such changes were seen as daring initiatives is an indication of the general lack of freedom in the press during the period. Nenashev himself was frank about the constraints on journalism under Brezhnev and in the early days of the Gorbachev administration (1987, p.11):

> Courageous journalists are found where you have a courageous editor; the support of the editor is in proportion to the measure of trust and support which he enjoys in the party committee.

Party policy was beyond criticism, despite the rights of every party member to 'freely discuss ... in the party press[48] questions of policy and the practical activity of the party' (*Rules of CPSU*, 1987, p.7). On paper, members also had the right to criticize any body of the CPSU (ibid.).

---

48 *Pravda, Kommunist, Partiinaya zhizn', Politicheskoe samoobrazovanie* and *Agitator* were the five main party publications.

It was easier for newspapers to be innovative under a liberal leadership. One journalist, Krivopalov (1988), described an incident of change that took place during the Khrushchev era at *Komsomol'skaya pravda* in 1957, though, again, the change was one of style more than substance.

Krivopalov was working as duty-editor in the news-room when a *TASS*[49] communiqué that would have filled an entire newspaper page arrived on his desk. Customary practice had been to print *TASS* communiqués in full, often, moreover, on the page and position on the page indicated on the *TASS* notice. About to proceed, Krivopalov was interrupted by the editor, Khrushchev's son-in-law, Adzhubei, who looked at the official notice and expressed his indignation at having to devote so much space to it. He then told Krivopalov to reduce the length of the notice by five times before printing it. Krivopalov, with grave misgivings, did so. The edited résumé appeared and neither Adzhubei nor Krivopalov were fired, a probable outcome prevented only because of Adzhubei's favoured status at the time, according to Krivopalov. Subsequently, other papers followed suit and soon *TASS* began to shorten their communiqués. Neither *Glavlit* nor any law had existed forbidding Adzhubei from taking such an editorial decision, though by his boldness he had broken the *de facto* law that precedents were not broken.

A similar example of 'change' comes from the early days of *glasnost'* under Gorbachev and also concerns *TASS*. According to Karpenko (see below, p.174), *Izvestiya* broke new ground in journalistic practice when, instead of using *TASS* reports, the paper's own correspondents covered an official visit by Gorbachev to Leningrad in 1987. The breaking with, and setting of, a precedent passed over without any repercussions for the initiators.

As *glasnost'* in the media grew, the changes made by daring editors became much more significant than stylistic tinkerings. Instead of challenging the system by changing the way certain authorized topics were dealt with, journalists began writing about new topics. Nevertheless, in the absence of a clearly defined legal position, the press still operated under the same 'law' of precedent, as one of the most

---

49   The official Soviet government news agency.

innovative editors of the initial *glasnost'* period explained (Yakovlev, 1987):

> Let us say that previously our press never wrote about prostitutes. Now, however, let's say one paper has written about prostitution, soon it's a case of let's all write about this, and with a special passion.

In his 1988 interview Boldyrev estimated that the number of state secrets had been reduced 'by a third' and that the curtailing of the list 'is still in progress and will continue in the future'. Among the 'dozens' of previously closed subjects about which it became possible to write at this stage of *glasnost'* were the pseudo-state secrets mentioned above, such as accidents, crime and health statistics and ecological issues.

Glavlit's duties were certainly reduced with the advent of *glasnost'*. According to the editor of *Sotsialisticheskaya industriya*, Alexander Baranov, prior censorship went out soon after Gorbachev came in (Steele, 1989). Baranov said there was still a censor in charge of security matters but that he did not know where the man's office was nor how he got to see the material his newspaper was planning to publish. Journalists from other publications expressed similar views around this time. A *Moskovskie novosti* deputy editor, Yevgeny Langfank, said that there were 'no closed zones' and that *Glavlit* was 'fading away' (*Moskovskie novosti*, 1988). The editor of *Ogonyok*, Vitaly Korotich, told this writer that he had yet to come across any 'forbidden zones', though others disagreed.[50] Zagal'skii (1987), a journalist with *Literaturnaya gazeta,* said that over a three-month period none of his copy had been interfered with,[51] while the head of the Moscow bureau of *TASS* (see below, Shestakov, p.190) said he had not spoken to the *Glavlit* representatives in his building for 'three or four months'. Zakharov, of *Nezavisimaya gazeta*, said that by 1989 the censors 'hardly read anything' (see below, p.197).

Thus, even before its formal abolition in 1990, for many journalists

---

50 See Yeltsin, 1990, p.170, who contradicted this by accusing Korotich of going to the party central committee to receive permission to publish an interview which *Ogonyok* had done with Yeltsin. According to Yeltsin, 'the officials vetoed its publication in the magazine'.

51 There had been no *pridirki* or *privyazki* (fault finding, nit-picking), which implies that his copy had been examined before being pronounced acceptable.

Glavlit had under Gorbachev become largely a dead letter. However, some topics, such as the current activities of the organs of state security and Soviet intelligence organs, remained state secrets. As in all areas of the media, there was less freedom from both *Glavlit* and party or state interference in the provinces, where the newspapers were kept on such a short leash by local party or state officials that there was little need for *Glavlit*. National media guidelines were applied in the narrowest way in the provinces, often leading to the sort of prohibition mentioned by Nenashev (1987, p.12):

> Having received a letter, I travelled to one particular region of the country. There it was categorically forbidden to show spades, pitchforks and any form of manual labour on the television screens. There was a theoretical basis for this: if we show something, then that means we are propagandizing it. ... I assure you that this type of thing is a real problem for provincial journalists.

Newspapers belonging to party and state organs felt the direct effects of official censorship in their coverage of events in the Baltic republic of Lithuania in December 1990, when Soviet troops shot dead thirteen unarmed people and left 140 injured.[52] It was, however, the unmonitored coverage of the same event in the influential non-state or party-owned *Moskovskie novosti* that triggered off a series of protests at a January 1991 sitting of the Supreme Soviet of the Congress of People's Deputies. The protests, which almost culminated in a suspension of the Law on the Press, were led by President Gorbachev.

Responding to the events in Lithuania, the front page of *Moskovskie novosti* printed a photograph, taking up almost the entire page, captioned 'Bloody Sunday'. The photograph showed a man carrying a Lithuanian flag running away from a Soviet tank.[53] Nine full pages of

---

52 Two graphic examples of the January 1991 crackdown in the official media, attributed to the intervention of the head of *Gosteleradio*, Leonid Kravchenko, are cited in a *Financial Times* article (Boulton, 1991). A presenter of a television news programme, Tatyana Mitkova, showed the *Financial Times* journalist a report which she had intended to read to viewers in early January 1991 after Soviet troops had seized Lithuania's television and radio stations and killed 13 unarmed citizens. Most of the text was crossed out with an editor's pencil. For a fuller account of this instance of television political censorship, see also Salykova, 1991. The second example is from the government daily, *Izvestiya*, which deliberately published its own reports side by side with distorted *TASS* stories the day after the television tower killings.

53 This edition of *Moskovskie novosti* (16 January 1991) failed to arrive at the offices of

coverage on what the editorial referred to as 'the crime of the regime that does not want to go away' were framed in black as a mark of respect to the victims. Reacting angrily in the Supreme Soviet to this edition of *Moskovskie novosti,* and to news coverage in general on events in Vilnius, Gorbachev proposed the suspension of the Law on the Press. He particularly attacked the newspaper's editorial.[54]

In the face of objections from the floor, Gorbachev later withdrew his proposal when it was decided instead that the praesidium and a special parliamentary commission on *glasnost'* would be charged with 'working out measures for the provision of objectivity in the coverage of events occurring in the country in the press, television and radio'. The result of the ballot taken on whether the commission should be set up (275 deputies voted for, 32 against, 30 abstentions) was a sobering reminder that even though the country's legislators might vote for a liberal press law, when the chips were down they still believed that they ought to be able to control the mass media.

Extracts from the Supreme Soviet debate[55] show just how close the

---

foreign subscribers on that date and was not available at news-stands (*Irish Times,* 1991).

54 The editorial read: '...today, when the last hours of the regime are close, it has started a decisive fight. Economic reform is at a dead end, censorship in the press and television has returned. And even more important, war has been declared on the republics....To preserve the Union, there is no need to turn it into a fraternal cemetery.' It was signed by a group of prominent liberals, including the economist, Nikolai Shmelyov, the mayor of Moscow, Gavriil Popov, his deputy, Sergei Stankevich, the sociologist Tatyana Zaslavskaya, and the deputy editor of *Izvestiya,* Igor' Golembiovskii. The events in Lithuania marked a turning point for the editor of *Moskovskie novosti,* Yegor Yakovlev, who until then had been a Gorbachev supporter. For Gorbachev, the negative coverage of the Lithuanian events meant he could no longer count on the uncritical support of the newspaper that had become the voice of the Khrushchev-era intelligentsia.

55 The debate took place on 17 January 1991. The following is an extract:
   Gorbachev: I would support the proposal that the Supreme Soviet should take control of all television and radio stations, all newspapers, so that they contain all points of view. [*Agitation in chamber*] That's what I suggest. That's it. ... People here talk about the Law on the Press. We can now take the decision to suspend the Law on the Press. The Supreme Soviet will provide full objectivity. The Supreme Soviet is fully empowered to decide this question. ...
   Yuri Karyakin [deputy]: The president has suggested that it is necessary to suspend the Law on the Press, if only for a month. I would remind you that we already suspended this law in 1918 and it took over 70 years to restore the law.
   Gorbachev: Allow me to react to my old, no, not opponent, but friend. ... I suppose I'm not really insisting [on suspending the law]. People are saying here that the Law on

Supreme Soviet came to suspending the Law on the Press. They also show that almost six years after the introduction of *glasnost'*, its instigator, Gorbachev, was still prone to reflex actions more characteristic of his predecessors. One exchange with a Latvian deputy revealed the president's understanding of 'objectivity'. The deputy asked the president how he could justify his call for objectivity. Gorbachev responded by peppering him with questions. 'Do you think your press was working normally? Do you think it was objective?', Gorbachev asked him. When the deputy responded 'Yes' to each question, Gorbachev said: 'That's because it expressed your point of view!' (*Irish Times*, 1991).[56]

Izvestiya's publishing of its own reports side by side with pro-government *TASS* reports on the events on the Lithuanian situation was certainly disturbing for the owners of the paper, the Supreme Soviet, whose patience was stretched to breaking point when the signature of the paper's first deputy editor, Igor' Golembiovskii, appeared in the notorious signed editorial of the 'Bloody Sunday' issue of *Moskovskie novosti*. There followed an ultimately unsuccessful attempt to force Golembiovskii to take up a post as the paper's Madrid correspondent.[57]

---

the Press prevents us from doing that. I would only like to express my point of view that the television stations — the '*Vzglyad*' [Viewpoint] programme and the first channel — should express a plurality of views and opinions. And not only the first channel, but the second, third, fourth and fifth ones, too. One minute now, I'll complete my thought! Not only television stations, but each and every newspaper, including *Pravda, Moscow News*, which you subscribe to, which said that today's regime was a criminal one and that the president was a criminal. So what I'd like is not only this point of view, that is, the *Moscow News* point of view, but that another point of view should be reflected in *Moscow News*. That all newspapers should carry society's opinions, and not those of political groups, all the more so of narrow groups.

Karyakin: So, if I understand you correctly, you are withdrawing your proposal to suspend the Law on the Press?

Gorbachev: I am not proposing [its suspension]....

56 For a snapshot view of Gorbachev's opinions on press freedom, see a report of his meeting with Western press baron, Rupert Murdoch, at which Gorbachev is reported to have said: 'Our journalists suffocate in oxygen.' He also told Murdoch that he thought the Soviet press was 'less manageable' than the Western press (Knight, 1991).

57 An edited transcript of a meeting of *Izvestiya*'s editorial staff concerning Golembiovskii is found in *Moskovskie novosti* of 10 February 1991, pp.8–9. ('*Kak dogovorilis' Anatolii Ivanovich s Nikolaem Ivanovichem*'). The transcript, and an accompanying commentary, explains the background to the Golembiovskii case and the roles played in

Two of the main players in the Lithuanian affair, Igor' Golembiovskii and Yegor Yakovlev, were later to figure in the two main
attempts to reimpose political censorship in the post-Soviet, Yeltsin
era. The first serious attempt took place in early 1992 when the
speaker of the Russian parliament, Ruslan Khasbulatov, in language
similar to that used by Mikhail Gorbachev a year earlier, called for
parliament to introduce measures to ensure the 'objectivity' of the
press. As with Gorbachev, Khasbulatov understood 'objectivity' to
mean uncritical support for the Supreme Soviet and himself.

Khasbulatov had been particularly unhappy with the unflattering
coverage he had been receiving in *Izvestiya*, formerly the organ of the
praesidium of the USSR Supreme Soviet, edited by Golembiovskii
since the newspapers's staff, having re-registered, fired Nikolai
Yefimov, the government-appointed editor, and re-registered with the
Russian press ministry as an independent periodical.

In what, according to reports in the admittedly pro-'reformist' and
anti-Khasbulatov media, became an increasingly bitter personal battle
between Khasbulatov and *Izvestiya*, the parliamentary speaker, with
the backing of the Supreme Soviet, attempted by a series of legislative
and legal means to make the country's main pretender to being a paper
of record, once again an organ of the Supreme Soviet (see below,
Pumpyanskii, p.232).[58]

At the end of April 1992 a Supreme Soviet committee on the mass
media headed by the pro-Yeltsin (and anti-Khasbulatov) Vyacheslav
Bragin was charged with preparing a report for parliamentary hearings
in July. In late May, however, by dint of complicated political
manoeuvring, Khasbulatov had managed to replace Bragin's committee with a new group headed by one of his then allies, Nikolai Ryabov.
In July 1992, Ryabov's committee presented the Supreme Soviet with
two draft resolutions. The first recommended the formation of a
parliamentary 'oversight council' with powers to make 'obligatory
recommendations' to the ministry of press and information on the

---

the affair by the incumbent editor, Nikolai Yefimov, and his predecessor, Ivan Laptev.
The meeting ended with a call for Yefimov to resign. For a more recent and more
detailed account of the whole affair, see the article written in the September 1991 issue
of the Journalists' Union magazine, *Zhurnalist*, by Pavel Gutionov (Gutionov, 1991).

58 For a detailed account of the *Izvestiya*–Khasbulatov battle see Gambrell (1992). See
also Brown (1992).

regulation of press, radio and television. The second resolution proposed that the press ministry re-register *Izvestiya* as an official organ of the Russian Supreme Soviet, said to be the proper heir to the praesidium of the USSR Supreme Soviet. Ryabov's report also claimed that the current staff at *Izvestiya* had been making illegal use of government property for private gain.

The reaction of the pro-Yeltsin (liberal) press was swift and extreme. On 15 July an open letter objecting to the committee's draft resolutions from editors of the leading liberal newspapers appeared in *Izvestiya*. On the following day newspapers from Moscow and St Petersburg put out a second, emergency issue of *Obshchaya gazeta* (General Newspaper), the first issue of which had appeared in August 1991 in defiance of the decree issued by the leaders of the coup imposing strict censorship on the press. On the same day, President Yeltsin met twenty editors and expressed his support for them.

Discussion at the Supreme Soviet on 17 July of the proposal to create an 'oversight council' was postponed until the autumn parliamentary session. On the question of re-nationalizing *Izvestiya* as an organ of the Supreme Soviet, on which parliament was obliged to vote before 23 August (one year after the newspaper had registered), 134 deputies voted for re-registration, 23 against and 12 abstained. As a result of the vote, the ministry of press and information was ordered to re-register *Izvestiya*. Comparing the percentages of deputies voting for the re-registration of *Izvestiya* with those who voted for the setting up of a watchdog body over the press in Gorbachev's all-Union Supreme Soviet in January 1991, Khasbulatov could rightly claim that the Russian Supreme Soviet was the successor of its Soviet counterpart.[59]

On 18 July Yeltsin was reported to be 'deeply concerned' and reaffirmed his commitment to 'defend the mass media'. Press minister Mikhail Poltoranin condemned the vote. At the end of July, a group of deputies requested the constitutional court to rule on the legality of the parliament's decision. The court agreed to hear the case, and, at the deputies' request, ordered the Supreme Soviet to refrain from any action until it had reached its verdict.

Given the polarization in the post-Soviet press between those in

---

59 The percentages in 1991 were 81.6 for, 9.4 against, 8.9 abstained; for 1992: 79.2 for, 13.6 against, 7.1 abstained.

favour of Boris Yeltsin's reform programme and those, such as Ruslan Khasbulatov, in favour of a less radical programme, the president's support for *Izvestiya* was to be expected. Though independent, *Izvestiya* was firmly allied with the president (see below, Ostal'skii, p.217) and, applying a variety of self-censorship, rarely investigated thoroughly the hardships brought by reforms. In the largely bi-polar post-Soviet press, negative reporting on the effects of the 'reforms' could be seen as deserting to the opposing, Khasbulatov camp, which had its own newspapers, chiefly *Rossiiskaya gazeta*. In fact, the Supreme Soviet deputies were in large measure correct in their perception that *Izvestiya* and, as we shall see below, the Russian and CIS television channels supported Yeltsin and ignored all but the most extreme, and therefore less dangerous, anti-Yeltsin views.[60]

On 23 August Yeltsin attempted to outmanoeuvre Khasbulatov by ordering *Goskomimushchestvo*, the state property company, to review the question of securing ownership of the *Izvestiya* publishing company's property in the name of the company itself.[61] Two days later the Khasbulatov camp struck back when the Russian federal property fund, controlled by parliament, issued a directive claiming ownership of the *Izvestiya* publishing company. On 27 August, the state property committee, headed by a Yeltsin-man, A. Chubais, issued its own directive, combining all the assets of the former USSR-owned *Izvestiya* into one 'government newspaper-publishing complex', naming Igor' Golembiovskii as acting director.

Because the state directive issued by Chubais took precedence over that issued by the Russian parliament, *Izvestiya* managed to avoid becoming a parliamentary organ. In May 1993 the constitutional court found that parliament's attempts to renationalize *Izvestiya* were illegal,

---

60 See Martin, 1993a: 'Only extremist anti-Yeltsin propaganda is allowed while more democratically-oriented opposition is silenced, thus giving the impression that all opposition to the President and his advisers is confined to the lunatic fringe.' The 'lunatic fringe', according to Martin, were the newspapers *Pravda, Den'* and *Sovetskaya Rossiya*, and the '*600 sekund*' (600 seconds) television programme presented by Alexander Nevzorov.

61 Meanwhile, *Izvestiya*, acting as an independent company, had announced a joint business venture with the *Financial Times* to publish from October 1992 a weekly eight-page Russian-language business supplement for its 300,000 Moscow subscribers, to be printed on pink paper and called *Financial Izvestiya* (*Financial Times*, 1992).

though the newspaper continued to be the subject of rows between the president and the Supreme Soviet.

Izvestiya's close association with the Yeltsin camp did not bode well for the newspaper's long-term independence. A clear result of the ownership tussle was a growing tendentiousness in the newspaper's domestic political coverage that reached its apogee in its totally pro-Yeltsin (anti-Khasbulatov) reporting of the president's unconstitutional dissolution of the Supreme Soviet on 21 September 1993. *Izvestiya*'s position as the leading liberal newspaper leading up to and during this period was assumed by *Nezavisimaya gazeta*, whose frequently convoluted political reports at least aspired to objectivity. In the two days following the storming of the White House during which preliminary censorship was restored, censors, who went through copy at the printing presses, excised two articles from *Nezavisimaya gazeta* as well as one from *Segodnya*, both belonging to the liberal camp. The official explanation for the reintroduction of censorship, which had been abolished along with *Glavlit* with the passing of the August 1990 press law, was the state of emergency declared by the president (Murray, 1993). More serious than the temporary reintroduction of preliminary censorship was the presidential decree closing down, in the days following the storming of the parliament, the ten most important opposition publications, including *Sovetskaya Rossiya*, *Pravda*[62] and *Den'*. By his draconian measures, Boris Yeltsin demonstrated that his understanding of freedom of the press was freedom for the pro-Yeltsin press. The decision to close certain newspapers was also a clear indication of the extent to which the post-Soviet press had polarized. It was ironic that Boris Yeltsin, representing the democratic forces in society, displayed the same instincts as the organizers of the August 1991 coup attempt. Having

62 On 14 October 1993 the Russian press and information ministry announced that the banning during the state of emergency of a number of the country's leading opposition newspapers was to be continued (Martin, 1993b). *Pravda* and *Sovetskaya Rossiya*, the two most prominent opposition newspapers, were given permission to republish only on the extraordinary condition that they re-register under different names, replace their present editors, and follow a different, presumably pro-Yeltsin, political line. The banned newspapers were accused by the ministry of 'substantially assisting in the de-stabilization of the situation during the mass disturbances in Moscow in late September and early October this year, and in the organization of the revolt'.

declared a state of emergency, both banned the newspapers that were inimical to their interests.

Another serious attempt to impose political censorship on the post-Soviet media did not initially concern the press in a direct manner, though its conclusion had implications for the entire media, including the press. During the summer of 1992, when the fate of *Izvestiya* was being decided, right-wing demonstrators protested for almost a month outside the country's television headquarters at Ostankino in Moscow. The director of the national television, the former editor of *Moskovskie novosti*, Yegor Yakovlev, was accused by the extremist leaders of the protest of ignoring the voice of the non-Yeltsin opposition. Coverage of the protest by the liberal press and a good portion, though not all, of the Western media tended to emphasize the clearly unsavoury personalities of some of the protest leaders, including the right-wing deputy Sergei Baburin and the editor of the fascist newspaper *Den'*, Alexander Prokhanov. The demands for airtime to be given to other than those who supported the president were not without foundation and found support among anti-Yeltsin deputies in the Supreme Soviet. Ryabov's July 1992 draft resolution recommending the setting up of an oversight committee was in part a response to what deputies saw as Yeltsin's monopolization of the country's most influential organs of the mass media, the first television channel and *Izvestiya*.

A meeting between the protestors and the director of central television, Yegor Yakovlev, the press minister, Mikhail Poltoranin, and the director of Russian television, Oleg Poptsov, led to an agreement guaranteeing the 'patriotic opposition' an amount of free airtime.

As editor of *Moskovskie novosti*, Yakovlev had been accused by one of his deputies of turning the newspaper into an uncritical organ supporting Gorbachev against criticism from both the extreme left and right (Remnick, 1992, pp.74–5). When Yakovlev finally deserted the Gorbachev camp after the January 1991 events in Lithuania, the paper lurched further to the left and gradually came to support the policies of Gorbachev's enemy, Boris Yeltsin. Yakovlev's somewhat dictatorial personality combined with his proven tendency to practice political loyalty made him a serious candidate for the post of director of state television following the collapse of the August 1991 coup and the sacking of Leonid Kravchenko. With Yakovlev in charge, Yeltsin could hope to have the support of what was easily the most powerful medium in the country, increasingly so as the rocketing price of newspapers meant that more and more people relied more and more heavily on television as a source of news.

Yakovlev, however, was sacked in November 1992 for not showing enough loyalty to Boris Yeltsin. Another Yeltsin placeman, press minister Mikhail Poltoranin, who was said to be involved in Yakovlev's sacking, allegedly urged Ostankino news editors, a day before Yakovlev was told to leave, to provide a more positive coverage of the president in his battles with the parliament (Wishnevsky, 1993, p.90). The subsequent change of personnel showed that the president, like his opponents in the Supreme Soviet, was more interested in securing political control of the media than defending its right to 'objectivity'.

Yakovlev was replaced by Vyacheslav Bragin, the deputy who had led the short-lived pro-Yeltsin parliamentary committee on the media. That neither Bragin nor his newly-appointed colleague, Kirill Ignatev, in charge of a new department set up within Ostankino to decide upon major personnel and administration questions, had any experience as journalists augured ill for the future of the national television station (Wishnevsky, 1993, p.90). Under the Soviet dispensation, the appointment of a politician to a top journalistic post flagged the leadership's desire to exert tighter control over the medium. By contrast, during liberal periods in the Soviet period, as under Khrushchev and Gorbachev, the appointment of journalists to leading positions signalled that the media could operate more freely.

Within two weeks of the new appointments the deputy chairperson of Ostankino, Igor' Malashenko, resigned, complaining that radical, pro-Yeltsin deputies had begun to visit the studios and lecture producers about how to make programmes in support of the Yeltsin camp. In particular, Malashenko claimed, Bragin had ordered Ostankino to ensure 'at all costs' the victory of Yeltsin at the April 1993 referendum.[63] The setting up in the following month of a Federal Information Centre headed by Potoranin and charged with supervising the work of the broadcast media, principally the CIS channel

---

63 See Wishnevsky, 1993, p.90. Wishnevsky gives examples of television's pro-Yeltsin bias in the months leading up to the referendum, which Yeltsin won.

Ostankino and the Russian Federation channel *Rossiya*, and the state-owned news agencies, *ITAR–TASS*[64] and *RIA*, was seen by many journalists as an attempt to reintroduce Soviet-style political control over the media.

The various attempts by both presidency and the legislature to use the media, including the press, as their own propaganda weapon show that changes in legislation have not been, nor, indeed, in such a short time could be expected to be, reflected in the mentality of politicians. The Soviet tradition of politicians having total control over the media combined with the innate desire of politicians everywhere to receive favourable media coverage combine to create a situation in which the continued existence of a free press is far from certain. That the post-Soviet press is itself highly politicized has not disabused politicians of their conviction that the press is in the fullest sense a participant in, rather than chronicler of, the 'news'.

Law on the Press
The Soviet Law on the Press which came into effect in August 1990 made the freedom of the press for the first time since the 1917 revolution a legal right rather than a privilege to be granted and taken away as seen fit by the all-powerful party. Although the liberal press complained that the law had not tackled the party's economic domination of the newspaper industry, it nevertheless opened up the Soviet newspaper world to hundreds of new, non-party or state-affiliated newspapers and publishers, thus laying the foundations for an independent press. Following the collapse of the Soviet Union, the Russian parliament passed its own law on the press in February 1992 which carried the liberal provisions of its Soviet parent even further.

Originally adumbrated in September 1986 (Wedgwood Benn, 1987, p.267), 1988 saw the publication of a long-awaited draft bill on the press which, *inter alia*, provided that only legally constituted and registered 'social associations' would be able to publish regularly.

---

64 During the September 1993 political emergency in the country following Yeltsin's decree dissolving the supreme soviet, an employee of *ITAR–TASS* informed this author that political reporters were told not to cover stories that were unfavourable to the President. Despite objections from the journalists, *ITAR–TASS* copy during the period reverted to Soviet-style biased reporting.

Criminal charges could follow any violations. The adoption of the bill in this form would have meant in fact a curtailment of freedom for the large numbers of informal groups which were at the time publishing bulletins more or less regularly all over the country and, because of the absence of any prohibiting law, were not liable to any penalty. Under pressure from editorial boards, to whom the draft bill had been submitted for consideration, the party decided that the bill would have to be redrafted. On the basis of another draft bill, published in December 1989 (*Proekt*, 1989), the Soviet Law on the Press and other Means of Mass Communication was finally adopted on 12 June 1990.

Under the new law, which became active on 1 August 1990, interference with the professional activities of journalists and even failure by officials to supply them with the information they needed, was deemed a criminal offence. As long as a newspaper did not advocate armed revolution, religious prejudice or racial persecution and did not reveal any state secrets, anyone was entitled to set up a newspaper, magazine or news service by registering with the authorities.[65] The first newspaper to register, *Izvestiya* (Cornwell 1990b), was, ironically, to become the object of a fiercely fought battle over its re-registration a year later as an independent newspaper after the August 1991 coup.

The adoption of the June 1990 press law was a victory for the liberals. This was evident in the law's provisions to abolish the censorship agency, *Glavlit*, and to permit individuals and parties other than the CPSU to set up their own newspapers or other media.[66]

The prior removal of two hitherto fundamental pieces of Soviet legislation was a prelude to and prerequisite for the press law. The first was the article in the criminal code on anti-Soviet agitation and propaganda, removed in July 1989 and replaced with a general article outlawing incitement to state subversion. This was followed in February 1990 by the removal of the section in Article 6 of the Soviet Constitution guaranteeing the preeminence of the party in all Soviet affairs. For the press, this meant that the party could now only control their own publications, and not those of non-party organizations, including those belonging to the state and new parties, which, with the

---

65 *Goskompechat'*, formerly *Goskomizdat*.
66 Whether or not to allow the individual to own a newspaper was, according to Shestakov (see below, pp.187–8), a contentious issue arising from the 1989 draft.

amendment of Article 6, now had the right to exist. Crucially, the amendment to Article 6 rang the death knell for the *nomenklatura* appointment system in the press (and elsewhere). In the meantime, Gorbachev had actively facilitated the publishing of the December 1989 draft law on the press that had foreseen the removal of the party's monopoly on the press. It was in this sense a stalking horse for the February 1990 removal of the amendment to Article 6. In a broader context the press law was an important part of Gorbachev's evident scheme to broaden the political and institutional base of society at the expense, perhaps unintentionally, of the party. By the time the Supreme Soviet had adopted the press law in June, non-party newspapers, such as the government daily *Izvestiya*, the radical *Moskovskie novosti* or the irreverent new arrival *Kommersant*, were already publishing materials critical of communist politicians and even of communism itself. While the law may have appeared, therefore, to be a formality, its great strength was to enshrine in legislation the right of the press to take issue with the party. This was no mean achievement for the reformists, given the ease with which the Brezhnev regime had been able to reverse the small progress made by the press under Khrushchev's 'thaw' without reference to any law or article in the Constitution.

As far as the liberals were concerned the great weakness of the 1990 law was its failure to address the issue of the state's monopoly on paper production and allocation and the party's near monopoly on publishing facilities. This meant that the party–state apparatus could still withhold newsprint from, or refuse to publish, non-party publications, especially if they were thought to be excessively critical of the party or government. It was, however, hardly in the scope of a law on the press to solve the burning political issue of party property[67] or, indeed, that of the disadvantages of state ownership in relation to the press. Nevertheless, representatives of the liberal press found fault with the law itself. For instance, a *Moskovskie novosti* journalist (Kabakov, 1990), commenting on the retention of the state monopoly

---

67   The question of privatizing or nationalizing the party's printing empire was of great concern to the organization not only politically, but, perhaps at this stage more importantly, financially. Apart from members' dues, most of the party's income came from publishing (Miller, 1993, p.90).

on the distribution of paper, compared the new law to the eman-
cipation of the serfs in 1861 when, he said, 'the serfs were liberated,
but they had been given freedom without land'. Summing up the
attitude of the anti-party section of the press world to the law, the
Russian press minister, Mikhail Poltoranin, said (Dobbs, 1990):
'Politically, it opens up great possibilities for the Soviet press, but
economically, the possibilities are limited.'

Liberals also complained that the authorities, especially in the
provinces, were refusing to register newspapers on political grounds.
This was, however, not the fault of the law, but of those enforcing it.
By February 1991, for example, the Russian deputy minister for
information, Mikhail Fedotov (1991), was able to point to such abuse
of the registration procedure:

> Powerful pressure is being exerted on local soviets and regional newspapers –
> previously published as organs of the soviets – to make them re-register as
> party–soviet organs, primarily as party organs. This process is especially active
> in the Krasnoyar' area, in Yakutiya and a lot of other areas. In Rostov-on-Don
> the regional Union of Journalists' organization announced that several party
> committees were interfering in newspapers and publications which were, as
> before, being censored.

Generally, though, the law was welcomed by liberal journalists (see,
for example, below, Zakharov, p.196 and the president of the Union of
Journalists, Sagalaev, in Vevers 1991b). Despite all, the law succeeded
in bringing in from a state of legal limbo the hundreds of hitherto
'unofficial' publications,[68] as well as paving the way for a veritable
explosion of new publications on to the market. *Kommersant*, for
example, had been successfully running as an independent newspaper
since the beginning of 1990, while the non-party or state *Nezavisimaya
gazeta* was set up in December 1990 according to the provisions of the
press law. The periodicals of fourteen new political parties were
among the 400 publications that registered during August and
September 1990 (Tolz, 1990, p.4), while about half of the approximately 8,000 newspapers and journals that had registered by spring
1991 were new (White, 1992, p.102).

Another consequence of the law was the opportunity it gave to

---

68 See Tolz, 1991a, June, p.15: 'An estimated 1,000 unofficial periodicals are now published in Russian alone.'

mostly liberal, pro-*glasnost'* publications to rid themselves of the bodies of which they were the 'organs'. *Ogonyok, Argumenty i fakty, Literaturnaya gazeta* and *Moskovskie novosti*, for example, managed to disaffiliate themselves from their founders (the *Pravda* publishing house, the *Znanie* society and the Soviet Writers' Union respectively) and register as independent publications, with their own working collectives becoming 'founders'.[69]

The function of the press in Soviet society changed in essence after the adoption of the press law. No longer could Gorbachev's policy of *glasnost'* be described as a public relations exercise for the party, nor could it be said any longer to be a safety valve for a society in a time of great upheaval nor even a weapon used by politicians both for and against reform with which to strike their opponents. It still served some of these functions, but, most importantly, the 1990 press law laid the foundations for the creation of a truly independent and free fourth estate.

That the post-Soviet, Russian Law on the Press, passed in February 1992, was based on the Soviet law was a tribute to its original drafters. The first version of a Russian press law, adopted in December 1991, was however less liberal than its Soviet predecessor.[70] As a result of liberal opposition to this initial draft, however, the legislation which finally came into force from 6 February 1992 was more liberal than the Soviet law, particularly in its provisions blocking the formation of monopolies and making prior censorship impossible.[71]

In sum, the Soviet and Russian press laws were among the most important pieces of legislation to come from the entire Gorbachev–Yeltsin period, doing more than any other single measure to ensure the incipient freedom of the press from political interference. The various attempts by the new post-Soviet rivals, the president and his parliament, each to gain some control over the press, disturbing as it appeared, was of a different nature to the party stranglehold on all

---

69 See Tolz, 1990, p.4, on the rights of a paper's founder (*uchreditel'*) to close down a periodical and dismiss its editor if unhappy with its editorial line.

70 See White, 1992, p.103. The first draft of the law, for example, obliged journalists to reveal their sources, an unwelcome departure from the Soviet law for journalists.

71 See Tolz, 1992, pp.7–8, 'by deliberately omitting any provision for funding censorship agencies, [the law] makes preliminary censorship by the government not only illegal [as provided for by the Soviet law], but impossible.'

forms of mass communications that was facilitated by the absence of any law protecting press freedom. The economic blackmail of the media by the party in the Soviet period, and by both the legislature and executive branches of the Russian state in the post-Soviet era, are for the press as much as anything an unhappy by-product of the trauma of switching from a planned to a market economy.

Union of Journalists
Even before the dissolution of the Soviet Union after August 1991 the old Soviet Union of Journalists had undergone so many radical changes in the period of *glasnost'* as to make it a body only distantly related to its pre-*glasnost'* namesake.

Prior to the Gorbachev reforms the main function of the union of Journalists of the USSR (*Soyuz zhurnalistov SSSR*) was the material concern of its members. Its function as party ideological watchdog and mentor was less evident in the domesticated press world of the Brezhnev era. As society and the press became more politicized the political complexion of the union's leadership was thrown into relief. Being part of the constellation of public bodies dominated by the party, it was unsurprising that the ideological currents emanating from the union's leadership should reflect the mood of the party. The president of the union had, as a rule, been the incumbent editor of *Pravda*, and, thus, a member and appointee of the party central committee. As it happened, that leadership at the time of transition reflected the conservative, basically anti-*glasnost'* views of the Ligachev camp. By the time the old union disbanded itself at its February 1991 congress to become the 'Union of Journalists of the USSR on a confederative basis' (*Soyuz zhurnalistov SSSR na konfederativnoi osnove*), it had already undergone a major 'reconstruction'.

The union's stability and fealty to the party inevitably came under pressure as part of the press itself changed from party servant to party assailant. It was also natural that most of the union leadership, selected according to the *nomenklatura* system on the basis of political reliability, should come under attack from members of the rank and file who, from a party perspective, supported an excessively radical and 'irresponsible' interpretation of *glasnost'*.

The fault-lines in the organization became very clear at its 1988 national congress when a keynote speech by one of the union's deputy presidents and editor of the conservative *Sovetskaya Rossiya*[72] newspaper, Valentin Chikin (Chikin, 1988), drew a hostile response from several members speaking from the floor (Plenary session, 1988). The congress showed up internal problems between some of the members and the union's leadership, the vulnerability of the regional press to party pressure, the difficult relationship between the national and regional press and the opposition of the party to *glasnost'* in the media.

Chikin's speech was criticized for paying lip-service to *glasnost'* and *perestroika* and bearing the hallmarks of conservatism. Aligning himself with the Ligachev camp, Chikin had spoken in favour of media criticism as long as it was 'ideologically progressive and spiritually rich in content' and contained 'constructiveness'.[73] He spoke against those newspapers that were 'sowing nihilistic moods' among the readers, and whose 'heads had turned' in their attempts to provide the readers with sensational stories.

One member, N. Cherkezishvili, editor of the Georgian newspaper *Zarya Vostoka* (Dawn of the East), criticized Chikin's speech for talking about 'negative phenomena' without giving 'concrete examples', instead relying on 'broad generalities' (ibid.). An *Izvestiya* journalist, V. Matveev, took issue with Chikin's positive assessment of the extent to which the government's main news agency, *TASS*, had reconstructed itself.[74] Matveev himself had not noticed any changes at all in the foreign coverage of *TASS*.

But the congress raised more important issues than the politics of the union's leadership. Members from all over the country spoke of how the party was attempting to silence the press. They also gave vent to their anger at the privileges enjoyed by the larger national

72 Afanas'ev (Yury) 1988, p.494, described *Sovetskaya Rossiya* as the most prominent national daily among those wishing to 'save Stalinism'. See also Shestakov's comments on Chikin, below, p.187. But for Chikin's very different earlier history as news editor of the same paper under Nenashev, see below, Shcherbachenko, p.243.

73 *Konstruktivnost'*. See also below, Korotich, pp.178ff.

74 Shestakov in 1990 said that not only had *TASS* not succeeded in 'restructuring itself' (see below, p.186), but that it was 'in alliance' with Chikin's newspaper, *Sovetskaya Rossiya*, which he called 'very conservative'. At this time the conservative Leonid Kravchenko was in charge of *TASS*. See also Karpenko below, p.174, complaining about *TASS*.

newspapers and the difficult conditions endured by the provincial press.

The editor of the national paper *Sotsialisticheskaya industriya,*[75] A. Baranov, was alarmed at mounting party opposition to *glasnost'* (ibid.):

> I should like to emphasize that my colleagues are not finding it easy to carry out their work. Opposition to the paper and to *glasnost'* has been strengthening recently from party activists and party leaders. If it's not one, then it's the other, sending official letters beginning: 'Dear Sir, I came under criticism in your article...'.

Other interventions at the congress made it plain that party officials from the provinces were less restrained in voicing their displeasure at media 'excesses'. The editor of one regional paper *Zarya kommunizma* (The Dawn of Communism) complained of local party opposition to all critical articles. 'They ask us who the author of such and such an article is, whether he has the right to express such and such a judgement and what sort of individual does he think he is anyway.' (ibid.). The smaller the paper, it seemed, the more difficult it was for the journalist to criticize the local administration. This was illustrated well by A. Tyutyugina, a journalist from a Tatar in-house newspaper[76] *Golos stroitelya* (Voice of the Builder) (ibid.):

> Let's be honest: the value of the word in small and big newspapers is not the same. The journalist from the capital arrives, makes his little bit of criticism and is off. The wind, as they say, is behind him. But the reporter from the factory newspaper has to criticize his own boss for the shambles he has created, or the person who is in an office on the floor below him, people on whom he himself depends. With the introduction of self-financing in our enterprises, the factory journalist will be subject to even harsher limitations. Why not deprive the journalists of their bonus? Why not deprive the paper of newsprint or machinery if it prints unwelcome criticism?[77] A lot of us accommodate ourselves to this situation and the result is harmless and bland articles. I will permit myself to draw the following conclusion: over the last three decades, in-house newspapers have not changed for the better one iota, because the problems they face have stayed the same.

75 This newspaper, along with *Stroitel'naya gazeta*, was later closed down by the central committee, the proprietor of both (O'Clery, 1990).
76 Known as a *mnogotirazhnaya gazeta* or, colloquially, *mnogotirazhka*.
77 The factory or enterprise which publishes the in-house newspaper finances the paper and pays the journalists.

A. Bavykin, editor of the Murmansk newspaper, *Polyarnaya pravda* (Polar Truth), gave the congress delegates a graphic example of how crusading journalism from the Moscow 'heavyweights' caused difficulties in the provinces (ibid.):

Asking oneself the question why there has been a rupture in relations between the central and regional press[78] (that the latter yields to the former in the sharpness of its criticism and in topicality is a fact), one cannot sidestep the relationship between party committees and the press. Let me give an example. *Polyarnaya pravda* wrote about an awful incident that took place in Murmansk. A pack of swine (there is no other word to describe them) began shooting around a war monument in the Valley of Glory. The hard-hitting article we published drew the attention of *Sovetskaya Rossiya*. At their request our journalist wrote an article in their paper. Then another national newspaper, the television and the magazine *Yunost'*[79] got interested. Two years have passed since then, but the reverberations are still felt. And what was the outcome of all this for the region? Without much investigation, the following conclusion was drawn: military-patriotic work in Murmansk has been allowed to fall into neglect. The Regional Party Committee (*obkom*) was forced to explain itself and to have answers ready. It is difficult to foresee the party committee reacting enthusiastically to criticism in the future.

Bavykin's tale also provided the outsider with a snapshot of the relationships between the newspaper world and the party. In an integrated hierarchical structure that incorporated the press and the party, the most important, though invisible, player in the saga was the party central committee, owner of the national paper *Sovetskaya Rossiya*. The next most important participant was *Sovetskaya Rossiya* itself, followed by the regional party committee. The weakest and most vulnerable position was occupied by the local paper. In such an environment the dramatic plea of the editor of another small paper, *Pravda Buryatii* (The Buryat Truth), was understandable: 'Comrades from the national press: help.' (ibid.) [80]

---

78 See below, Grigoryants, p.171, on *glasnost'* being especially noticeable in the national press.

79 A monthly magazine published by the Writers' Union.

80 The powerlessness of the regional press to withstand party pressures was a problem that had surfaced at the 1987 union congress. The editor of a small paper, *Novaya zhizn'* (New Life), G. Lazarev, told the delegates: 'If it appears in the national press then [the word of the party] is more or less important and carries weight, while if it appears in the regional press or, let's say, a wall-newspaper, it's not worth a farthing. Excuse my bluntness, but that is the way things really are. As things stand, we have different truths:

A by-product of party pressure preventing the local press from engaging in serious criticism was, according to Mikhail Poltoranin,[81] a fall in its circulation and an increase in the circulation of the more powerful national papers (*Perestroika*, 1988, p.8).

The complaints of party harassment by the union's members did not, however, fix the matter. The union may have become a genuine forum for expressing members' grievances, but the press was still subordinate to the party. Members' contributions at a plenary session of the union in January 1989 showed that the situation had not improved (Radov, 1989):[82]

> We are experiencing growing pressure on the organs of the press, especially in the regions. There are many incidents of efforts to command and manipulate the press. There are cases of persecution because of criticism, cases where editors and journalists have been punished severely without sufficient cause, where they have been removed from their posts. ... Recently the assistant editor of the Voronezh paper *Molodoi Kommunar* (The Young Communard), V. Kolobov, was sacked for disobedience, as was Kirillov, the news editor of the Tula youth paper. But the *mnogotirazhki* (in-house newspapers) are having an especially difficult time of it. The latest instance took place on the steamship *Maksim Gor'ky* where, during the cruise itself, Il'in, the editor of the paper, was removed from his post while the ship's administration took over the paper. In its own image and likeness, it must be said.

It was not until its February 1991 congress that the union finally discarded its old structures to become 'the Union of Journalists of the USSR on a confederate basis'.[83] In the spirit of the times, the new

---

one for the national press, another for the provincial press and a third for the regional press'(*S"ezd*, 1987, p.21).

81 See Yeltsin, 1990, pp.92–4, on how Poltoranin, editor-in-chief of *Moskovskaya pravda* when Yeltsin was Moscow party secretary, was removed from this post because he published stories unacceptable to the political establishment. In August 1990, Poltoranin was appointed minister for information in the cabinet of the government of the RSFSR, under the presidency of Yeltsin. He was fired from Yeltsin's cabinet in 1993 as a concession to the conservative majority in the congress of people's deputies. Following his dismissal in 1993, Poltoranin was made head of the Federal Information Agency.

82 See also Bovin's example of a journalist from *Stavropol'skaya pravda* being victimized (*Perestroika*, 1988, p.8).

83 In the course of 1991 two other journalists' associations were set up: the Independent Trade Union of Journalists, headed by Sergei Grigoryants, and the Association of Journalists with Parliamentary Accreditation (Tolz, 1992, p.30).

president of the revamped union, Eduard Sagalaev, was a product of the *glasnost'* revolution. For the first time in its history the president was an active, working journalist. Sagalaev was director of the fourth television channel, which he co-owned with Ted Turner, the owner of CNN (and husband to Jane Fonda). Sagalaev was also the initiator of several controversial and hard-hitting television programmes, including the very popular '*Vzglyad*' (Viewpoint), banned, just before Sagalaev's election to the presidency, by Leonid Kravchenko, director of the state broadcasting organization, *Gosteleradio*, and previously head of *TASS*. In electing Sagalaev, who described himself as a 'left democrat'(Vevers, 1991a), the union had shown that its political inclinations now lay with the anti-establishment and iconoclastic wing of the media (see Trapeznikov, 1991).

The first section of the new union's constitution (*Dogovor*, 1991, p.2) stated that it would be 'independent from political parties', and organized on a confederative basis in order to give each branch a large amount of autonomy. In an interview given to the NUJ (National Union of Journalists[84]), the new president said that the most important result of the February congress had been the creation of the new confederate structure which 'in many ways reflects and foresees the political changes in our country'[85] (Vevers, 1991a). Two months after the founding congress, one new branch, the Moscow Association of Journalists, flexed its muscles by expelling Leonid Kravchenko from its organization.[86]

---

84 The trade union for journalists in Britain and Ireland.
85 The confederative structure of the new union indeed reflected the fractious tendencies of some republics in the country at the time. Attending the February founding congress were 732 delegates from eleven of the fifteen republics. Georgia, Lithuania, Latvia and Estonia sent observers (Trapeznikov, 1991).
86 Eduard Sagalaev himself was not behind Kravchenko's expulsion, although, because of Kravchenko's part in taking '*Vzglyad*' (Viewpoint) off the air, he might have had good reason to be. The *Novosti* news agency reported Sagalaev as saying that, while the Moscow Association of Journalists was an independent body entitled to make all kinds of decisions, Kravchenko's primary (i.e., branch) organization had not been consulted and that the decision to expel him had been made without any formal accusations or evidence against him. Sagalaev was also reported as saying that, while the due process of the law must be adhered to, Kravchenko had violated the press law by limiting public access to information and impairing journalists' work. Kravchenko's expulsion was not unexpected. He was criticized by many speakers at the three-day congress for his part in the taking off the air of '*Vzglyad*' and for the reintroduction of old-style, pre-*glasnost*' censorship on state television (*Guardian*, 1991). At the February congress many dele-

Kravchenko's role as director of *Gosteleradio* in presiding over the assaults on *glasnost'* in the early part of 1991, arising directly out the treatment in the Moscow liberal press of the Soviet army crackdown in the Baltics, had made him a *bête noir* for the liberal media.

Sagalaev also committed himself to dealing with the problem of journalists' pay, an issue which he regarded as central given the huge rise in the cost of living in the early part of 1991. In his concern for journalists' financial welfare, Sagalaev was fulfilling his function as representative of journalists in the economic and social sphere.[87] However, given the new situation of an emerging independent and privately-run press that had to fight for survival in a harsh economic climate, the union's concern for the material welfare of its members was not much more than an aspiration. The main function of the union, Sagalaev said, was 'to defend the policy of openness and objectivity as well as the social protection of individual journalists' (*Guardian*, 1991). The importance of this was emphasized by the statement made to delegates at the February congress by a surprise guest to the congress, Anatoly Lukyanov, speaker of the Soviet parliament. Lukyanov assured delegates that the August 1990 press law would not be suspended, as had been suggested in a moment of anger by Mikhail Gorbachev the previous month in reaction to some newspaper coverage of events in the Baltic republics. Ominously, however, Lukyanov reported that the presidium of the congress and the parliamentary committee on *glasnost'* formed in January 1991 would discuss the application of the law with the aim of enhancing the media's precision and balance in reporting (Trapeznikov, 1991). In the highly-charged atmosphere of the time, the desire to 'enhance the precision' of the media bespoke the desperation of a party losing control of what was once its most faithful lieutenant.

Even in the heyday of *glasnost'* the old Soviet journalists' union

---

gates had demanded that he be recalled from the Congress of People's Deputies, where he had been elected on the ticket of the journalists' union, and that he be expelled from the union. The question of his expulsion, however, was not resolved at the congress, the decision being left to the Moscow Association of Journalists (Trapeznikov, 1991). On 25 April, thirteen days after his expulsion from the union, Kravchenko was recalled as the organization's representative in the USSR Supreme Soviet.

87 Section iii, paragraph 3 of the union's new constitution refers to its role in defending the 'material, professional and social rights of the journalist' (*Dogovor*, 1991, p.2); Paragraph 4 also refers to the union's aim to provide material benefits for members.

was never the channel through which the press made most of its gains. The admittedly lively debate at the latter congresses of the old union was tempered by the continuing conservative leadership of the organization.[88] Thus, the union became a talking-shop for journalists, but in this was no different from practically the entire periodical press in the *glasnost'* period, except that its official voice became pro-*glasnost'* very late in the day. It was only in the course of 1991 that the union's monthly magazine, *Zhurnalist*, began to reflect the anti-establishment views of members.[89] As the once-focused ideological force of the party became diffuse, so the union's role as the party's watchdog in the press became less effective, though even in the Brezhnev period this function was more formal than actual. The formation of independent newspapers and the aspirations of officially owned newspapers to become independent, all now beginning to compete for readers in the marketplace, engendered in newspapers and journalists a dog-eat-dog mentality that had less and less time for trade union politics. Unlike in Western Europe, there was no natural animosity between staff and management. A prevalent attitude to the union was one of barely hidden disdain. One experienced journalist who worked for several Soviet newspapers under Brezhnev told this writer that the new union was ignored by most journalists. The annual journalists' ball, he said, was the only important event in the union's calendar. The handing out of awards to outstanding journalists at the ball, previously an important occasion, was now, he said, a minor event. Access to a good restaurant in *Dom zhurnalista* ('House of the Journalist'), the organization's headquarters, was the other advantage of being a member of the union.[90] The union's president, Sagalaev, he

---

88 Yegor Yakovlev, then editor of the radical *Moskovskie novosti*, commenting on his failure to gain election to the Supreme Soviet by the journalists' union, said the organization was 'still dominated by utterly untalented people from the provinces' (Cohen and vanden Heuval, 1989, p.208).

89 Tolz (1991b, p.14) reported that on 17 June 1991 the *Pravda* publishing house had revoked its status as the magazine's founder, thereby depriving it of access to the printing presses. The publishers were unhappy, Tolz suggested, with an interview in the magazine that reported violations of the press law by Soviet officials, as well as criticism of all-Union television under the directorship of Leonid Kravchenko.

90 See below, Shcherbachenko, p.249. A younger *ITAR–TASS* journalist expressed an identical view to this author.

said, was busy running his television channel. A younger journalist working with *Moskovskii komsomolets* also told this writer that the union was now an irrelevancy.

3. News Fit to Print

The newspaper as teacher

Among the fundamental tasks which the bolsheviks set themselves after the 1917 revolution was the need to transform the ethical and moral outlook of the largely peasant population.[1] In Marxist terms this meant raising the ideological consciousness of the rural and urban masses eventually and ideally to a level equal to that of members of the vanguard of society, the party. As a means of bridging the enormous gap between the masses and the party intelligentsia, Lenin encouraged the widest use of all means of mass agitation and propaganda. For a largely illiterate population, the emphasis was at first placed on spoken agitation. As literacy became more widespread, the emphasis shifted from the 'unsystematic' (Mickiewicz, 1985, p.45) spoken word, to the more reliable printed word, later on to radio, cinema and television.

From the outset, Lenin and the bolsheviks understood the value of the newspaper as means of schooling the public in the basics of Marxist ideology and, more practically, of casting in a favourable light selected government policies. It is no accident that many of the prominent early members of the bolsheviks were themselves journalists, or, at least, prolific contributors to newspapers (Lenin, Trotsky, Stalin, Bukharin, to name but a few). While newspapers played a very important role in the dissemination of Russian socialist ideas before the revolution, the rapid bolshevik monopolization of the press soon after the revolution[2] hugely expanded the propaganda potential of the press for the party. The bolshevik press could now spread its message every day to a mass readership without tsarist interference. As the liberal, non-bolshevik socialist and other newspapers were closed down, soon the only voice heard was the bolshevik one.

Such was the importance attached to the responsibility of journalists

---

1 See Pethybridge, 1966, p.234 on the educational level of the population at this period.
2 See above, p.1.

to educate the public in the 'right' way that until well into the *glasnost'* period the majority of journalists were party members[3] supposedly bearing the message of Marxism–Leninism. Hence the view of a leading Soviet press analyst, Grigory Solganik (1980, p.25):

> The newspaper for us is not an impartial instrument for communicating the news, rather it is an organ of the party, upholding the ideas and views of the progressive class and the party.

Soviet students of journalism were trained to present events in accordance with this world view and its accompanying scientific logic. Put at its crudest, for the Soviet journalist there was only one correct perspective on any news story. While synchronically an incident might be assessed on its subjective merits or demerits, all events diachronically fitted into a larger picture, forming part of a progressive, forward-moving political momentum. Thus all Soviet newspapers, as indeed did most Western ones, portrayed the world as divided into two antagonistic camps, one socialist, the other non-socialist (Solganik, 1976, p.12). The Soviet view held that each camp, though for the present at different stages of development, was destined to become communist in the fullness of time.

The role of the Soviet press, however, was not simply to report in accordance with Marxist–Leninist logic. The journalist also had a duty actively to participate in the construction of the future society. Thus, for example, the press always supported party and state economic campaigns. In Western terms, the press was the party's publicist. As for the Western publicist, so for the Soviet press, 'news' was anything that reflected favourably on its 'client', not the rapid reporting of current events.

So integral to the Soviet newspaper was the idea of the press as teacher that it became its defining feature, and the one from which all others derived. It was something of an historical irony that in this area the bolsheviks had revived the liberal press tradition that went back to the nineteenth-century publicists (*publitsisty*), Herzen and Belinskii,

---

3 See above, p.40, on the percentage of journalists in the party. See, also, above, pp.40ff on the selection procedures for senior positions in the media. See, also, Korotich below, p.178, and his attempts to reconcile editorial independence with party loyalty.

and which, until the 1917 revolution, had been rapidly giving way to a mass-readership popular press.[4]

Home news coverage

Home news prior to *glasnost'* was treated variously. Even during the *glasnost'* period the press still gave full coverage of very long speeches given by high officials of the government and party, illustrating the newspaper's role as an instrument for conveying politically enlightening knowledge.[5] This slavish adherence to a fundamental Leninist principle turned much of the newspaper into a dry official gazette, devaluing its function as an organ of popular propaganda. Among the easiest targets for criticism in the initial period of *glasnost'*, even by conservatives, were these same speeches which were not especially well written and often passed over by the newspaper reader, as senior editorial staff of *Izvestiya* and *Pravda* admitted (Karpenko, 1987 and Afanas'ev, 1986, p.4). Thus, from a Western perspective, the Soviet newspaper failed to serve the requirements of both the consumer (the reader) and the advertiser (the party) for attractively packaged and easily digestible information.

The press under Brezhnev went through the motions of mobilizing the population to meet economic goals by means of devoting endless column inches to lauding industrial achievements. Much 'news' amounted to appeals for higher productivity and lavish praise for those who overfulfilled plan targets. As will be seen in this chapter, the greater the strides made by *glasnost'*, the less this type of 'news' appeared. In *Izvestiya*, for example, the brief reports on economic achievements had by 1988 all but disappeared from their former prominent position on the first page (see below, Karpenko, p.173), though the page-one 'production-photographs' (*proizvodstvennye portrety*)[6] of enthusiastic workers lasted longer.

Criticism in the press under Brezhnev and in the early days under

---

4 See Louise McReynold's excellent account of the development of the pre-1917 Russian mass-circulation press, especially Chapters 5 and 11 (1991).

5 See, for example, *Pravda*, 25 April 1989, where the full speech of the Chairman of the all-Union *Profsoyuz* organization is given, occupying almost five entire broad-sheet pages.

6 See below, Chapter 4, *passim*, on the decline of traditional Soviet genres during *perestroika*.

Gorbachev was mostly very low level, the most frequent targets being 'bureaucratism, excessive observance of formalities, suppression of criticism, anti-social phenomena such as drunkenness, bribe-taking, black-market dealing, idleness and obsequiousness' (*Resolution,* 1987). At this period uniformity of opinion on broad political and economic issues in the press was still the order of the day. All official Soviet newspapers, for example, professed to support *perestroika.* Journalists refrained from criticizing Gorbachev, or other powerful figures in the leadership, leaving it instead to politicians, whose speeches, under a relaxed censorship regime, were dutifully published in the press.

Following the introduction of *glasnost'* in 1985, the Russian press went through several stages of development. Though the changes in the press constituted a continuum, some rough division of the process is possible. The first period began in 1985, after the formal introduction of the policy of *glasnost'* at the April plenary session of the central committee. This period, which lasted until around the beginning of 1988, was marked by a gradual realization among journalists that *glasnost'* was more than mere rhetoric, and was in fact supported by Gorbachev and other elements within the leadership. A second phase in the evolution of *glasnost'* was discernible early in 1988 when the press began to feel its strength and lose its fear of the conservative elements in the leadership who now regularly expressed in a threatening manner their discontent with the destructive nature of *glasnost'.* The view of *glasnost'* as a political weapon used by Gorbachev to discredit his political enemies was generally applicable up to 1989. Until then much of the investigative reporting of a newly-invigorated press made it possible for Gorbachev to purge the party leadership of the Brezhnev rump whom he saw as an impediment to his reform programme.[7] After 1988, a part of the press began to publish critical articles independent of the views of the leadership. The third phase in the development of *glasnost'* began in August 1990 with the coming

---

7   Hill (1989, p.320) saw *glasnost'* as a political weapon which enabled Gorbachev to '[undermine] the positions of those, such as Grishin and Kunaev, who had been closely associated with the Brezhnev era. By allowing the mass media to expose the corruption that had taken place during their trusteeship of (in those cases) Moscow and Kazakhstan, rather than confronting them behind the closed doors of the Politburo's meeting room, Gorbachev was able to make defence of their position impossible'.

into effect of the Law on the Press, which gave the press a legal protection from party interference and abolished the state censorship agency, *Glavlit*. The next phase coincided with the collapse of the Soviet Union and the acceleration of the Westernization of a now independent press. It was in this last period, too, that the press experienced grave economic difficulties as it was forced to operate in a market situation. As the certainties of the old system crumbled, so the country entered a state of flux, reflected in the variety of newspapers that appeared in the post-Soviet world. The regulating 'system' had ceded its authority to a multiplicity of individual voices. Instead of addressing itself to one idealized readership, the Russian newspaper now catered for several readerships. Thus the newspaper world acquired its share of down-market tabloids, 'heavyweight' liberal newspapers, a thriving pornographic press and a combative nationalist press as well as scores of publications representing sectional interests. Amidst the flux it became clear that the philosophical void left by the shattering of the Soviet model of journalism was being filled by Western models.

Sensationalism

One of the consequences of the bolshevik insistence on using a high-brow press to get across their message was a complete rejection of sensationalism. With the exception of the worst forms of hyperbole in the Stalinist period, the Soviet press usually presented a staid face to its reader. The 'spirit of sensationalism' was 'alien' to the Soviet press, wrote one media analyst, Pel't, in 1985 (p.7). The Soviet newspaper took pride in not providing its readers with what it regarded as an undesirable trait of the bourgeois press. For the Soviet journalist, at least in theory, news ought to inform, and not entertain.[8] Sensationalism, gossip and advertising were all considered examples of 'secondary' news, opposed to the 'primary' variety characteristic of the Soviet press (ibid., p.7). According to Pel't (ibid., p.38), Soviet newspapers covered 'socially important, vitally significant new facts and phenomena' while 'striving to be always genuinely interesting for

---

8 Pel't (1985, p.38) distinguished between the principles of *razvlekatel'nost'* (enter-tainment-ness, entertainment-worthiness) and *interesnost'* (interest-ness, interest-worthiness).

a broad circle of readers'. The Western press, on the other hand, was said to be more concerned with entertaining its readership with 'the off-beat, the fortuitous … the rare happening'. Quoting the impressions of a former *Izvestiya* foreign correspondent who had worked in Britain, France and the USA, Pel't concluded that the bourgeois journalist, for whom the most important thing was to be 'the first to report a fact', wrote 'in a primitive manner' (ibid., p.6).

In fact, the conceptually sophisticated Soviet press often left the average reader behind in its attempts to communicate that which presumably fell into the category of 'socially important' news. Critics claimed that readers could not understand much of the complex conceptual vocabulary that appeared on the pages of all newspapers (Groys, 1983). A Soviet survey carried out in Taganrog during the Brezhnev era, for example, found that about 25 per cent of informants did not know the meaning of 'colonialism', about 40 per cent could not explain 'dictatorship', around 50 per cent could not understand 'imperialism' while almost 66 per cent did not understand 'leftist forces' (Mickiewicz, 1985, p.47). Despite this, the Soviet press machine continued to churn out ideologically motivated 'news' at the expense of day-to-day reporting on life in the country. There could be no question of a newspaper publishing sensational, let alone sensationalist news. The only sensations found in the Brezhnev press were those embedded in dull-looking, often cryptic, lines that made sense only to *cognoscenti*. It was not a popular press.

Since the immediate publication of 'hot' news, be it sensationalist in content or not, creates a sensation of sorts, the predominance of old news in the press during the pre-*glasnost'* period was an indication of the authorities' distaste for even such minor disruptions to the carefully constructed picture presented by the press of a country where surprises, particularly unpleasant ones, did not happen. The rejection of the 'spirit of sensationalism', and the fear of the Soviet authorities that unchecked and unverified news might create public disquiet, meant that stories did not, as a rule, 'break'. Furthermore, in the absence of competition between papers for sales, newspapers did not vie with one another to be the first to 'break' a story, nor indeed was this possible under the highly controlled pre-publication vetting structures.

So, the fear of causing sensation was the main reason for the reluctance of the pre-*glasnost'* press to publish fresh news. Based on a study of the content of Soviet newspapers for 1976, for example, one investigator calculated that a mere 15 per cent of news had happened the previous day (Mickiewicz, 1985, p.37). Because news was received, processed and digested before publication,[9] when, at length, it did appear, it was often something more akin to a thoughtful, not infrequently rambling essay than to a Western-style news story or even news feature. In Western terminology, the Brezhnev press, and to a lesser extent the Gorbachev and Yeltsin-era press, was plagued by editorializing.

This patronizing, teacher–pupil relationship with the reader started to weaken as official controls began to lose their force under *glasnost'*, though this was a slow process. Solganik (1987) observed in 1987 that the press was moving away from the old-style instructive article which, he said, bore the hallmarks of *direktivnost'* (a commanding tone) and *imperativnost'* (imperativeness).[10] *Izvestiya*'s policy in the early *glasnost'* period of printing fewer and fewer editorials, either replacing them with signed 'opinion' columns or dispensing with them altogether, was an example of one paper's desire to shed its didactic persona. It was also a reflection of the paper's new-found freedom not to publish unnuanced propagandistic 'news' that was, as Karpenko put it, read by 'a few individuals out of millions' (1987).

Nevertheless during the early years of *glasnost'* important stories were still by and large sensibly and responsibly 'broken' to readers who were told how they ought to react to that news. This was even the attitude of the most daring publications of the time, such as *Ogonyok*, whose editor was adamant in 1988 that no criticism of Lenin should appear on the pages of his magazine in case it might end up 'destroying the whole temple' (see below, Korotich, p.180).

---

9   See Ostrogorsky (1988) on the general lack of flexibility in radio programming and the consequent inability to react quickly to stories that have broken. See also Roxburgh, 1987, pp.64–5: 'The basic shape of each day's *Pravda* is decided well in advance. It is little wonder that the finished product is such a polished article.'

10   Mickiewicz (1985, p.37) reported on a Soviet survey carried out before the *glasnost'* period which found that instructional television programmes were among the least popular. The same was probably true of instructional newspaper articles.

The elephantine Soviet press was consistently 'scooped' in both home and foreign stories by foreign radio stations broadcasting into the Soviet Union, known as 'enemy voices' (*vrazhskie golosa*).[11] This was because in the pre-*glasnost'* period Soviet journalists were forbidden from covering many foreign stories, in particular those which portrayed unfavourably Soviet foreign policy. As regards domestic news, foreign journalists, often Soviet émigrés working for the 'enemy voices', had the advantage over their Soviet colleagues of being free to report bad news and indulge in political commentary and speculation. Broadcasts from the US government-sponsored Radio Free Europe, for example, tended to emphasize the bad news coming out of the Soviet Union. Since the possibilities of the Soviet press were so limited, it was easy for the foreign radio stations to provide sensations for the news-hungry Soviet listener.

One such sensation happened in 1987, when most newspapers were still timid and untrusting of the new policy of *glasnost'*. On 28 May of that year a deranged young German, Mathias Rust, landed his small plane in the middle of Red Square. While the Western media, including foreign radio stations, revelled in the sensation, only the daring *Moskovskie novosti* printed a picture of Rust's plane on the square. However, at this early stage in the progress of *glasnost'* the 'freedom' to publish what others avoided was relative. Unlike other newspapers, *Moskovskie novosti* was to an extent indemnified against official reprimands since its editor, Yegor Yakovlev, was, and realized he was, a Gorbachev *protégé*.[12]

In the absence of not only a reliable news service, but one that refused to provide 'sensations', it was not surprising that foreign radio stations enjoyed large audiences. Different surveys taken in the Brezhnev period and the initial and final periods of *glasnost'* showed that a sizeable number of people listened to foreign radio broadcasts. One survey carried out between 1977 and 1980 found that about a

11 The main foreign stations broadcasting in Russian were The Voice of America, Radio Free Europe, BBC World Service and Deutsche Welle.
12 See Yakovlev interview in Cohen and vanden Heuval, 1989, p.206. See also Schillinger and Porter, 1991, p.130, who report that Yakovlev was appointed editor at Gorbachev's behest, and that his appointment was confirmed by the party central committee, as, indeed, were all *nomenklatura* appointments.

third of the Soviet adult population 'was exposed to Western radio broadcasts (though not necessarily news broadcasts) in the course of a year, about one fifth in the course of a typical week' (Mickiewicz, 1985, p.57). More recent findings suggested that about 67 million people (23 per cent of the Soviet population) listened to foreign radio programmes in the late 1980s once jamming was lifted.[13] Of these, 18 million listened to the BBC (White, 1992, p.78). Figures published in June 1991 showed a slight decrease in audience numbers, though about 18 per cent of the population, and a much higher figure in large cities, was still tuning in to foreign stations (Tolz, 1991, July, p.14). During the August 1991 coup, when the Emergency Committee attempted to take control of the press, television and radio, people turned to foreign radio stations for news. Many were slightly taken aback at the casual admission by the Soviet President and party general secretary that he, too, listened to the 'enemy voices' while in captivity in his Crimean dacha (Gorbachev, 1991, p.27):[14]

The best reception was from the BBC and Radio Liberty. Later we managed to pick up the Voice of America. My son-in-law Anatoli managed to listen to a Western station on his pocket Sony. We started to collect and analyse the way the situation was developing.

Even under normal circumstances, Russian listeners continued to listen to foreign stations because their level of professional competence was seen as higher than those of native stations, which, though more pluralist than their Soviet predecessors, were not necessarily more competent. In 1993, for example, this writer observed that Soviet people still listened to foreign stations for an alternative view of events in the country, displaying the loyalty of listeners to a service that had served them regularly over a period of many years.

In the post-Soviet press there was no longer any avoidance of the sensational. The gradual 'de-sovietization' of news-reporting was

13 Jamming of Russian-language broadcasts of the BBC was lifted in January 1987, of the Voice of America's Russian language programme, in May of the same year.
14 The dissemination of anti-Soviet propaganda was a crime under Soviet law. Since such propaganda often took the form of transcripts of foreign radio broadcasts, tuning in to such programmes, while not a crime, was viewed by the KGB as suspect and an anti-Soviet activity. Listening to foreign stations was, therefore, done in secret.

already apparent in 1987 when all the main stories were 'broken' by Soviet reporters who, in a reversal of roles, provided sensations to their Western colleagues. Foreign correspondents in Moscow now regularly filed stories that were frequently picked off from the Soviet media. In this period of *glasnost'* so great was the area of taboo topics that it was easy for newspapers to provide sensations.

Unlike the Mathias Rust incident, a sensation according to any definition, most of the 'sensational' news of around this period was sensational only because it had never previously been covered by the Soviet press. For example, articles began to appear acknowledging the existence of drug-addiction[15] and prostitution.[16] At this period, also, retrospective *glasnost'* created many sensations, such as the publishing of previously banned or disapproved works of literature. Anna Akhmatova's series of poems on the Stalinist terror, *Requiem*, was published in the March issue of the journal *Oktyabr'*, while another monthly journal, *Druzhba narodov*, began the serialization of Anatoly Rybakov's *Children of the Arbat*, also on the Stalin theme. Whether or not people read the articles or works of literature, the fact of their having been published was, in the Soviet context, a sensation.

In the post-Soviet period, sensations no longer come from the filling in of 'blank spots' in the history of the Soviet Union. Instead, the Yeltsin-era Russian press, in borrowing the Western understanding of 'sensationalism', dealt a mortal blow to the old pedagogic Soviet understanding of newsworthiness. A 'pointless', from the old Soviet point of view, personality feature on tennis player Boris Becker's[17] new girlfriend that appeared in *Nedelya* in 1993 became a typical post-Soviet article, providing a minor sensation of no obvious significance or use to the reader. That the article was more or less 'lifted' from a Western source (it was by-lined 'Tamara Bulanova. Based on materials from *Stern* magazine') showed the Western source of the

---

15 *Pravda*, 6 January 1987; *Izvestiya*, 13 May 1987.
16 *Sovetskaya Rossiya*, 13 March 1987.
17 *Oni prosto schastlivy'* (They're simply happy), *Nedelya*, N° 17, 1993. See also *'Katarina Vitt kon'ki poka ne otbrosila'* (Katarina Witt has not yet hung up her skates), *Argumenty i fakty*, N° 16, 1993. The article, which mentions Boris Becker as the skater's one-time suspected boyfriend, was by-lined 'A. Bryukhanova, Based on materials from *Paris Match* magazine.'

new way of writing. The Russian press now looked to the West to relearn the skills of popular journalism. The teacher became a pupil.

Accidents

As well as shunning Western-style sensationalism, the Soviet media had avoided covering accidents or natural disasters within their own boundaries, while being quick to pick up on mishaps outside the country.[18] As we have seen earlier, the explanation for the shying away from reporting on domestic calamities originated in the post-revolutionary idea that the new Soviet republic was in a besieged position, surrounded by enemies and detractors eager to seize on any misfortune as ammunition for the anti-Soviet propaganda battle. What began life as an emergency reaction to extraordinary circumstances became institutionalized under Stalin's reign of terror when the publication of unfavourable news might be construed as reflecting badly on the leadership (for example, the 1930s famine).[19] It was under Stalin, too, that readers got used to reading of accidents, disasters and catastrophes as only happening abroad. At a stretch, the refusal to make public such 'bad' news was also fitting with the pedagogic function of the press. Why teach the pupils 'bad' examples? By contrast, 'up-beat', good news was emphasized in the Soviet press in the belief that it was not only opinion-forming, but character-forming, though even before *glasnost'* there was evidence that readers' opinions were not being shaped by the monotonous diet of positive news which they knew through their own experience and other sources, such as the foreign radio stations, to be only partially true (see Mickiewicz, 1985, p.55). The veto on reporting bad news became first and foremost a device used by the apparatus to block at source any public criticism of its failings or inadequacies.

It was against this history of secrecy and hush-ups that the Soviet authorities failed to report the April 1986 nuclear accident at Cher-

---

18 See White (1992, p.77), on how the Soviet press gave almost no details of a major earthquake in Tadzhikistan in October 1985, but provided extensive, on-the-spot reports of an earthquake that had taken place in Mexico at around the same period.

19 On 8 February 1990 *Izvestiya* published an article that spoke of the political causes of the 1930s famine in Ukraine. Neither the accident nor the famine had received press coverage at the time.

nobyl. That the Soviet press would report the accident without the permission of these authorities was unthinkable. Since the nature of the accident made it impossible to hide – the Swedes were the first to report increased levels of radiation – the next priority of the Soviet establishment was to minimize its gravity. The first official response to the world's largest known nuclear accident came in the form of a minimalist statement from the Soviet council of ministers[20] after two days of silence:

> An accident has occurred at the Chernobyl nuclear power station. One of the atomic reactors has been damaged, but measures are being taken to eliminate the consequences of the accident. Aid is being given to the victims and a government commission has been set up.

The statement was broadcast on a Radio Moscow home service news programme as the fourth item, and the eleventh item on Radio Kiev. Soviet television's main evening news programme, *Vremya*, also covered the announcement as the twenty-first item in their bulletin for which the lead story was a statistical update on figures for cardboard production (Whelan, 1992).[21]

The coincidence of the introduction of a policy of media *glasnost'* and the impossibility of covering up the Chernobyl accident combined to fatally weaken the principle of never reporting 'bad' news. Though a natural calamity and not an accident,[22] the immediate and extensive Soviet press coverage of the 1988 Armenian earthquake was a measure of the progress of *glasnost'* in the intervening period of less than two years. The extent and nature of the reportage and commentaries on the

---

20 The statement was monitored on 28 April 1986 by the BBC Summary of World Broadcasts.

21 In a fascinating study, Whelan (1992) charts the spare Soviet coverage of the accident that quickly became the most important story in the world. While *Pravda* filled its columns with articles proclaiming the arrival of spring in Ukraine, the Western media had gone into overdrive reporting the movements of the radioactive cloud over parts of Europe, as well as rumours that a second reactor had caught fire. Four days after the accident, Boris Yeltsin, attending the West German communist party congress, condemned the bourgeois media for concocting scare stories about the accident. The aim of such scaremongering was, he said, to 'step up anti-Soviet hysteria' and 'drive a wedge in the Soviet Union's relations with other countries'.

22 For journalists writing in the pre-*glasnost'* period, natural calamities and disasters caused by human error amounted to much the same thing.

Armenian earthquake stood in contrast to the tight-lipped and grudging official communiqués on the Chernobyl accident. According to one Western Moscow correspondent, the disaster was covered in the Soviet press 'almost as fully and honestly as anyone could wish' (see Steele, 1988, for examples of coverage of different papers; also see *Observer*, 1988). In 1986, the media were still tightly controlled by the party-state apparatus. By 1988, newspapers felt free enough to carry reports from the scene of the calamity, as well as articles critical of the authorities. *Izvestiya*, for example, provided moving eye-witness accounts of the earthquake as well as criticizing the country's civil defence for its lack of preparedness to react to the earthquake. The national dailies and weeklies showed 'sensational' front-page pictures from the disaster area of women weeping over child-sized coffins.[23]

In spite of the new-found freedom to report on calamities, Western correspondents in the Soviet Union noticed signs of the old journalism in coverage of the earthquake (Steele, 1988):

> After all the emphasis on nationalism during the recent Supreme Soviet debates on the constitution, it is as though a general press advisory has gone out in order to try and counteract it. Stress the multi-national solidarity. Show that we are all one Soviet family, or as an eight-column headline put it, 'There is no such thing as someone else's grief'. As a result of this coverage, reports of something less than solidarity in Azerbaijan have been suppressed.[24]

---

23 National dailies did not, however, publish the 'sensationalist' rumour, which reached the ears of Western correspondents covering the 1988 earthquake, that Raisa Gorbacheva was not only a Muslim, but that Gorbachev was her fourth husband (*Irish Times*, 20 December 1988).

24 Western journalists also noted how the media were being pressed into action to launch a 'vehement campaign' against the Armenian nationalist 'Karabakh Committee' (O'Clery, 1988c). O'Clery also reported an attempt by the main party newspaper, *Pravda*, to use the earthquake as an opportunity to give a bad press to the nationalist Estonians: 'It turned out that an article in *Pravda* had pointedly drawn attention to the fact that members of the Estonian Popular Front had been to Leninakan some months ago to advise pro-reformers there but no Estonians had been there since the earthquake. "People reacted with great anger to the article," said Mr Indrek Toome, chairman of the Estonian Council of Ministers.' *TASS* somewhat restored the reputation of the Estonians by carrying a report the following day on Estonian construction designers working in Spitak and Leninakan. One *Moskovskie novosti* commentator (Ostrogorsky, 1988) compared unfavourably the Soviet national radio coverage of the earthquake with that of the much more flexible Radio Free Europe (*Svoboda*), which changed its schedules specially and offered listeners use of its frequencies to help locate friends and relatives in the disaster area: 'And what was our own radio doing at the same time? It was broad-

Nevertheless, while press coverage was still subject to official guidance, there was no denying that the taboo on covering accidents and calamities had been well and truly broken. The abandonment of the veto on covering bad news of all sorts, not only accidents, was an important step in the progress of the press away from the Soviet model of journalism on its way to a more Western approach to newsworthiness and methods of coverage. Factual reporting from the scene of catastrophes, for example, was bound to be sensationalist. Liberal editors, however, insisted that such reporting was primarily informative, and not sensationalist. For the editor of the liberal *Moskovskie novosti* newspaper, Yegor Yakovlev, 'sensation' in the news was a concept which bureaucrats 'drag out into the light when they are accusing us of something that is displeasing to them' (Yakovlev, 1987).

The freedom to report in a totally unencumbered manner only came about with the emergence of an independent, non-state or party press in the course of 1990. The process was gradual and happened in conjunction with a series of legislative measures culminating in the 1990 press law. The post-Soviet press showed no trace of the old taboo. Accidents were now reported in the same way as in the West. In the new situation, while Russian journalists had to fight against the instinct of institutions to hide negative news, the institutions themselves were no longer part of a monolithic party–state apparatus to which the press was subordinate.

Polarization

The changes in format and presentation in the press that began in earnest in 1987 could not have come about without the encouragement of the party. On several occasions during that year Gorbachev and the head of the party propaganda department, Alexander Yakovlev, urged the media to embrace *glasnost'*. On 31 March Yakovlev told representatives of the media to be more open and critical. The caution shown by editors at this time was understandable given the contradictory

---

casting the normal programmes of concerts and features, scheduled, apparently, long before the tragic event. What were they waiting for? Instructions from above? Or were the special programmes making their way on to the airwaves along the long ladder of permits which are the norm for our radio?'

signals coming from the party hierarchy. Already in March 1987 the future standard-bearer of the conservative faction within the party, Yegor Ligachev, had expressed displeasure with the destructive nature of *glasnost'*, saying that there had been achievements even during the Brezhnev period, which Gorbachev had derided as the 'era of stagnation' at the 27th party congress in February 1986. This incipient splitting of the party monolith into, broadly speaking, conservative and reformist camps was reflected in a growing polarization of the press along similar lines. The emerging divisions between what was to become a pro- and anti-reformist press only became absolutely clear around 1988. Before that the entire media machine had enthusiastically supported what appeared to be a crusade for *glasnost'*. Such unanimity of response to the initiative of the general secretary was only to have been expected from an institution that had since the time of Stalin been the mouthpiece of the party. Neither was it particularly odd that, despite several important personnel changes,[25] the arrival of *glasnost'* had not been accompanied by any wholesale replacement of older journalists by younger ones untainted by the Brezhnev era. Instead, the entire journalistic community, old and young alike, predictably weighed in behind the latest government campaign and immediately ceased writing and thinking (on paper) in the old way.

The language of the press in the Soviet Union, in some ways the same as anywhere else, soon purged itself of old clichés for fresh replacements more in spirit with the times. The new discourse of *glasnost'* was endlessly presented to the reader by the most diverse publications. But the *glasnost'* campaign was different from the others. Behind the rhetoric of renewal uttered by all and sundry lay deeply different interpretations of what *glasnost'* actually meant.

Almost everyone was eager to praise 'the fresh air of *glasnost'*' (Lakshin, 1987) and criticize the Brezhnev press. Among the most

---

25 Some of the key appointments made in the media were: June 1986, Vitaly Korotich, a minor Ukranian writer, appointed editor of *Ogonyok*; August 1986, Yegor Yakovlev, a quasi-casualty of the Khrushchev era, appointed editor of *Moskovskie novosti*; August 1986, Sergei Zalygin, a noted writer who was not a party member, appointed editor of *Novy mir*. Between 1985 and 1986 new editors were also appointed to the following national newspapers: *Trud, Krasnaya zvezda, Sovetskaya Rossiya, Sotsialisticheskaya industriya* and *Sovetskaya kul'tura*. The former editor of *Sovetskaya Rossiya*, Mikhail Nenashev, was appointed director of the state publishing committee (*Goskomizdat*).

vociferous in their denunciation of the old-style journalism were those who themselves were past-masters of that same style. The editor of *Pravda* and president of the union of journalists,[26] Viktor Afanas'ev, called on his colleagues to root out 'empty verbiage, mediocrity, high-flown rhetoric and primitivism'. He railed against 'clichéd reports', 'over-long articles of official news which you willingly don't even read up to half-way' and articles which resembled 'technical instructions for the specialist'. He continued (Afanas'ev, 1986, p.2):

> We have not yet rid ourselves of the harmful habit of giving approximate, general evaluations instead of business-like language. We have not yet rid ourselves of our passion for high style rhetoric, the tinsel that clutters up the clear and accessible language that should be the hallmark of our press.

Appointed in the Brezhnev era, Afanas'ev had expressed a contrary view in 1977 when he praised Soviet journalism for its 'high level of craftsmanship, clarity and depth of content, its accessibility and clearness of form' (Afanas'ev, 1977, p.4).

Ivan Laptev, the editor of *Izvestiya* and a deputy president of the journalists' union, who, unlike Afanas'ev, turned out to have liberal tendencies, repeated almost exactly the sentiments of *Pravda*'s editor. He spoke against the 'ostentatious, triumphant speech-making style' which characterized the past (Laptev, 1987, p.1). Laptev's subordinates at *Izvestiya* spoke the same *glasnost'* phrases as their editor. L. Korneshov, a deputy editor, denounced 'high-sounding phrases' as 'phenomena associated with the period of stagnation' (Korneshov, 1987, p.4); he was against 'standard articles in which there are a lot of correct words, but few fresh ideas or exceptional solutions' (ibid., p.6).

In a book written according to Gorbachev's new thinking, Mikhail Nenashev, the then editor of the, for the time, innovative *Sovetskaya Rossiya*, perceived an 'urgent necessity to overcome the existing glorification in coverage of vitally important issues' (Nenashev, 1986,

26 See Remington, 1985, p.498: 'It is likely that the selection of the editor of the party's leading newspaper [*Pravda*] as chairman of the Journalists' Union is an institutionalized practice.' This practice changed in 1991 with the election of Eduard Sagalaev.

p.89). The journalist, Nenashev wrote, must avoid the 'standard slogans: 'to strive for', 'to strengthen', 'to improve' (ibid., p.18) and generally reject the 'declarative approach, with its wide use of general slogans and appeals, its exaggeration of successes, victories and absence of necessary criticism'. This 'declarativeness and formalism' led to a 'dangerous gap between the word and the deed, when sometimes on the pages of the newspapers one reads of one thing and in life one sees something completely different' (ibid., p.18). The journalist must 'learn to speak from the pages of the press in human language' (ibid., p.43).

There were few publications that would not give space to Soviet journalists mercilessly lashing the inadequacies of the old canon. In an article 'Do our heroes really speak like that?', which appeared in the monthly magazine of the journalists' union, *Zhurnalist*, the author made fun of a fellow journalist's recreation of dialogue written in the old fashion (Kozhemyako, 1986, p.14):

> In the evening as he strolled along the sea-front his comrade asked him: 'What do do want most in life?' And, as if awaiting that very question, without pausing for thought, he replied: 'To become a victor in socialist competition!!!' In that very way, with three exclamation marks.

Despite the pro-*glasnost'* rhetoric, however, by 1988 the authorities were worried that the wave of public criticism released especially during 1987 seemed to be growing. The crises thrown up by the failures of *perestroika* to produce any tangible benefits, notably in the economy, were feeding into a press that was growing ever more bold and self-confident. At a meeting between Gorbachev and representatives of the press held in January 1988 several journalists bemoaned the absence of 'propaganda of positive experience' (Laptev, quoted in *Vstrecha*, 1988, p.2) in the press. Still thinking in Leninist terms of the propagandistic role of the press, *Pravda*'s editor spoke in the past tense of the 'first phase' of *glasnost'* that had concentrated on 'blunders, mistakes and deficiencies'. The second phase, he said, ought to focus on 'the search, dissemination and support for the positive' (*Vstrecha*, 1988, p.3). Chikin, the editor of *Sovetskaya Ros-*

siya,[27] spoke about the 'quite insistent demands of the readers ... for positive experience to be shown' (*Vstrecha*, 1988, p.2; see also Chikin, 1988). The circulation figures for those publications specializing in sensationalist exposés of 'blunders, mistakes and deficiencies' seemed to contradict, or at least place a question mark over Chikin's implication that people really wanted to read positive news.[28]

A newspaper's policy on retrospective *glasnost'* was at this period an indication of its position on *glasnost'* in general. The more conservative publications typically called for more care to be taken and greater respect to be shown to figures from the past, while the more pro-*glasnost'*, 'liberal' ones attempted to widen the scope of criticism. Thus, for example, the editor of the forward-looking, though still orthodox, *Ogonyok*, Korotich, called for the rehabilitation 'of those who merit it' to be carried out 'more intensively' (*Vstrecha*, 1988, p.2),[29] while the editor of *Sovetskaya Rossiya*, Chikin, was upset that some newspapers were 'blaspheming' against figures from the past. 'We ought to ease up on our historical strivings and concentrate on everyday affairs.... There seems to be a kind of frenzied activity in the area of history', he said (*Vstrecha*, 1988, p.2).[30]

Underlying the objections from within the party to critical and invariably negative reassessments of the Soviet Union under Stalin and Brezhnev lay the fear that *glasnost'* was rapidly running out of control

27 See below, Shcherbachenko, pp.242–3, on Chikin's days as daring and innovative news editor of *Sovetskaya Rossiya* under Nenashev's editorship in the late 1970s.

28 Politicians from all systems dislike newspapers when they write articles that reflect badly on themselves. See, for example, Douglas Hurd, the British Foreign Secretary, appealing to the British press to strike a better balance between 'achievement and criticism' (White, 1993).

29 See also below, Korotich, p.177, where he says that his readers supported the publication of 'negative' articles.

30 Chikin was in fact objecting to an article which appeared in *Moskovskaya pravda* after the politburo decision to change the name of the town Brezhnev to Naberezhnye Chyolny (its original name) and the Brezhnev district in Moscow to the Cheryomushki district. The article in question suggested renaming Voroshilovgrad and Kaliningrad, both names glorifying figures who had been at least partially discredited in the public eye as a result of newspaper articles critically reassessing their role in the early history of the Soviet state. While managing to avoid naming the 'guilty' paper, Chikin let his opposition to the article be known. In the process he succeeded in condemning publicly the editor of *Moskovskaya pravda* in the presence of the general secretary, an example both of disloyalty to a colleague, and loyalty to what he perceived as the correct party line. *Moskovskaya pravda* was subsequently forced to recant on the offending article.

and would soon consume the present leadership. And, indeed, the critics were correct. The press had smelt blood and was no longer willing to avert its basilisk stare from the incumbent party–state establishment. A journalist from *Literaturnaya gazeta* expressed a widespread feeling among a section of the media that the 'hierarchy of the [party] apparatus' was an area 'closed to criticism' (*Perestroika*, 1988, p.8). The situation had progressed a long way in the two years since Nenashev, calling for 'party criticism' (Nenashev, 1986, p.25), had understood the term to mean criticism coming from within the party. A modernized form of Leninist self-criticism (*samokritika*), however, would no longer satisfy an increasingly large element of the media.

As *glasnost'* threatened to engulf more and more areas of Soviet society, so it became more and more obvious who did and did not support Gorbachev's reforms. The decision of a senior *Izvestiya* editor not to cover reports that the newly-formed cooperative restaurants were overcharging customers put the government daily into the Gorbachev camp. *Izvestiya*, he said, supported the cooperative movement (Karpenko, 1987). Shestakov of the Moscow *TASS* bureau gave a similar explanation for his decision to refuse to sanction publication of articles on the same topic by one of the journalists working under him (see below, Shestakov, p.189). As well as showing support for Gorbachev, the actions of these editors led to a polarization of the press into pro- and anti-Gorbachev camps. In the old Stalinist way, the pro-Gorbachev newspapers would suppress news that reflected poorly on their faction, while the opponents of reforms concentrated on blaming the state of the country's economy on the Gorbachev reforms, in particular on *glasnost'*.

Chief among the supporters of the conservative, pro-Ligachev camp was *Sovetskaya Rossiya*, which published a letter on 13 March by a Leningrad school teacher, Nina Andreeva (Andreeva, 1988),[31] who pined for the past and railed against the changes brought about by *perestroika*. That an important national newspaper that was an organ of the party central committee[32] should devote an entire page to

---

31 Published in *Sovetskaya Rossiya*, 13 March 1988, as well as in several regional newspapers (see *Perestroika*, 1988, p.8).
32 *Sovetskaya Rossiya* was an organ for the party central committee, as well as the Russian

publishing so blatant an attack on *glasnost'* and *perestroika* was a sign that Gorbachev had split the party and, as a consequence, the once monolithic press.

In what appeared even at the time as a slightly anachronistic form of politics-through-letters, the Andreeva letter was generally understood to be a manifesto for Yegor Ligachev, while the response on 5 April in *Pravda* was understood to be Gorbachev's voice (*Economist*, 1988b).[33]

The response of a *Novosti* journalist, Alexander Levikov, to the Andreeva incident was revealing (*Perestroika*, 1988, p.8):

> But one might ask: if our press was completely reconstructed (which I strongly doubt), then why, right until 5 April, when *Pravda* printed an editorial on it, could all the influential newspapers not make up their minds to print even a reader's letter objecting to Andreeva's letter? I, for instance, was only able to print my letter objecting to it on 23 April and then only in *Moskovskie novosti*.[34] The other newspapers were waiting for instructions or permission.

Levikov indirectly acknowledged that newspapers at this period used readers' letters as proxy editorial statements which they were too afraid to print as leader articles. It also showed that the important *Sovetskaya Rossiya* newspaper could only be 'trumped' by another, more powerful newspaper, in this case the leading organ of the party central committee, *Pravda*.

The furore created by the Andreeva letter and its aftermath was an indication of the importance of readers' correspondence in the Soviet press, even during *perestroika*. National newspapers traditionally ran large correspondence departments to handle, sort and summarize the contents of the vast amounts of mail received. In the absence of a developed mediation network connecting the citizen with the ruling party–state apparatus, both the public and the authorities were aware of the importance of the letter to the editor. In the Brezhnev period, for example, every month *Pravda* prepared a dozen or so summaries of its editorial mail for distribution to members of the party central

---

Federation Supreme Soviet and council of ministers.

33 The Andreeva letter was reprinted in East Germany's *Neues Deutschland*: see *Economist*, 30 April 1988, p.54 and 9 July 1988, p.18. The actual author of the response to the letter was rumoured to have been Alexander Yakovlev (Miller, 1993, p.97).

34 Not, therefore, considered an influential newspaper.

committee (Mickiewicz, 1985, p.46). All letters sent to national news-papers were said to have been answered. On assuming office, general secretaries ritually called for more letters from the public, in the apparent belief that they were a true 'barometer of public opinion' (Konstantin Chernenko, quoted in Mickiewicz, ibid., p.27).

One early fruit of *glasnost'* was a huge increase in the amount of mail received by the press.[35] As the press began to polarize, the cor-respondence columns were transformed from being a forum for 'nationwide approval' to one expressing a 'rag-bag' of viewpoints (Nenashev, 1987). In the new atmosphere it was possible for the editor of *Sovetskaya Rossiya* to publish the Andreeva letter, while the editor of the pro-reform weekly, *Ogonyok*, could reveal his policy of publishing 'purely controversial' letters (see below, Korotich, p.177).

The boom period in correspondence abated once newspapers were allowed to use the services of public opinion polls, a more scientific method of ascertaining the views of the population. The trend in the post-Soviet press was for the more pro-reform newspapers, such as *Moskovskie novosti* or *Argumenty i fakty*, to use opinion polls more than the increasingly marginalized conservative publications, such as *Pravda* or *Sovetskaya Rossiya*, which still resorted to the device of the reader's letter to make an editorial point partly due to tradition, partly because they were less able to afford the services of professional pollsters.

Foreign news coverage

In another manifestation of the newspaper as teacher, the Soviet press had since its inception portrayed the capitalist Western world as a decaying, corrupt and unjust system. Reports were imbued with the view that the capitalist way was philosophically wrong. Thus, for example, mass unemployment in Western Europe was looked upon

---

35 Such was the increase in the amount of mail *Ogonyok* received that it had to expand its letter department (see below, Korotich, pp.182–3 and also Karpenko, for *Izvestiya*, p.173). The letter department of *Moskovskaya pravda* had 'expanded its register of themes in response to an increase (and increase in variety) of 10,000 letters over the last year [1986]' (Mostovshchikov and Loshak, 1987), while Nenashev noted an increase in the number of letters concentrating on 'negative phenomena', and on 'the activity of party collectives, government bodies and inadequacies in industry and agriculture' (Nenashev, 1986, p.92).

with *Schadenfreude* as a visible crack in the edifice of capitalism while industrial strikes were seized upon as an example of the working class rising up against its capitalist overlords.[36]

In spite of the negative press the West received, surveys carried out in the Soviet Union under Brezhnev showed that, cutting across all levels of education and occupation, foreign news was the most popular amongst readers. One survey carried out in 1977, for example, found that most *Pravda* readers turned first to the foreign page (Roxburgh, 1987, pp.93 and 279). The preference for foreign news may have been a reaction against the usually bland and watered-down presentation of home news. By contrast, Soviet foreign correspondents took pains to be as searching as possible in their criticism of capitalist countries. The reports, often written in confrontational language, satisfied the reader's craving for sensationalism. Also, readers so cut off from the outside world were curious to see what was happening beyond the borders of the Soviet Union. Finally, in spite of propaganda which placed the West politically behind the socialist world, the Soviet citizen looked towards the West as the source of progressive ideas and things modern. The West, for example, set the fashion in popular music and fashion.

Soviet coverage of capitalist countries was marked by a superior and sarcastic attitude such as that in the 'Gold fever' (*Zolotaya likhoradka*) report of *Pravda*'s London correspondent, A. Maslennikov, in 1979. Maslennikov reported on 21 September that the 'foreign exchange money markets of the capitalist world once again find themselves in the grip of a "gold fever".'

Unlike the generally hostile coverage from the capitalist world, reports filed from fellow socialist states normally emphasized their fraternal relations with the Soviet Union. Most importantly the reporter was never a critical outsider, rather a well-intentioned, benignly predisposed visitor to a friendly country. Dissident movements in the fraternal countries were condemned in the same way as were analogous groups in the Soviet Union. Coverage of maverick socialist

---

36 See Jacobssen, 1969, p.20, on the rubric in the trade union daily, *Trud*, called *Na frontakh klassovoi bor'by* (On the front-lines of the class struggle). Van den Bercken (1980, p.169) viewed the Marxist–Leninist philosophy behind the anti-Western bias as a rationalization of a centuries-old negative attitude to the West.

countries showed plainly the malleability of the Soviet press. Since the founding of the People's Republic of China in 1949, for instance, Peking's relationship with the Soviet Union had run the full gamut, from 'eternal friendship' during the 1950s to 'permanent enmity' during the 1960s and 1970s.

Pre-*glasnost'* foreign coverage was a finely-tuned instrument capable of distinguishing between several classes of country. An analysis of *Izvestiya*'s coverage of foreign countries between 1970 and 1979 distinguished four such classes (van den Bercken, 1980, p.172):

> The first one is denoted by the terms 'unity and fraternity' and applies to communist countries maintaining relations with both the government and the communist party of the Soviet Union. The communist countries are also designated by the special group labels 'socialist commonwealth' and 'socialist world system'. The second type of relationship is a 'special friendship', and is applied to countries which are both non-aligned and neutral. The third relationship, 'friendship' or 'good neighborship', applies to countries which are non-aligned. The fourth relationship, 'business cooperation', applies to capitalist countries which belong to NATO.

What foreign news actually appeared on the pages of the pre-*glasnost'* Soviet press was ultimately determined in the most direct way by the party. According to a KGB defector who worked in the press,[37] foreign reports appeared in the newspapers in the following manner (Dzhirkvelov, 1987, p.369):

> Every morning Zamyatin,[38] who in 1978 was made head of the International Department of the party, issued instructions to the editors of the national news-

---

37 Another KGB defector, Vladimir Kuzichkin (1990, p.117), wrote that the KGB and GRU (Soviet military intelligence) commonly used *Novosti*, *TASS* and various newspapers as cover organizations for their agents 'Only Pravda, the newspaper of the Party Central Committee, is not used as a cover organization by the intelligence services. This has been forbidden by the Central Committee', Kuzichkin wrote (ibid.). V. Ignatenko, former editor of *Novoe vremya* and press secretary to President Gorbachev who became head of *ITAR–TASS* from August 1991, openly admitted that *TASS* employees were divided between 'them' [i.e., the KGB] and 'us'. He said that soon after his appointment he dissolved the 'special secret mail' service (*osobo zakrytaya pochta*), the function of which was to gather information on domestic politicians. The first document they presented to him, he added, was a denunciation (*donos*) of Eduard Shevardnadze (Ignatenko, 1992). A Soviet foreign correspondent admitted that any of his colleagues would be able to name a dozen journalists in different media who 'combined jobs' (i.e., also worked for the KGB) (Kryuchkov, 1991).
38 Later Soviet ambassador to the United Kingdom.

papers and periodicals, the *TASS* and *Novosti* agencies, and the editors of radio and television news, about what to publish and broadcast concerning events in the Middle East, the policies of the American and British governments or the situation in Afghanistan or Poland. He told them which events they were not to report if they revealed the Soviet Union in a bad light. According to Zamyatin and people like him, Soviet people are not supposed to learn about such events. What the Soviet press will publish about international affairs is now decided by the Department of International Information in conjunction with the International Department of the Central Committee. In this way there will be no unpleasant surprises in the press.

When I was working in the *TASS* agency on the foreign news desk I had to attend a briefing every morning at which we were told which international events to devote most attention to, what emphasis we were to give them and which ones to ignore altogether.

Under *glasnost'* the old journalistic stereotypes that passed for foreign news began to be attacked. *Izvestiya*'s influential political commentator, Alexander Bovin,[39] caught the spirit of the time at a congress of the journalists' union when he complained that foreign coverage consisted of sarcastic epithets rather than hard facts (*S"ezd*, 1987, p.23):

Let's say our minister is travelling to Australia, we write 'trip' (*poezdka*). If a Western minister is going to Peking, we write 'journey' (*voyazh*).[40] We think that these words *poezdka* and *voyazh* solve some kind of problem. In fact they solve nothing. If we write 'bad' or 'slanderous',[41] these words in themselves do not solve anything if behind them there is no serious, well-argued and proven analysis of the facts.

As *glasnost'* became more established, foreign reports from the capitalist camp became less openly hostile. Under Brezhnev, for example, *Izvestiya*'s coverage of elections in the West had 'stressed the manipulation by elusive powers' (van den Bercken, 1980, p.170). An analysis of Soviet newspaper coverage of the 1988 US presidential elections found that 'while the old themes of capital and its faithful puppet, the mass media, are still conspicuous, they are tempered by a sense of balance' (Daly, 1988).

Change, however, was not fast. In 1988 Bovin again bemoaned the

39 Later Russia's first ambassador to Israel.
40 '(Obs. or iron.) journey, travels', Wheeler, 1978.
41 *Klevetnicheskii*, a word often found in foreign copy on unfriendly countries.

'minimal' changes in foreign coverage (*Perestroika*, 1988, p.3)[42] with particular reference to reporting news from the fraternal countries (ibid., p.9):

> By not telling our readers and listeners about what is going on, for instance, in Romania or Angola, or Iran or Mozambique, Lebanon or North Korea ... we ourselves are pushing people into listening to the 'Voice of America' and other 'voices'.

In fact, even when reports from abroad were imbued with the spirit of *glasnost'*, the voracious public appetite for domestic news meant that they might pass largely unnoticed. According to the editor of the leading foreign affairs weekly, *New Times* (*Novoe vremya*) the Soviet reader during the heyday of *glasnost'* was obsessed with domestic news and interested in foreign news only if it had a bearing on home news (see below, Pumpyanskii, pp.207, 232; see also below, Shestakov, p.194).

Coupled with the problem of exciting the interest of a public focused on internal matters, Soviet foreign correspondents encountered other difficulties not shared by their home-based colleagues. Before the collapse of the Soviet bloc in Eastern Europe, the position of the Russian correspondent covering the 'fraternal' socialist countries had become ever more difficult, in particular for those reporting from countries which had not followed the Soviet path of reconstruction and media openness. Until the removal from office of Todor Zhivkov in November 1989, Soviet correspondents filing reports from Bulgaria found themselves in a delicate position. On the one hand the Soviet reader, now used to frankness in home news, had begun to demand the same standards in foreign news. On the other hand, any report critical

---

42 See also White, 1992, pp.77–8. The author refers to the extensive coverage in Soviet press of foreign disasters, as opposed to silence on internal ones. He also quotes a reader who said he knew in detail what was happening in various African countries, but only had 'a very rough idea of what was happening in his own city'. See also the hidden 'disaster chronology' of the Soviet Union from 1935–87 in Oberg, 1989. Speaking to Western scholars in 1989 (Cohen and vanden Heuval, 1989, p.222), Bovin said: 'We can criticize what happened before 1985 – the deployment of SS–20 missiles in Europe and the invasion of Afghanistan, for example – but I can't disagree with what Foreign Minister Eduard Shevardnadze said today, yesterday, or last year. And the reason is the old habit, yours and ours, of associating everything that appears in Soviet newspapers with the Kremlin.'

of Bulgaria that might appear in an influential Soviet newspaper, such as *Izvestiya* or *Pravda*, was seen by the Bulgarian communist party as Soviet interference in Bulgarian affairs, especially considering the popularity and influence of the Soviet press sold in Bulgaria itself. Since Soviet–Bulgarian government and party relations at that time were officially good, criticism of the Bulgarian government under Zhivkov in government or party newspapers tended to be indirect.

One example of criticism directed obliquely at the Bulgarian regime came in the form of a lengthy article which appeared in *Izvestiya* headlined 'Everything is available in Turkey' (Zakhar'ko, 1989). The author gave a glowing account of what he saw as an economic miracle taking place in Turkey. According to his description, in Turkey one could buy everything 'from figs, olive oil and dozens of varieties of salami, to videos, cars and personal computers'.

The Bulgarian reader would have noticed that the author of the article, before becoming Istanbul correspondent, had been *Izvestiya*'s man in Sofia. The Soviet reporter was criticizing the official anti-Turkish Bulgarian policy of the time not by explicitly condemning Zhivkov and his government, but, instead, extolling the virtues of the country which the Zhivkov regime was denigrating.

News coverage from Afghanistan during the Soviet military occupation, the foreign story that had the most relevance for Soviet readers, was far from comprehensive and heavily censored. A lengthy and penetrating article dealing with coverage of the war appeared in the August 1989 edition of the journal *Novy mir*. Public discussion of many important questions concerning the war was still taboo when Bovin had spoken in April 1988 on less immediately relevant countries such as Mozambique.

The author of the *Novy mir* article, a senior *Izvestiya* political commentator, Stanislav Kondrashov, recounted how he had been asked on 26 or 27 December 1979 by *Izvestiya*'s editor at the time, P. Alekseev, to write an article justifying in advance the imminent Soviet entry into Afghanistan.[43] Kondrashov refused on the grounds that Afghanistan was not his area, an act, he said, of 'passive resistance made by a powerless serf of whom is demanded blind obedience

---

43 Note that the editor of *Izvestiya* already knew of the politburo decision to send the Soviet army into Afghanistan.

to the baron and an irrational love for his country' (Kondrashov, 1989, p.191). A few days later, *Izvestiya* published an article written by one of Kondrashov's colleagues on the same theme headlined: 'Intrigues of imperialism repulsed. Revolution in Afghanistan enters new phase' (ibid., p.191).

During the course of the nine-year occupation, Kondrashov wrote, readers sent letters to the newspapers requesting information on the number of casualties and deaths from among what the Soviet media described euphemistically as a 'limited contingent of Soviet troops'.[44] Readers also asked who had given permission to the ministry of defence to send in troops to a country on which war had not been declared. The press did not publish these letters (ibid., p.187).

The Soviet reading public had to wait a long time before it was told how many soldiers were stationed in Afghanistan (ibid., p.187):

> Eight and a half years after the commencement of Soviet military acts in Afghanistan and three years after the April 1985 Plenum of the Central Committee of the CPSU; after the conclusion of the Geneva accords on the withdrawal of Soviet troops and after the beginning of the first phase of withdrawal; only then did our people learn through the media that the 'limited contingent of Soviet troops' was about 100,000 strong. Although in the rest of the world the mass media had long cited such a figure and reported that hidden under the pseudonym of the 'limited contingent of Soviet troops' was the 40th army.

It was at this time that the Soviet people first learned of the extent of Soviet losses from the war in Afghanistan (ibid., p.187):

> When, where and how were these figures made public? ... 22 May 1988 in the press centre of the ministry for foreign affairs of the USSR, [an institution] aimed more at the foreign press corps than our own, in the context of preparation for the forthcoming Soviet–American summit, the head of the main political department of the Soviet Army and Navy, General A.D. Lizichev, reported that in May 1988 the number of Soviet deaths in Afghanistan was 13,310, there had been 35,478 serious injuries and 311 lost without trace. Until this announcement Soviet people had to make do, through listening to foreign broadcasts, with exaggerated figures (40,000–50,000 dead). The official figures on the number of losses, naturally, went around the world and, moreover, were reported more widely abroad than in the Soviet Union. Soviet newspapers consigned the painful figures to the inside columns, tucked inside the official report on the

44 *Ogranichenny kontingent sovetskikh voisk (OKSV)*.

press conference. It is worth noting that this happened not in the era of stagnation, but under *glasnost'*.

Foreign news coverage changed drastically following the collapse of state controls on the press. In the Yeltsin period as a result of economic difficulties and a change in philosophy, the liberal press began to lean very heavily on Western sources for the bulk of its foreign stories. Since the August 1991 coup, for example, *Izvestiya* began to rely almost exclusively for its daily foreign news-brief column on Western agency reports.[45] The borrowing of this genre is but one example of how the Western way of treating news was imported into Russia after the disintegration of the old power structures. These foreign news items, mostly translations from English, were composed according to a Western model that excluded the old Soviet-style presentation of news. They reflected a Western understanding of what constituted news that completely undermined the moralistic and didactic approach of the Soviet school of journalism. A 1987 *Izvestiya* headline, 'Is Uncle Sam's umbrella necessary?' (11 March), for example, would have looked out of place among a typical non-judgemental headline from *Izvestiya* in 1993 'Bosnian Serbs accept peace plan' (Reuter, 21 January 1993).

---

45 Over a 30-day period between December 1992 and January 1993, for example, of 198 such news items, only 48, or 24 per cent, were written by Russian correspondents, the vast majority, 150 or 76 per cent, were translations from Reuters, AP and AFP. See below, p.157.

4. Language of the Soviet Press

Development of Soviet press language under Gorbachev

The language of the Soviet press during *perestroika* underwent changes directly related to a change in political thinking. At a deeper level, this change in political thinking undermined the didactic principle of the Leninist press.[1] The resulting absence of this guiding principle meant that several typical Soviet newspaper genres lost their *raison d'être* and became redundant. In some cases, newspapers reacted by attempting to alter the style and content of the old genres to fit the new criteria. In others, the genres proved resistant to such manipulation.

A study of the development of the language and content of the *zametka, fotoreportazh* and editorial (*peredovaya stat'ya*), three front-page genres that gave the Soviet newspaper its distinctive face, reveals the dynamic and modalities of change during the early years of *perestroika*. We shall be examining the changes that took place in these genres in the former government newspaper, *Izvestiya*, in 1979 and 1987. The articles from 1979 are typical of the pre-*glasnost'*, Brezhnev era, while those of 1987 belong to a transitional period between the introduction of *glasnost'* in 1985 and the close of the period in August 1991.

Zametka

Perhaps the genre considered most typical of the Soviet newspaper under Brezhnev was the short front-page news item, or *zametka*.[2] This genre came to the fore under Stalin's vigorous campaigns in the 1930s to industrialize the country[3] and continued essentially unchanged in

---

1 See, for example, Brian McNair, 1991, pp.16–17.
2 Literally 'note', or 'news brief' in Western journalistic parlance. The Soviet *zametka* was also referred to as '*proizvodstvennaya informatsiya*' (industrial information item), '*pervopolosnaya informatsiya*' (page-one information item), *khronikal'naya informatsiya*' (chronicle information item) and, informally, as '*informashka*'.
3 D'yachenko, 1987, p.8, without explicitly referring to Stalin, notes that 'the industrial (page-one) genre was formed in the years of the first five-year plans' during which time,

style and content in all the main Soviet newspapers, including *Izvestiya*, until around 1987. After this period its prestige declined and it gradually disappeared altogether as a genre.

The fundamental philosophy behind the genre was didactic: the publishing of successful news stories from the industrial, agricultural and construction fronts was intended to present to the reader exemplary instances of success which ought to be emulated.

D'yachenko described the typical, unreconstructed *zametka* as a bearer of 'joyful tidings' and 'happy occurrences'.[4] Based on the notion instilled in journalists since the early 1930s that success was to be judged predominantly according to 'quantitative assessments and indicators',[5] these short news items of around a hundred words each in length consistently produced a series of data denoting, above all, size. Typically, such data came in the form of comparative statistical information on increases in productivity or over-fulfilment of production quotas in record time.

This genre was extremely resistant to changes in political and economic thought under *perestroika*. The content of the *zametka* and its linguistic expression had become so linked to the Stalinist quantitative economic philosophy and the instructional role of the press in promoting it, that adapting it to the new economic thinking of *perestroika* eventually proved impossible. Thus, despite the changes that had taken place in the press by 1987, two years after the formal introduction of *glasnost'*, the *zametka* that appeared in *Izvestiya* in that year had much the same form as its 1979 counterpart. Ultimately, because it proved impossible to 'reconstruct', the genre was done away with altogether. By the end of the Soviet period it no longer appeared in *Izvestiya*, or any other important newspaper.

Though still present in 1987, the *zametka* was already beginning to appear with much less frequency than in 1979. Featuring almost daily

---

he continues, the breaking of records had a real meaning in the context of the feverish attempts to build up industry in the country. D'yachenko's article suggested that the genre, and its accompanying language, were not appropriate in 1987.

4   Ibid., p.7. The two-line poem which D'yachenko quotes – '*Nasha rodina prekrasno i tsvetyot kak makov tsvet. Okromya yavlenii schast'ya, nikakikh yavlenii net*' (Our Motherland is blooming beautifully. Apart from happy events, nothing happens) – summarized his attitude to the *zametka* in its traditional form.

5   Nenashev, 1986, p.119.

in June 1979, frequently under the rubric *SSSR – Novosti* (USSR – News), it formed an integral part of the typical front page of *Izvestiya*.[6] When *zametki* appeared in 1987, they normally found themselves transplanted from page one to the second page, no longer meriting a separate rubric even there. Such, however, was the philosophy behind the genre that when they did appear in 1987, they reported exclusively good news. On this evidence, the *zametka* seemedunreformable.

The diminution of their frequency of appearance on page one (and overall), as well as their relegation to page two, showed that they had become less prestigious as a genre. At a deeper level, however, this pointed to a negatively critical reassessment of their value as effective propaganda, sometimes expressed by the party general secretary himself: 'One does not need millions of tons of steel, millions of tons of coal as such. What one needs are tangible end results.'[7]

The fall of the old-style *zametka* was directly related to the new economic policy in industry for which quality, not statistically measurable as easily as quantity, was deemed to matter more.[8] In 1987 the quantitative approach was consistently cited as the cause of many of the ills of Soviet industry. It is not surprising, therefore, that the *informashka*, which serviced the quantitative approach, was also equally openly criticized.

So, while the fading away of the *zametka* in its own way reflected the latest economic policy of the leadership, it was impossible to predict in 1987 that it would eventually disappear. At that time, influential voices periodically called for *glasnost'* to shift its focus from

6   *Zametki* appeared on 23 of the 25 days examined in June 1979, with more than one such item – from two to 11 – appearing on each of the 23 days. The average number of *zametki* appearing on any one day was over five. In stark contrast, only on ten of the 29 days counted in November 1987 did they appear, in numbers ranging from one (on four days) to five. Their total number came to 25, meaning an average number on the days they appeared of 2.5 and less than one over the 29 days (83.3). *Izvestiya* was not alone in publishing fewer *zametki* than previously at this time. D'yachenko observed that *Pravda* published 'fewer and fewer' of this type of article, though not everywhere was the trend visible (ibid. p.8): 'Some newspapers continue literally to stuff the first-page columns with "shock information" (*udarnaya informatsiya*), written according to the old clichés.'

7   Gorbachev, 1988a.

8   A state quality-control body, *Gospriyomka*, which had the power to reject poor quality goods and reduce the pay of those responsible, was introduced in early 1987 (White, 1992, p.144).

muckraking journalism to articles containing at least 'constructive' criticism and 'progressive experiences' (Chikin, 1988), both code-words for the type of positive propaganda promoted in the *zametka*. In retrospect, the decline and final fall of the *zametka* was linked to the failure of those set against economic reform to wrest political power from those in favour of change.

The *zametka* was eventually replaced by a new type of article that had very little in common with it. This replacement was found in a new rubric called *Panorama novostei* (News Panorama), of which three were published in November 1987. The rubric included three genres: the *fotoreportazh*, the official photograph and the *zametka*. The new *zametka* was not restricted to reporting good news. Unlike the old articles, written either in an anonymous style or in the faceless prose characteristic of *TASS* reports, the individuality of the reporting journalist was apparent in the new genre. Importantly, though, this individuality was expressed as if by default. The vacuum left by the absence of old-style clichéd language was necessarily filled by a language which drew from a greater referential field, so expressing the news by means of a more individualized authorial language which, paradoxically, was less 'subjective' (or judgmental) than the old-style formulaic language. These new 1987 *zametki* serve as a good example of a genre brought about by the collapse of the old certainties in journalistic philosophy as well as being a consequence of the internal *perestroika* of *Izvestiya* brought about by the advent of *glasnost'*. They were a halfway house to becoming a new genre combining elements of both the analytical economic article and the *reportazh*. In Western journalistic parlance, the new genre which finally developed from the transformed *zametka* would be called, simply, a news story.

The instructional philosophy behind the traditional form of the *zametka* predetermined its content, as well as the language[9] in which

9   Articles analysed for language analysis of *zametka*:

	1979		1987	
Article N° 1	5.iii.1979	N° 57[19122]	17.iii.1987	N° 77[21884]
Article N° 2	12.iv.1979	N° 88[19153]	1.iv.1987	N° 92[21899]
Article N° 3	3.v.1979	N° 105[19170]	22.v.1987	N° 143[21950]
Article N° 4	4.vi.1979	N° 130[19195]	5.vi.1987	N° 157[21964]
Article N° 5	3.ix.1979	N° 206[19271]	5.ix.1987	N° 249[22056]
Article N° 6	9.x.1979	N° 237[19302]	31.x.1987	N° 305[22112]

the content was described. Because the typical exemplary industry or enterprise was traditionally measured in quantitative terms, the *zametka* contained a profusion of linguistic expressions of production figures and rates of production. The expression of production figures manifested itself lexically as often very large numbers, while rates of productivity were described by a variety of linguistic means to express the comparative degree. Often, the comparisons were 'false', since they were compared to nothing.[10]

Frequently, a constellation of these linguistic features appeared, creating an impression that the *zametka* was written according to a set formula, or series of formulas, appropriate to the *genre*. In other words, these formulas, manifested in, for example, a large number or an expression containing a comparative degree, were taken from a finite source of formulas. Thus, it was common to find examples of both large numbers and comparative degree appearing side by side:

> ... the country received over a million tons of oil. As a result of this two million roubles worth of production was produced over the plan (both 22 December 1979);
> Their application will increase sevenfold ... rates of productivity (5 March 1979).

The linguistic expression of the economic planning system resulted in a series of words and phrases from the economic sphere denoting economic plans, their fulfilment or overfulfilment, and the means of competition under Soviet socialism:

| Article N° 7 | 19.xi.1979 | N° 271[19336] | 10.xi.1987 | N° 315[22122] |
| Article N° 8 | 22.xii.1979 | N° 299[19364] | 2.xii.1987 | N° 337[22144] |

10 D'yachenko (1987, p.8) found that many of the record figures achieved by 'heroic' workers and hailed as success stories were often incomplete, superficial and hollow reports of 'superficial success' stories. Nenashev spoke of the 'contradiction between statistics and real life' (Nenashev, 1986, p.119). Indeed, it appears that these reports themselves were sometimes written with the purpose of fulfilling a quota of positive news. See, for example, Johnstone, 1987, p.22 (the author was a member of the British communist party's executive committee and of the editorial board of *Marxism Today*): 'One of the editors of *Moskovskie novosti* told me recently: "The population were told that victorious socialism was bringing rising grain production and falling crime rates. In fact the statistical curves swung in the opposite direction."' See also D'yachenko's 'factional' account (1987, p.9) of how *zametka* stories were gathered by journalists.

> They completed the four-year plan ahead of schedule (3 September 1979); ... a socialist competition developed for the fulfilling of the plan ahead of schedule (13 July 1979).

Again, it was not unusual to find combinations of features in one sentence, as, for example, below, where a term from the sphere of economic planning appeared alongside language to do with production and rates of productivity:

> She completed a personal five-year plan task by producing 661 tons of twisted thread, of which 56 tons were over the plan target (12 April 1979).

Fotoreportazh

The fall of the *zametka* was due to its inherent inability to re-form itself to the new requirements of the time. Another genre that characterized the Soviet press under Brezhnev and lasted well into *perestroika* was the front-page *fotoreportazh*. Unlike the *zametka*, the *fotoreportazh* proved to be more susceptible to adaptations required by the changing political philosophy of the time. In the end, however, it, too, suffered the fate of the *zametka*, and disappeared from the pages of the mainstream press.

Under Brezhnev, the *fotoreportazh* consisted of a 'lead picture', usually portraying a model worker, or group of workers, accompanied by a short text. As *glasnost'* gained more ground, the nature of the *fotoreportazh* changed. No longer featuring an élite group of heroic figures from the workplace, the protagonists depicted in the photographs became more flesh-and-blood characters, while the nature of their exemplary activity changed in accordance with the new economic priorities of *perestroika*. With the widening of the definition of what constituted a role model, the genre aimed to appeal to a more average, non-heroic, worker, who could identify, and be identified, with an idealized role model.

By the time of the August 1991 coup, the *fotoreportazh* had as a genre disappeared, replaced by what Western journalists would call a 'news picture', or simply a photograph illustrating a prominent page-one story, often the lead story.

The reasons for the disappearance of the Soviet-style *fotoreportazh* are not unlike those for the *zametka*. The function of both the *zametka* and the *fotoreportazh* was to present an ideal[11] and idealistic picture of Soviet life.[12] The *zametka* should provide readers with examples to be emulated of successful enterprises of all sorts, while the *fotoreportazh* was to give the reader an individual role model. The same undermining process of this fundamental didactic principle of the Leninist press, which resulted in the ultimate eclipse of the *zametka*, had the same effect on the *fotoreportazh*. Once its propagandist role had been discredited, the genre served no real purpose. A *fotoreportazh* without a purpose was merely a news or mini-feature story with a picture.

A comparative count of the frequency of the *fotoreportazh* in 1979 and 1987 showed that there was no significant change in its rate of appearance.[13] However, by 1987 the 'heroic' credentials of the subject had been modified to fit into the mould of the exemplary Soviet citizen fashioned according to the philosophy of *perestroika*. Typically, then, what was brought to the attention of the reader was a financially, rather than ideologically, stimulated worker. In a survey of the *fotoreportazh* for 1987 there were fewer pictures of hero-workers, shock brigades, and so forth, and more showing, for instance, an industrious family working and earning a good living in a contractual agreement with the collective farm.[14]

It was only after 1987 that the already modified *fotoreportazh*, different from its Brezhnevite counterpart in degree rather than in

---

11 According to the chairman of the all-Union commission on photography, G. Koposov (*Sezd*, 1987, p.21): 'What we get on the pages of our newspapers and magazines are clichéd photographs, interminable smiles that say nothing.'

12 In Vomperskii, 1970, p.7, the prerequisites for the *zametka*, or short news item, also pertain to the *fotoreportazh*: 'For the journalist and rural correspondent it is always important to take note of and display the framework of things that are new and communist, to provide coverage of the patriotic deeds of the toilers and to provide information on the most important achievements of the Soviet people.'

13 Of the 29 counted issues for November 1987, 25 contain a *fotoreportazh*. On two days there are two, bringing the total to 27. Out of 25 days in June 1979, the *fotoreportazh* appeared on 20 separate days.

14 While the majority (seven out of ten) of the *fotoreportazhi* in the period examined for 1987 revealed a a genre in evolution, the remaining three, from 1 April, 5 September and 5 June 1987, bore the hallmarks of the earlier Brezhnev period.

kind, began to be replaced by the news picture, or topical photograph. The change in function of the *fotoreportazh* from propaganda tool to bearer of a Western concept of 'news' was, however, very gradual. An article published in a 1988 edition of *Sovetskoe foto*, touching on the topic of the '*problematic*' *fotoreportazh*, or photographs showing the negative side of Soviet life, reported that photo-journalists were more constrained than reporters. According to the author, while a reporter could write about a queue, the photographer was 'condemned to avoid' such negative phenomena of Soviet life.[15]

Despite the gradualness of the change, the language[16] used in the *fotoreportazh* of 1987, compared to 1979, reflected the changes which the genre was undergoing. With hindsight, it is plain that the stylistic register of the 1987 *fotoreportazh* was drawing closer to the spoken language. This was achieved principally by omitting the type of politico–economic language that typified the 1979 *fotoreportazh*, as well as by the introduction of colloquial speech.

15   See Vyatkin, 1988, p.16. *Moskovskie novosti, Ogonyok* as well as other of the more daring publications, led the way in using photographs which could only be called problematic. See, for example, the dead body in the snow shown on the front page of *Moskovskie novosti*, 24 January 1990, a victim of the Armenian–Azerbaijani conflict over Nagorny–Karabakh. Lev Sherstennikov, staff photographer for *Ogonyok*, was (in 1988) encouraged by the new freedom to take 'negative' photographs, evidence that the editorial freedom given to photographs varied from publication to publication: 'It is of course encouraging that, unlike the old *Ogonyok*, today's *Ogonyok* is not preoccupied with the smoothing over and beautification of negative photographs.' (Quoted in Chudakov, 1988, p.16). The large circulation dailies moved more slowly. The head of the illustrations department of *Izvestiya*, Vladimir Shin, wrote of the new attitude to the role of the photographer in covering 'problematic' news stories. Echoing the sentiments of Vyatkin (above), Shin reported: 'Usually in those cases, photojournalism has tended to stay in the shade, occupying a secondary position.' (Quoted in *Sovetskoe foto*, 1988, p.9.)

16   Articles analysed for language analysis of *fotoreportazh*:

	1979		1987	
Article N° 1	5.iii.1979	N° 57[19122]	17.iii.1987	N° 77[21884]
Article N° 2	12.iv.1979	N° 88[19153]	1.iv.1987	N° 92[21899]
Article N° 3	3.v.1979	N° 105[19170]	22.v.1987	N° 143[21950]
Article N° 4	4.vi.1979	N° 130[19195]	5.vi.1987	N° 157[21964]
Article N° 5	3.ix.1979	N° 206[19271]	5.ix.1987	N° 249[22056]
Article N° 6	9.x.1979	N° 237[19302]	31.x.1987	N° 305[22112]
Article N° 7	19.xi.1979	N° 271[19336]	10.xi.1987	N° 315[22122]
Article N° 8	22.xii.1979	N° 299[19364]	2.xii.1987	N° 337[22144]

The balance of stylistic features for the 1979 *fotoreportazh* was indicative of the specific 'literary' pretensions of a genre which typically contained biographical details of the heroic subject's life or work, often embellished by a figurative language. The content of the text usually established a link between these details and the attainment of an economic goal, often expressed with the aid of one of the stock of current affairs clichés and large figures or statistics. The heroes of the *fotoreportazh* were as a rule shown to possess ideological motivation, usually expressed in clichéd socio–political language.

Thus, for instance, the 'Cotton of Uzbekistan comes on stream' *fotoreportazh* (9 October 1979) contains *zametka*-like raw statistical information – the attainment of the goal – as well as figurative clichés applied to the work undertaken and to those who have undertaken the work:

More than 1.8 million tons of 'white gold' has been dispatched.

Throughout the piece, aspects of the actual work are continually referred to in what for the Soviet reader was clichéd language. The cotton harvest is the 'white harvest' (*belaya zhatva*), the harvesters 'cotton-growers' (*khlopkoroby*), while the combine-harvesters are referred to as 'blue ships' (*golubye korabli*). 'Competition', meaning socialist, ideologically driven, competition, is thrice mentioned as a motivating force behind the workers' enthusiasm.

The reader is also provided with impressive-looking numerical data which, because of the absence of information essential to put it into context, is meaningless:

13,235 cotton-harvesting machines will take part in the cotton harvest.

The heroic credentials of the human heroes featuring in the 1979 *fotoreportazh* are very often linguistically manifested in a combination of an ideological or economic cliché, and the name of their profession. Thus, the 3 September 1979 article features a 'progressive machine operator', the hero for 3 May 1979 is a 'progressive *Komsomol* electrical fitter' and for 5 March 1979, in a combination of two clichéd expressions, 'progressive workers of socialist competition'.

The 'plumbers–assembly workers' are also referred to as 'toilers' involved in an 'uninterrupted creative search', both current affairs clichés. And just as the Uzbek cotton harvest is portrayed as a massive operation, so the 'metal workers–assembly workers' work in 'one of the largest enterprises in the country', while their high level of output, for which they have been awarded the 'state Mark of Honour', is a realization of their desire to 'translate into life the decisions of the XXV [party] Congress', the latter phrase being a classic cliché.

Another device employed to attribute heroic qualities to the subjects of the *fotoreportazh* is the use of a stylistically high-sounding word when referring to their profession. The 12 April 1979 hero is dubbed a 'noble weaver'[17] while the tractor-builders who figure in the same report are referred to as 'creators of mighty tractors'. The 'noble weaver' also has the desired and appropriate political and moral qualifications to merit her heroic status:

> Being [*yavlyayas'*] a member of the Executive Committee ... the noble weaver ... is [*yavlyaetsy]*) a mentor for the youth.

Worthy of note is the appearance twice in one sentence of the bookish *yavlyat'sya*, a variant of the verb 'to be' (*byt'*). In the Brezhnevite press adherence to the stylistic norm of avoiding the same word, especially a stylistically-marked one such as *yavlyat'sya*, in one sentence was less important than the journalist's duty to ensure that considerations other than stylistic were observed. In this example these considerations consisted of an inventory of the subject's official attributes. In similar fashion, the 5 March 1979 hero, a work collective, was the recipient of an award, the full-blown, officious-sounding title of which was supplied without regard to the strains it imposed on the article's readability:

> [The collective] has been presented with the Red Banner challenge award of the Central Committee of the USSR, the Soviet of Ministers of the USSR, the All-Union Central Council of Professional Unions, the Central Committee of the All-Union Leninist Communist Union of Youth, and will be entered into the All-

17 See Shmelyov, 1977, p.285 on the 'workers' dynasty' (*rabochaya dinastiya*) in Russian journalese.

Union board of honour at the Exhibition of Economic Achievements of the USSR.[18]

Occasionally, the journalist's attempts to introduce the hero in a casual manner generated a pseudo-literary style. Thus, the opening lines for the 4 June 1979 article, 'Hot days, June days', preceded an article replete with examples of large figures and comparisons that were, outside a context, largely bereft of meaning:

> ... over 60 combine-harvesters have been brought out on to the field; the grain-growers ... are faced with the prospect of gathering in cereals from an area of 17,250 hectares; hundreds of fodder-procuring detachments have taken to the fields; here they intend to get no less than five crops of hay.

The language of the 1987 *fotoreportazh* is marked by the presence of colloquial lexicon, first-person narration, parenthetical words and phrases, and particles, all linguistic features characteristic of informal Russian[19] and absent from the 1979 *fotoreportazh*. These features often appear in clusters, complementing each other to create a less clichéd variety of *fotoreportazh*. Gone for the most part is the *pere-dovik* (front-rank worker), the heroic focus of the 1979 *fotoreportazh*. The new hero is the family, the single most frequently encountered subject of the 1987 count. The shift in policy, from bestowing glory on an individual hero (*peredovik*), or group of heroes such as the 'brigade of progressive workers', or 'progressive brigade', to the family, reflected the political mood of the leadership of the time, especially in the area of agriculture. Two of the headlines, 'Family farm' (17 March 1987) and 'Family lease farm' (2 December 1987), show the

18 See also an example of scrupulous adherence to the reproduction of official nomenclature, connected to the predilection of the then general secretary, Leonid Brezhnev, for imposing and lofty-sounding titles. In the following instance from a 1979 *fotoreportazh*, the announcing of part of Leonid Brezhnev's official title prefaces an oblique official quotation: '21 September 1978 will remain forever in the memories of the toilers of the factory. Visiting them was the General Secretary of the Central Committee of the CPSU, the Chairman of the Supreme Soviet of the USSR, Leonid Ilyich Brezhnev. He valued highly the toil of the collective, gave good advice and best wishes.' (*Izvestiya*, 9 February 1979).

19 On the relationship between informal language and particles and parenthetical words and phrases see, for example, on particles: Miloslavskii, 1987, p.43, E.A. Zemskaya, 1987, p.91, and A.N. Vasilyeva, no date, p.6 and passim; on parenthetical words and phrases, see Zemskaya, passim, op. cit. and Kapanadze, 1983, pp.142–72.

government's backing for the family farm unit.

The innocent-looking change in headlines masked a much deeper shift in policy. The government initiative to encourage peasants to lease land from the collectivized farms was an indirect challenge to the wisdom of the collectivization campaign of the 1920s and 1930s. Public condemnation at this period of both the means by which agriculture was collectivized and of the failures of the collectivized system to meet the country's needs was not possible, especially in the government's own daily. Nevertheless it was impossible to avoid noticing the new emphasis in the press on the non-ideologically stimulated, small collective of an emotionally close-knit and preferably large family that might include grandparents and grandchildren. Thus the chatty and familial style in the 31 October 1987 *fotoreportazh*:

> The Pisar' family home was always full of people. In the village they'd say that this gave Il'ya and Nadezhda so much happiness that you could borrow some of it.

In six of the ten months counted, the family unit is the focal point of the *fotoreportazh*, with its members depicted in the accompanying photograph. This centring on the family was accompanied by a lowering of the register in which the articles were written. Authors appeared to be attempting to reproduce the language of the home. The highly stylized politico-economic rhetoric characteristic of the 1979 *fotoreportazh* had been largely replaced by domestic language, or, at least, the journalist's attempts at its recreation, bound by his or her own literary talents and the limitations imposed by the unchanging, fundamentally propagandistic philosophical intent which lay behind this front-page genre.

The 1979 *fotoreportazh*, despite its monotonous expository style, read smoothly. By contrast, the stylistic awkwardness of some of the 1987 pieces was a result of using non-heroic, domestic language in a genre that was essentially heroic. The awkwardness was also a result of journalists' inexperience in writing in a new manner, as well as readers' inexperience in reading such language.

The emphasis on the family generated a domestic language. The very nomenclature used in describing the family members helped transport the heroes out of the world of the 1979 *fotoreportazh*. For instance, the members of the Shatokhin family (17 March 1987) were 'papa', 'mama' and the 'kids' (*rebyata*). The father was said to be known in the area as 'the cleverest craftsman in the village'. The Shatokhin 'kids', Walton-like, prepare the rustic, home-cooking 'potato cakes'[20] for their hardworking parents. The model father of the 22 May 1987 *fotoreportazh*, Fyodorov (22 May 1987), loved his 'bunch of kids' (*rebatnya*). The reporter stands in awe of Fyodorov, who is asked how he manages with 'four children!'.

The reader is told in similarly conversational language that Nikolai Gretskii, hero of the 10 November 1987 *fotoreportazh*, is a busy man: 'Nikolai Dmitrievich Gretskii, you could say (*mozhno skazat'*), has practically no spare time (*vremya v obrez*)'. The parenthetical ('you could say') immediately informs the reader that the information is being communicated in a non-categorical, relaxed fashion, an impression bolstered by the colloquial *vremya v obrez*. Vladimir Ivanovich (2 December 1987) is so occupied that when people tried to count how many professions he had, 'it turned out to be somewhere between 6 and 10'. The lack of exactitude and the use of the colloquial-sounding disjunctive conjunction to express the number of professions the hero manages to hold simultaneously (*ne to 6, ne to 10*), combine to impute heroic characteristics to an otherwise ordinary subject in a non-dogmatic way. Super-dad Fyodorov uses a very non-heroic register to describe his wonderful children (22 May 1987):

> And this bunch of kids brings such an amount of joy! And, incidentally, they're growing up interested in electronics.

Sometimes, in an effort to present the news informally, journalists submerged their own authorial voice and took on that of the hero. Thus the 17 March 1987 *fotoreportazh* had no direct speech, yet the piece

---

20 '*Kartofel'nye deruny*'. Here, in an attempt to achieve a relaxed, informal style, the journalist resorts to the Byelorussian word for potato cakes. The use of a foreign word, which sounds rustic to educated Russians, is also an example of the national press giving its readers a bird's-eye view of life throughout the Soviet Union, homing in on one family. In fact, as a genre the *fotoreportazh* served the function of providing the reader with a picture of life in seemingly randomly chosen areas of the country (see Henry and Young, 1983, p.26).

described the Shatokhin family in a language used by people like the Shatokhins. This resulted in the appearance of many features typically found in the spoken language. This technique of assuming the language of the subject was used to present a serious political message (for example, 'make money') in a non-didactic way. The same way, it was thought, in which the heroes of the *fotoreportazh* and their like would communicate:

> The Shatokhins give a fair amount of milk to the collective farm, and at a cheap price. And the earnings on the family farm aren't bad either.

In the 1987 *fotoreportazh*, instead of bludgeoning the reader with a barrage of unfathomable statistics, the journalist tried a softer approach in the hope that the message would seep into the reader's consciousness. It was enough to tell the sophisticated reader that the Shatokhins sold 'a fair amount' of milk to the *kolkhoz*. It was not necessary to spell out either the amount or the price. Suffice to say that the family's earnings 'aren't bad', without going into figures. In the language of advertising, the 1987 'copywriter' (journalist) was rephrasing the message of the 'client' (party) for a far more subtle and intelligent 'consumer' (reader) than in 1979. The 'consumer' is being subjected to a 'soft-sell' technique.

Another 'family farm' *fotoreportazh* (2 December 1987), though written in an informal style and showing an abundance of colloquial features, also contained some 1979 characteristics, in particular the use of large figures and quantitative comparisons. While the article appeared to be anachronistic, it was significantly different from its 1979 ancestor. Of the two figures, one gave the yearly milk yield of one family set against a named average yield. The other figure gave the average monthly earnings of one family. In the first case, the reader was given the information necessary to make the comparison meaningful, while in the second instance, although no comparative figure was provided, the average reader would have found it easy to understand that the monthly earnings of the family, 1,100 roubles, were for the time exceptional. The implied compared unit, the average monthly earnings of a collective farm-worker, was common knowledge. Both figures were presented in a relaxed and informal style, devoid of demagogy:

So it's not difficult to compare them by results. While the average milk yield per cow on the collective farm is 2,680 kilogrammes, the Gus'kovs' yield is 5,123.

The monthly earnings of the family are introduced with the aid of a parenthetical phrase, 'it is true' (*pravda*), used to soften the delivery, by means of delay, of the numerical data:

Earnings, it's true (*pravda*), are good: an average of 1,100 roubles per family.

The parenthesis also serves as a device to create understatement, perceived in 1987 as an effective rhetorical device for propagandizing one's message.

Typical also was the open-ended manner in which the Fyodorov (22 May 1987) *fotoreportazh* concluded: 'All their toys are electronic...'.[21] The use of a series of dots to complete a piece had the effect of presenting the information as not very out of the ordinary, rather as a common occurrence in the lives of fairly average individuals, an event plucked from, and then dropped back into, the stream of everyday life.

So, it is clear that the introduction of the policy of *perestroika* led to changes in the language of the *zametka* and the *fotoreportazh*, two of the most distinctive and prominent genres of the traditional Soviet press. In the new conditions of *perestroika* these genres could not survive. In a further progression from their 1987 intermediary form, both the *zametka* and the *fotoreportazh* went on to become in the post-Soviet press more and more indistinguishable from the Western news story and news picture.

The quintessentially Soviet 1979 *zametka* was bound to become redundant as the party redefined its relationship to industry and agriculture. So linked had it become to the heavy-handed didactic and moralistic approach that it proved impossible to reform. Once the party under Gorbachev decided that the average reader was patently not being inspired by this technique, the old-fashioned *zametka* was eased away from page-one prominence and, ensconced for a while in the inside columns of page two, the genre gradually disappeared. In its

21 Another 1987 *fotoreportazh* article (17 July 1987) ends in the same way 'Life goes on ...' (*Idyet zhizn'*).

place on the front page came the news story. The eclipse of the *fotoreportazh* by the non-propagandistic news picture was a more drawn-out process. Initially it was thought that the genre could be re-vamped in order to express and support the political and economic policies of *perestroika.* However, this genre, too, was destined to dis-appear as it became clear that its underlying propagandistic principle no longer served as the linchpin of the Soviet news machine.

The language of both genres under Brezhnev and Gorbachev reflected the different political priorities of both periods. The language of 1979 was composed largely of clichés, mostly from the economic sphere, while that of 1987 was distinguished most clearly by the absence of clichés and their replacement by a fresher style that drew from a larger referential field including conversational, or informal Russian. These changes were also reflected in the transformation under *glasnost'* of the editorial.

Editorial

As with most Western newspapers, Soviet newspapers, including *Izvestiya,* regularly published an editorial which was the voice of the newspaper. As the government's main organ, the *Izvestiya* editorial had the status of official policy. The editorial as a genre leaves no room for self-doubt or questioning. By its very nature it is categorical and opinionated and, as such, was one genre that the bolsheviks could carry over into the new Soviet press without subjecting it to much stylistic modification. For the Soviet press, as for the Western press, the editorial was an instructional sermon delivered in an authoritative voice. The drastic reduction in the frequency of appearance of editorials in 1987 compared to 1979 is therefore both surprising and indicative of a deep change in the philosophy of the Soviet press having taken place between both years. During the whole of Novem-ber 1987 only one editorial appeared while out of 25 numbers examined in June 1979, nine editorials appeared.[22]

This decrease in the number of editorials was one of the most striking features of change in the appearance of *Izvestiya*'s front page during this stage of *perestroika.* The Soviet editorial had traditionally

22   Twenty-nine days in November 1987 were counted, 25 days in June 1979.

contained ideological rhetoric, much of which was, according to one influential newspaper editor, mere repetition of political speeches reproduced in a 'pretentious and declaratory' fashion. According to the same author, neither the original speeches themselves nor the derivative editorials were read by the public (Nenashev, 1986, pp. 39–40). The same author complained that the editorial, the 'most important element' of the paper was not answering the 'demands' of the readership (ibid., p. 89). Indeed, it was clear that the Brezhnev-era editorial lacked the 'dynamism, topicality and relevance'[23] (Solganik, 1981, p. 4) which the textbooks claimed the genre ought to contain. Nenashev also reasoned that a readership with a greater cultural and educational level was simply no longer prepared to accept 'general phrases written in a language deprived of passion' (Nenashev, 1986, p.40).

Stylistically the 1987 editorial employed a less imperative tone than its 1979 counterpart while the subject matter of the *perestroika*-era leading article tended to be treated in a more concrete and less diffuse manner. If in June 1979 it often proved difficult to decide whether the main thrust of an editorial had to do with political, economic or ideological questions, in November 1987 there was no such confusion. On economic issues, for example, the 1987 editorial was more likely to focus on one problem without necessarily providing solutions. The high-flown, sometimes military-sounding, exhortatory rhetoric characteristic of the 1979 editorial on economic issues was avoided in 1987. On the other hand, editorials in 1987 dealing with what Solganik called 'socio-political themes', for example, patriotism, still produced the high-flown language found in 1979 articles on the same topic (see Solganik, 1981, p. 5).

In November 1987 *Izvestiya* introduced two new occasional columns, 'Notes of the Commentator on Public Affairs' and 'On the Theme of the Day',[24] which had no equivalent in 1979. The new columns replaced the slot once occupied by the editorial. For the month of November 1987, three 'Notes of the Commentator on Public Affairs' and two 'On the Theme of the Day' were published. The

23 *Operativnost', zlobodnevnost', publitsistichnost'.*
24 *Zametki publitsista* and *Na temu dnya.*

columns shared common features. Both, for example, were shorter than the November 1987 editorial, but about the same length as the June 1979 editorial. They usually consisted of two articles, 45 to 50 lines long, in two columns and in bold print. They were normally positioned one above the other along the left-hand side of the page, where the editorial was found. Each article was headlined and embellished by a rubric title. Like the editorial, they dealt with broad issues relating to home affairs (for example, industry, agriculture, patriotism) or foreign questions (peace, NATO, the Warsaw Pact). Unlike the editorial the articles were by-lined and contained what was expressed as the author's personal opinion, though in 1987 this rarely if ever deviated from the established line in *Izvestiya*.

As a rule, the new columns were lighter in general tone but more polemically aggressive than the editorial. Writers appeared more as journalists in the Lenin mould, intellectually sharp and combative, emotive in exposition, unashamedly opinionated, and convinced that right was on their side. Thus, while the greater number of writers being permitted to give their opinions on major policy issues had increased, these opinions, however novel in presentation and style, were still official in content. The re-emergence of signed leading articles (editorials were signed in the 1920s) pointed to an attempt to personalize official policy and signalled a move away from the anonymity of the old, edict-style editorial. It was an effort to reach out to the readership by portraying a human hand behind the news. The intent behind the genre may not have changed much, but the medium certainly had.

As with other genres, the language of the 1987 editorial differed from that of its 1979 counterpart. The change in subject matter and a different presentation of the editorial were the most noticeable differences. The 1979 editorial, similar to the *fotoreportazh* and *zametka* of the same period, often focused on the achievement of an economic feat executed by model workers. Again as in other genres, this stereotyped theme was accompanied by a constellation of linguistic features that characterized a large amount of the language of the press in 1979.[25] These features included the frequent recourse to political

25 Articles analysed for language analysis of editorial:

and economic words and phrases that had lost their impact through excessive, uncritical and seemingly automatic use in conventional contexts. The much more sharply focused 1987 editorial, by contrast, was marked by a much greater variety of themes expressed in a less monotonously conventional language. Inevitably, the 1987 editorial also showed examples of new, *perestroika*-inspired clichés. Overall, though, the language of the 1987 editorial was less tightly structured and more free of the thematic and linguistic constraints evident in 1979.

A theme central to three of the four editorials from 1979, and to Soviet newspapers under Brezhnev in general, was the heroification of the worker. As in the *fotoreportazh*, individuals who featured in articles were endowed with exceptional qualities, often expressed in well-worn phrases (Article N° 3, 1979):

...far beyond the boundaries of the area the name is known of fitter G. Smirnov, Hero of Socialist Labour, Honoured Worker of the Russian Federation, he is a genuine ace in the field of tools.[26]

The same article is also peopled by 'progressive' and 'first-class' workers,[27] as were the heroes of the N° 4, 1979, editorial:

It was from that very background that the following talented mentors of the younger generation have emerged: Hero of Socialist Labour, Leningrad worker S. Vitchenko, bearer of the orders of the October Revolution and the Red Banner of Labour, Moscow spinner E. Koryakina, bearer of the Order of Lenin, Zaporozhe plumber V. Aleshin and tens of thousands of others.

	1979		1987	
Article N° 1	14.viii.1979	N° 188[19253]	17.iii.1987	N° 77[21884]
Article N° 2	4.ix.1979	N° 206[19271]	5.ix.1987	N° 249[22056]
Article N° 3	10.x.1979	N° 237 [19302]	31.x.1987	N° 305 [22112]
Article N° 4	22.xii.1979	N° 298 [19363]	2.xii.1987	N° 337 [22144]

26 Note the mixture of the heavy official nomenclature alongside the chatty 'genuine ace', followed by the official-sounding circumlocution 'in the field of tools' (*v instrumental'nom dele*).

27 See also Article N° 1, 1979, where the harvesters are variously referred to in laudatory language as 'our best farmers' and 'toilers of agriculture'. In Article N° 3, 1979, we read of 'a large detachment of agricultural toilers'.

In the 1979 editorial, the workforce was often driven to great deeds by a moral imperative, not by the prospect of material gain. Again, just as many of the descriptions of the workers themselves degenerated into clichés, so, too, did the linguistic expression of their motivation. In Article N° 3, 1979, for example, motivation was supplied by a spontaneous 'rush of creativity'. 'Competition', meaning socialist and therefore ideologically driven, was the impulse 'for the attainment of high final results' (Article N° 3, 1979).[28] Competition was between collectives, never between individuals.

The description of moral qualities also gave rise to an elevated and bookish style. The hero-workers of Article N° 2, 1979, for example, possessed 'moral strength' as well as the 'finest human qualities'. According to the article their 'professional qualities are just as irreproachable as their high level of consciousness'.[29]

The application of an elevated style to fairly unremarkable topics created a stylistically jarring juxtaposition between theme and language. For the farm-workers of Article N° 1, 1979, for example, the sugar-beet harvest was a 'test of [their] skill, courage and moral qualities'. To complete the picture of a heroic workforce working hard for the right motives, the 1979 editorial frequently heroified the work itself. The gathering in of the sugar-beet harvest was said to 'crown (*venchaet*) the labour of the farmers'. Twice the harvesting was described as a 'struggle' (*bor'ba*), a vintage cliché. In the first example, the 'struggle' is followed by another military cliché:[30]

> Now in the struggle to bring in the harvest we have to storm the main position,...before us lies a hard struggle to reduce losses of raw material and sugar.

Alongside the clichés directly associated with the description of the whole area of work, the 1979 editorial also yielded some more official-

28 See also Article N° 2, 1979: 'the attainment of maximum results', Article N° 1, 1979: 'to aim for excellent results' to be carried out 'at the fastest rates' (Article N° 1, 1979, twice), or the analogous 'at the optimum rates' (Article N° 1 ,1979), in Article N° 3, 1979, the 'rates' are 'higher than last year's'.
29 Article N° 4, 1979, for instance, mentions 'many examples of self-sacrificing, skilled work'.
30 In Article N° 2, 1979, the work is described as an 'honourable task' (*pochyotnaya zadacha*).

sounding, bureaucratic expressions. Official language appeared when the editorial was paraphrasing or referring to an official utterance or directive. Article N° 1, 1979, spoke of all sorts of measures to be taken ('internal measures', 'all measures', 'additional measures'; 'a series of concrete measures'). Passive constructions were frequent, such as in Article N° 2, 1979, where official pronouncements were twice 'emphasized' (*podchyorknuty*).

A good example of how the 1979 editorial reflected the political situation of the period was the use of quotations from the then party general secretary, Leonid Brezhnev. The lengthy citing of the leader was in itself an expression of the campaign to build a personality cult around the Brezhnev persona. However, no less reflective of the era was the turgid, official language in which the country's leader spoke. In the following example from Article N° 2, 1979, Brezhnev was describing the qualities of the progressive Soviet worker, a theme expanded throughout the article in similar clichéd language:

> The progressive worker today is someone in possession of profound knowledge, a broad cultural outlook, and a conscientious and creative attitude towards labour. He feels himself to be the owner of [the means] of production, a person responsible for all that is happening in our society.[31]

The language used in a Brezhnev quotation in the area of foreign policy showed the official attitude towards foreign countries held at the time (N° 4 , 1979):

> We intend in the future to continue to strengthen friendship and co-operation with the liberated countries, with the countries in the non-aligned movement and with the peoples who are fighting for their freedom and independence.[32]

The same article also contained the emotive and judgemental language of the Soviet press to refer to countries, and their activities, unfavourable to the Soviet Union. For example, this article alone

---

31 In the same article Brezhnev used the officialese clichés 'to devote special attention to' (*udelyat' pervostepennoe vnimanie na*) and 'to show constant concern over' (*proyavlyat' postoyannuyo zabotu o*).

32 See above, p.109 on how the Brezhnev press classified foreign countries.

mentioned 'fierce imperialist opposition', 'gross interference', 'economic blackmail', 'colonial regimes' and 'imperialist circles'.[33]

While official language could be said to be the main characteristic of the 1979 editorial, the 1987 counterpart, especially in its two variations,[34] was marked by a greater use of different linguistic registers. This was partly because the 1987 editorials dealt with more themes. In Article N° 4 (2), 1987 (On the Theme of the Day), for instance, the author attempted to reproduce colloquial speech:

> I don't understand!... I set about fixing up my flat but was too busy to do it myself, so I got in some tradesmen to do the wall-papering. They stuck it up this way and that, bubbles all over the place.... I told them to re-paper it properly, and that I'd pay extra if necessary. And then it became clear. They wanted to do it properly, they tried to, but they weren't able to! How can this be![35]

The colloquial style of the syntax in the above example contrasts with the relatively complex structure of the following extract, from a 1979 editorial (Article N° 2):

> The honourable task of mentors is to attract youth on a wide scale to participation in the national socialist competition for the achievement of maximum results in labour, to the study and mastering of progressive experience, [and] to the search for the reserves of economizing measures in each working place.[36]

33 References to friendly countries, and their relations with the Soviet Union, were, however, rendered in positive formulas, for example, 'friendly cooperation', 'fruitful cooperation', 'with profound understanding', 'profound allegiance to peace and freedom', 'to follow the path of progress', 'to follow the path of industrialization', 'genuine and true friends', and so on.

34 *Na temu dnya* and *Zametki publitsista* .

35 '*Ne ponimayu.... Zateyal remont v kvartire, no samomy nedosug – priglasil masterov oboi nakleit'. Sdelali vkriv' i vkos', puzyry sploshnye... Govoryu: perekleite kak sleduet, doplachu, esli nado. I vizhu: khotyat lyudi, starayutsya, a ne mogut! Kak zhe eto!*' The colloquial effect is in part achieved by the paratactic conjunction of subordinate clauses to main clauses, as in '*govoryu: perekleite*' (lit. I say: re-paper) and '*I vizhu: khotyat lyudi*' (lit. And I see: they want to). Also, the absence of the personal pronoun is characteristic of spoken Russian.

36 '*Pochyotnoi zadachei nastavnikov yavlyaetsya shirokoe privlechenie molodyozhi k uchastiyu vo vsenarodnom sotsialisticheskom sorevnovanii za dostizhenie maksimal'nykh resul'tatov v trude, izucheniyu i osvoeniyu peredovogo opyta, poisku rezervov ekonomii na kazhdom rabochem meste.*' In this compound phrase the noun head, '*privlechenie*' (lit. the attraction), is modified by the adjective preceding it, '*shirokoe*' (wide); the noun head is qualified by another noun '*molodyozhi*' (youth); this modified

Another 1987 editorial, Article N° 1, 1987, was written in a style more appropriate to 1979. The article, which set out to show the necessity of linking the current 'restructuring' with the 1917 revolution, yielded a series of clichés from the political–ideological sphere, such as 'the spiritual bankruptcy of bourgeois society', 'socialist construction', 'the continued growth of popular well-being' and 'the continued flourishing of the economy and culture'. This editorial also threw up clichés from the area of work and its idealization mentioning 'genuine Stakhanovites', 'heroes of labour', 'labour honour', 'raising the economy to the highest level in the world' and 'bearing the banner of socialist competition'. The article concluded that the 'address of the Central Committee of the Party found a profound response in the hearts of people'.[37]

The use of the question and answer technique in the 1987 editorial-type article contrasted with a more categorical, imperative tone often found in the 1979 editorial. In the N° 4, 1987, 'On the Theme of the

---

and qualified head noun is further qualified by four prepositional phrases. One preposition '*k*' (to, towards), governs the four phrases. The first of these '*k uchastiyu*' (to participation), itself syntactically governing a compound noun phrase – '*vo vsenarodnom sotsialisticheskom sorevnovanii za dostizhenie maksimal'nykh rezul'tatov*' (in the national socialist competition for the achievement of maximum results). Here the noun head is '*sorevnovanie*' (competition), modified by the adjectives '*vsenarodnom sotsialisticheskom*' (national socialist), and qualified by the prepositional phrase, '*za dostizhenie maksimal'nykh resul'tatov*' (for the achievement of maximum results), itself made up of a preposition governing a compound noun phrase whose noun head, '*dostizhenie*', is qualified by the compound noun phrase, '*maksimal'nykh rezul'tatov*' (maximum results), an adjective modifying a noun head. The second and third dependent prepositional phrases '(*k*) *izucheniyu i osvoeniyu*' ((to) the study and mastering), both govern a modified noun phrase '*peredovogo opyta*' (progressive experience); the fourth, '(*k*) *poisku*' ((to) the search), governs a noun phrase qualified by a noun '*rezervov ekonomii*' (lit. reserves of economizing), itself qualified by a prepositional phrase, '*na kazhdom rabochem meste*' (in each working place), made up of a preposition, '*na*' (in), and a head, '*meste*' (place), modified by two preceding adjectives, '*kazhdom rabochem*' (each working).

37 This 1987 editorial also showed examples of emotive word order (Krylova and Khavronina, 1988, p.112) more characteristic of the 1979 editorial, for example, 'majestic are our achievements'; lit. 'A profound response in the hearts of people found the Address of the Central Committee of the party to the Soviet people' and 'great is our beetroot field' (*velichesvenny nashi dostizheniya; Glubokii otklik v serdtsakh lyudei nakhodit Obrashchenie Tsentral'nogo Komiteta partii k sovetskomu narodu; veliko nashe sveklovochnoe pole*), all examples of inversion where the rheme, or new information, precedes the theme, or given information. In non-emotive speech the theme precedes the rheme (Krylova and Khavronina, 1988, p.12; see also Bivon, 1971, p.30).

Day' article there were numerous examples of question–answer constructions, for example, 'What do you call that type of prize-giving? An empty formality, nothing more!'. The question and answer sequence in Russian is much more common in speech than in writing. It has been described as one of the 'most salient differences' between these two types of expression (Comrie and Stone, 1978, pp. 125–6). In a text, the sequence is 'an obvious way of making [the text] more expressive, closer to the spoken language. ... [It] can serve to create a closer rapport between writer and audience' (ibid.).

The primary prescriptive function of the 1979 editorial was usually carried out in the mode of official discourse. Linguistically, this was expressed using impersonal imperative constructions[38] such as those in the following phrases from Article N° 1, 1979:

> In worrying about today's harvest, one must not [*nel'zya*] forget about tomorrow's harvest; And it is very important [*ochen' vazhno*] that progressive experience should become the property of all machine-operators.[39]

Article N° 1, 1987 editorial, 'October in our affairs', which deals with a sacrosanct theme of the October revolution, not unexpectedly contains instances of the editorial edict, for example,

> One must not [*nel'zya*] ignore ...; One should be[(*prikhoditsy*)] reminded of this – it is necessary [*nuzhno*] to be reminded ...

In 1987 the stern and forbidding voice of the leader-writer was toned down. The 'Swiftly changing world' editorial (N° 3, 1987), issued a relatively mild admonition – 'one should not' (*ne nado*) (compare '*nel'zya*', one can not, it is not permitted), modified by the colloquial use of 'only' (*tol'ko*) – which appealed to, rather than commanded, the reader: 'Only one shouldn't fool oneself with illusions...'

As the N° 1, 1987, editorial showed, the language of *perestroika*, though containing fewer clichés than in 1979, could produce its own

38 That is, without the presence of a dative semantic subject.
39 See also Article N° 3, 1979: 'And it is very important (*ochen' vazhno*) to think now about the person who gathers and transports the harvest'; 'It is essential (*neobkhodimo*) to ask rigorous questions'; and Article N° 3, 1979: 'One must (*Nado*)... make decisive efforts.'

crop of set expressions directly inspired by the current political circumstances:

> the essentially revolutionary transformation of all aspects of Soviet society; the revolutionary cause of *perestroika*; one must fight for *perestroika*; *perestroika* must be defended ... *perestroika* is necessary for the people who are supporting the cause, who are impatient with bad management; each step on the path of acceleration (*uskorenie*); many are transferring to a system of self-financing and full cost-accounting (*samofinansirovanie i polny khozyaistvenny raschyot*).

The new *perestroika* rhetoric also included an armoury of anti-bureaucratic words and phrases, for example,

> to produce paperwork (*plodit' bumagi*); report-making mania (*raportomaniya*); embellishment (*priukrashivanie*) of the true state of affairs; there should be no verbal blether (*slovesnaya treskotnya*); a breaking of hardened methods (*lomka zakosnelykh form*); to 'administrate' (*administrirovat'*)

In the following paragraph from the same editorial, the style is composed of old-style current affairs clichés 'stapling' together the new set phrases of *perestroika*:[40]

> The [success] of everything hangs on a *swelling of the ranks* (old) of those who are *struggling* (old) for the *renewal* (new) of society, for *perestroika* (new), not by *words and assertions* (new), but by *pioneering, conscientious toil* (old). We have embarked upon a *profound* (old) *restructuring* (new) of our society. We are *perfecting* (old) the *economic mechanism* (new). The *transfer to self-financing* (new) makes of *each worker* (old), technician and designer an *economist* (new) and zealous *owner of* [the means of] *production* (new). The introduction of the *State quality control mechanism* (new) has shown *how grave is the problem* (old) and how much one can do if one is serious about the *elimination* (old) of our accumulated *deficiencies* (old).

Article N° 3, 1979, provided a classic example of the set phrases employed for the writing of a typical low-level critical article in 1979.

---

40 '*Delo za tem, chtoby mnozhilis' ryady tekh, kto boretsya za obnovlenie obshchestva, za perestroiku, – da ne slovami i zavereniyami, a novatorskim, dobrosovestnym trudom. My nachali glubokuyu rekonstruktsiyu narodnogo khozyaistva. Sovershenstvuem khozyaistvenny mekhanizm. Perekhod na samofinansirovanie delaet ekonomistom, rachitel'nym khozyainom proizvodstva kazhdogo rabochego, tekhnologa, konstruktora. Vvedenie gospriyomki pokazalo, kak ostro stoit problema kachestva i kak mnogo mozhno sdelat', esli vseryoz zanyat'sya ustraneniem nakopivshikhsya zdes' problem.*'

After an initial positive assessment of whatever was about to be criticized, the negative criticism was introduced by means of highly stylized clichés:

At the same time (*Vmeste s tem*) ... one must not close one's eyes [to the fact that] (*nel'zya zakryt' glaza*); However, far from everywhere (*Odnako, daleko ne vezde*) are people acting like this. Unfortunately (*k sozhaleniyu*) ... not everything is well (*ne vsyo blagopoluchno*) ...

Zametki publitsista

The first of the two 'Notes of the Commentator on Public Affairs' in Article N° 2, 1987, urged the reader to remember the victory of the imperial Russian army over Napoleon at Borodino in 1812. As all material dealing with patriotic matters was treated in a solemn manner, the language of this article was full of high-style words and rhetorical devices appropriate to the exalted theme. The article used three Russian words to stand for the Russian empire: *Rodina* (Motherland), *Otchizna* and *Otechestvo* (both Fatherland), of which the first is neutral in register, the second high style and the third moderately high style, all printed as proper nouns. The battle itself was referred to in glowing terms as belonging to the 'glorious chronicle of the Fatherland'. The author used the rhetorical device of listing words in groups of three:

Geographical names that have become monuments to the people's patriotism, the people's courage and the art of commanding an army; Because without memory, without respect for the past, history and traditions the people lose their roots, strength and future; ...towards evening it lit up the road to Waterloo. To the turning-point, the defeat, the downfall of such a brilliant career of an emperor, [a career] which was destroyed when it came up against the love of freedom and unbending will of the defenders of the Fatherland.[41]

41 Of note here also is the rhetorical device of compounding by means of continuing one sentence in the following sentence. In the third example, the second sentence is a continuation of the indirect object complement of the direct object of the governing 'lit up (the road) to' (*osvetilo (dorogu) k*) of the first sentence. In the following passage, the three sentences are syntactically interconnected: 'They shall come in order to pay their debt to people of different rank and generation but who were able equally strongly and effectively to love the Motherland. In order to feel at one with those who remained here forever in 1812. And with those who spilt their blood at these monuments in October 1941, who blocked the road to Moscow from the fascist invaders.' Here the 'in order to' (*chtoby*) of the second sentence is subordinate to the main verb 'They shall come' of the

The theme in the second of the 'Notes ...' (Article N° 2, 1987), concerned the movement for peace on the planet. The language was earnest, abstract and elevated, containing a large number of learned words. In the first paragraph alone, for example, there appeared seven words ending in abstract suffixes: allegiance, danger, safety, power, tonality, understanding, possession and thinking.[42] Occasionally, the language becomes pseudo-literary, as, for example, when the reader is told that 'sprouts of comprehension are breaking through the asphalt of slumbering prejudices'.

The second article in the 'Notes ...' (Article N° 3, 1987), though it deals in part with the October revolution, was written in a forthright, challenging and pugnacious style. The author created a demon in the form of a generalization that the West believed that 'the February revolution without [the] October [revolution] could quite easily have turned Russia into some sort of (*edakoe*)[43] flourishing democratic society'. The demon is slain in the next sentence, which appealed to the reader's chauvinism ('But we [more than most] know (*Uzh my-to znaem*) our country and what happened in it).[44] The use of the collo-quial particles[45] (*uzh* and *-to*) emphasized the author's unapologetic

---

previous sentence, while the 'And with those' of the third sentence is the indirect object complement of 'to feel at one' governing the verb phrase of the second sentence. The thematic linking of the 1812 victory to the 1941 victory over the encroaching Nazis is mirrored in the syntactical linking of the two final sentences.

42 *Priverzhennost', opasnost', bezopasnost', vlast', tonal'nost', ponimanie, obladanie, myshlenie.*

43 The pejorative and colloquial 'some sort of' (*edakoe*) conveys sarcasm.

44 '*Uzh my-to znaem svoyu stranu, chto i kak v nei bylo*'.

45 One important element in the informal style of discourse in newspapers is the particle. These are syntactic words in Russian that have no word for word English translation. They are predominantly a feature of the spoken, rather than written, language (Zemskaya, 1987, p.91). According to V.V. Vinogradov's definition, particles are 'words which, as a rule, have no completely independent real or material meaning, but for the most part introduce additional shades into the meanings of other words, phrases or sentences' (quoted in Vasilyeva, no date, p.9, from Vinogradov's '*Russkii yazyk*', 1947, p.663 (Moscow). In a very broad, but useful, definition of the functions of the particle, Miloslavskii writes that it 'can indicate a question (*razve, neuzheli, li* (surely, really)), affirmation (*da, tak* (indeed, so)), negation (*ne, net, vovse ne* (not, not at all)), reported speech (*mol, deskat', yakoby* (they say, supposedly)), emphasis (*zhe, dazhe, ved'* (even, but surely)), comparison (*slovno, tochno, budto* (as if)). Among particles one also finds those graphically separated: v*ryad li, kak raz, chto za* (hardly, just) etc.' (Miloslavskii, 1987, p.43). The increased use of the particle in 1987 compared to 1979

stance. This was not the solemnity of the 1987 editorial 'October in our days' (N° 1), rather a confident and combative personal view.

Article N° 4, 1987, contained two pieces under the rubric of 'On the Theme of the Day'. In common with the 'Notes...', both articles were signed and bore the linguistic marks of an authorial hand, rather than those of a collective authorship. The signed articles, while expressing support for the same pro-*perestroika* policies as those promoted by anonymous editorials, communicated the message in a more personalized manner. The 'On the Theme of the Day' pieces were written in an unequivocally colloquial style, with extensive use being made of the colloquial particle,[46] and the interposed, (parenthetical) phrase, for example, 'probably', 'at least', 'of course', 'for instance' and 'for example'. These have an opposite function to the imperative words characteristic of the 1979 editorials, suggesting, because they show that the article was written by an individual, human fallibility rather than the magisterial certainty of the anonymous editorial. (In the second of the two pieces, the author writes in the first person.)

One feature of Articles N° 3 and 4, 1987, was their occasionally critical use of official slogans. In the first instance, a Brezhnev-era slogan, 'The economy should be economical',[47] was quoted by the author, and then debunked:

> About ten years ago, commenting on the slogan which was popular in those years 'the economy should be economical', one of the participants at a meeting organized by the newspaper, sighing, said: 'An economy should above all be an economy'.

The change in rhetoric brought about by changing political exigencies of *perestroika* was not that intended by those who introduced

---

was part of a stylistic realignment of press language away from the anonymous, formal, clichéd and distancing rhetoric of the Brezhnev era towards the speech of educated speakers of Russian.

46   For instance (particles in bold), '*Vot kak im vospol'zovalis'*...' (That's how they used them...); '*Chto zhe tut novogo? A tol'ko to, chto, esli ran'she...*' (So what's new there? Only that if earlier...); '*No pri chyom tut konstruktory? Ved'* na postavki neposredstvenno povliyat' oni ne mogut.' (But what do the designers have to do with it? Sure, they have no direct influence on deliveries.); '*I ved'* tozhe staralis'...' (And they also tried...); '*Tol'ko budem po-leninski otkrovenny.*' (Only let us be frank in the manner of Lenin.); '...*tak i ne udalos'*...' (...but it didn't succeed...).

47   '*Ekonomika dolzhna byt' ekonomnoi.*'

the new policy. Gorbachev and his colleagues wished the press to write in a responsible manner. By this they meant that journalists should replace the obviously ineffective old-style Soviet discourse with a reinvigorated, though still essentially propagandistic, rhetoric of *perestroika*. Instead, the linguistic freedom to write in a personalized style became a licence to think independently of the party line. It proved impossible simply to alter the rhetoric while preserving the philosophy that lay behind it. While the growing autonomy of the press from the dictates of the party could only have happened within the context of an increasingly less authoritarian atmosphere in Soviet society as *perestroika* progressed, it is also true that the most powerful fuel for that progress was the emancipated language of the press.

5. Westernization of Press Language

The language of the Russian press since the decline and fall of the Soviet Union is qualitatively different from Soviet press language. As the structure of traditional Soviet newspaper genres began to break down as a result of the upheavals in the press caused by *perestroika*, so the conventional language of the genres began to adapt to meet the new requirements. In this way the language of Gorbachev's *perestroika* period was to a greater or lesser extent, depending on the suitability of the old genre to new demands, a development and modification of an earlier style. The post-Soviet period, by contrast, was in general not an extension of the Soviet tradition, instead drawing its inspiration from a Western tradition that was in its fundamentals alien to the spirit of the Leninist press. For some mainstream newspapers, such as *Kommersant* and *Nezavisimaya gazeta*, the adoption of Western models, especially of news reporting, predated the formal collapse of the Soviet Union in December 1991.

The most salient feature of the language of the post-Soviet varieties of some of the country's most important newspapers, such as *Izvestiya* or *Komsomol'skaya pravda*, is its aspiration to appear neutral and objective. The presentation of the news story, the corner-stone of a Western-style serious newspaper, is now on the surface devoid of both the blatant propagandistic formulas of the Brezhnev- era press and the more subtle attempts at persuasion of the press during *perestroika*. The political preference of a newspaper in the Yeltsin era is now more determined by editorial selection of what news to cover, rather than how it is covered. In other words, the methods of reporting have changed. In the highly politically polarized press of the Yeltsin era, however, much political news, while possessing some of the external attributes of the Western news story, is on closer examination quite crude propaganda for the political grouping which a particular newspaper supports.

The language of some genres has changed more drastically than others. The foreign news story, for example, has nothing in common with its distant and many times removed Soviet relative. For a variety of reasons, chief among them economic, Russian newspapers now rely almost entirely on Western European and American news agencies to fill their columns of foreign news briefs. In other areas, the modern version of the pre-Soviet political and social commentary, usually more wide-ranging than its Western counterpart, remains intact. Criticized by some as unwelcome editorializing, for others it is a forum for the thoughts of the country's intelligentsia, of which leading journalists consider themselves an important element.

The language of the news feature has become more permissive of the discourse of previously marginalized and suppressed subjects. The language of youth culture is now represented in the press, as is that of sex and religion. Finally, the appearance of advertising has been a vehicle for the import of scores of Western words including brand names and words with Russian equivalents that are used because they sound Western.

Because the language of the new Russian press draws heavily on Western models, Russian newspapers now show a far greater variety than the enforced sameness and resultant monotony in both language and content of the Soviet press. Instead of addressing itself to one idealized readership, the Russian newspaper now caters for several readerships. The emerging newspaper world has many varieties of language and register, including the new, Western liberal style (*Izvestiya, Nezavisimaya gazeta*), the old Soviet style (*Pravda, Sovetskaya Rossiya*), a new, ultra-nationalist discourse (*Den'*), and the language of the new, Western-inspired, pornographic press (*Mister Iks*).

Western objectivity

The two foundations of the pre-revolutionary Russian liberal press, factual reporting and sensationalism, were repugnant to the bolshevik journalistic creed and formed no part of the canon of Soviet journalism. For the Soviet journalist, as we have seen, the purpose of the newspaper was not to communicate the news impartially, but to defend the interests of the party, of which most Soviet journalists were members. Forbidding newspapers to cover certain stories altogether while at the same time demanding that the stories that could be covered should be covered in a particular way led to a press that was little more than an extension of the all-powerful system. The language of the Soviet news story, as illustrated by the *zametka* and *foto-reportazh*, was in turn a reflection of the newspaper's subordination to the party.

Following the collapse of the Soviet power structures and the liberation of the press from the party stranglehold, Russian journalists turned to the Western press to find a replacement ideology for the discredited Leninist creed. This has taken the form of genre-borrowing, a process that is proving much more influential than word-borrowing in shaping the emerging Russian press. The appearance of non-Soviet genres in the press has facilitated the introduction into the public discourse of words which previously did not appear in the pages of the press. Most of these words, while new for the press, are not new to Russian, though in the Soviet-era they received sparse if any coverage in less public genres. Obvious examples would be words to do with sex and capitalist economics.

Home news stories

The domestic news story is the most important area where genre-borrowing from the West has taken place. The contrast in language and tone between a Soviet, *perestroika*-era language and that of the post-Soviet period is made plain by comparing a triumphant headline from *Izvestiya* in 1987 (1 April), 'We have reached the billionth tonne!',[1] with a typical sober headline in the same paper in 1993 (18 January), 'Fall in oil production takes on steady character'. The first headline concentrates on a grandiloquent achievement and, with the help of an exclamation mark, shows the journalist's approval of the feat. The second headline focuses on bad news and does not betray the journalist's opinion on the story. It is unlikely that a 1987 news editor would have deemed the 1993 story newsworthy, just as a 1993 editor would probably not have covered the 1987 story.

A further comparison of *Izvestiya* headlines for news stories over the years 1987, 1990 and 1993 shows a trend away from both propagandistic ('Fashionable footware from Kaluga') and cryptic ('A second for all') headlines towards the much more informative ('Who is in charge of Russia's ministries?') headline to the headline that is itself a

---

1   *'Est' milliardnaya tonna!'*.

synopsis of the story ('Buryatiya does not intend to leave Russian federation'):

> *Izvestiya* (20 December 1987, p.1), 'News panorama': 'Fashionable footware from Kaluga'; 'In the cosmos and on earth'; 'School of co-operators'; 'Personal inn not superfluous'; 'Winter beckons tourists'; 'A second for all'
>
> *Izvestiya* (9 July 1990, p.2) 'Direct link; *Izvestiya* journalists report': 'Who is in charge of Russia's ministries?'; 'The working week; one hour less'; 'Another new party'; 'Failed test of reforms'; 'March for survival'; 'Emergency situation on railways'
>
> *Izvestiya* (28 January 1993, p.2): 'Buryatiya does not intend to leave Russian federation'; 'Government strengthens social support for invalids'; 'Transfer of Russian military installations to Estonia continues'; 'Avalanches in North Ossetia lead to loss of life'; 'Forgers rendered harmless in Moldova'

Both the 'Fashionable footware from Kaluga' and 'School of co-operators' headlines are essentially propagandistic messages of the *perestroika* era that reflect *Izvestiya*'s support for the new economic thinking of the period. The 'Kaluga' story concerns a Soviet–Italian joint enterprise to produce footware, while the 'cooperators' article deals with those working in the cooperative, or private, sector. Both joint enterprises and the cooperative movement[2] were Gorbachev initiatives. The 'Kaluga' headline is a toned-down product of the 'We have reached the billionth tonne!'-school of journalism. The primary aim of the headline and the story is to impart the message of the party such that it might be emulated, at least admired, by others. The content of the other articles is masked by the opaqueness of their headlines. One can only judge that none is 'hard news', except the 'In the cosmos and on earth', which reports on the progress of a Soviet space mission. In fact, none of these front-page headlines is immediately recognizable as reporting the essence of an event of some immediate significance that has just occurred, the approximate definition of a Western news story.

By 1990, roughly a year before the August 1991 coup and one month after the press law was passed, there is a definite change in the way headlines are being written. Here the reader is confronted with a Western-looking headline that promises some hard news of immediate

---

2 The Law on Cooperatives was passed by the All-Union Supreme Soviet on 26 May 1987.

relevance. Whereas none of the 1987 headlines signalled bad news, all but two, 'The working week ...' and 'Another new party', of the six 1990 headlines are harbingers of unhappy content. 'Who is in charge...' suggests no one is in charge of Russia's ministries, 'Failed test ...' is self-evidently bad news for the subject in question, while 'March for survival' and 'Emergency ...' are dramatic headings to what must be desperate situations. The combined images of administrative chaos, economic failure and desperation form a completely different picture from the 1987 portrayal of steady progress towards economic reform. Of the remaining two headlines, one, 'The working week...', is of general interest to all those who work and would merit inclusion in a Western newspaper, while the other, the announcement of the formation of another new party, was of great significance in the Soviet Union of that period, only six months after the party central committee amended the constitution to allow other political parties to exist. In summary, all six headlines are informative, report on events that have just occurred and are not obviously in favour of one or other political party. They are neither triumphant nor condemnatory in content and have pretensions to being descriptive rather than prescriptive.

The 1993 set of headlines has moved even further away from the Soviet model than those of 1990. Two years after the collapse of the Soviet Union, *Izvestiya* is no longer an organ of the parliament. It is an independent newspaper that is accused by opponents of excessive kow-towing to the executive branch of the government and of unfairly portraying the activities of the Russian parliament in a poor light. Despite the newspaper's undoubted political bias in favour of President Boris Yeltsin, the language of its news story headlines extracted above are not obviously tendentious. Their main feature is informativeness. The tantalizing quality of the 1990 headlines, such as 'Another new party', 'Failed test of reforms' or 'March for survival', has been brushed aside in favour of the clarion clarity of the headline that encapsulates the essence of the story. Each of the 1993 headlines follows the full sentence model found in the 1987 headline 'Who is in charge of Russia's ministries?'.

The stories beneath the headlines are written according to a strict formula. The headline is followed by a short sub-headline in bold print elaborating on the headline, and then a single paragraph giving more details to the story. Sometimes the headline is followed directly by the details of the story. The 'Buryatiya ...' story is a good example of the first variety:

BURYATIYA DOES NOT INTEND TO LEAVE RUSSIAN FEDERATION

Sovereign Buryatiya does not intend to leave the Russian Federation and the draft of Buryatiya's new Constitution never contained any provision for its secession from Russia. This was announced at a press conference by the leader of the working group of the republic's Supreme Soviet constitutional commission, Oleg Khyshikutev.

The subjective elements of the story are here extra-textual, and not linguistic. The selection of the news itself is an editorial decision, as was the decision of the reporter to select one particular aspect of the press conference. Given those elements, the language in which the news is reported is neutral. The article contains no authorial suggestion of approval or disapproval.

In obvious but noteworthy contrast to the practice in the Brezhnev era, *Izvestiya* page-one stories now regularly report accidents, both natural ('Avalanches in North Ossetia lead to loss of life') and caused by human error ('More miners die').[3]

If these brief news stories are now written very much in the Western mould, another variety of news story, the lead story, is often written according to a different model. The 3 February 1993 lead story in *Izvestiya*, with a banner headline – 'Crisis in food production not a threat to Russia, fall of output of goods temporarily halted'[4] – is a good example of how the news story is now written according to Western formulas. Underneath the synopsizing headline is a 17-word intro-duction, printed in bold face, to the content of the story, which is really an exposition of an official report:

Experts from the Russian Ministry of agriculture and food have analysed the state of food production and consumption for the beginning of the year.

3 '*Snova gibnut shakhtyory*', *Izvestiya*, 28 January 1993, p.1.
4 '*Prodovol'stvenny krizis Rossii ne grozit, spad proizvodstva produktov priostanavli-vaetsya.*'

The journalist has made clear his main source from the outset, referring to it once again in the first paragraph ('According to Ministry of agriculture information ...'). Embedded in that first paragraph proper, which extracts statistical findings of the ministerial report, the journalist refers to unnamed experts ('according to specialists' predictions ...') whose forecast that there is no imminent food crisis forms the headline. Since the source of this prediction is unnamed, the story loses some of its impact. It is as if the reporter believes that the Western-sounding 'according to reliable sources' cliché will impart verisimilitude to the opinion of anonymous specialists. The rest of the article cites no named sources apart from the ministry itself. There is no attempt to question the sources of the ministry, or to quote a contrary or sceptical opinion on the ministry's figures from a spokesperson for any of Russia's sectional groups, most noticeably from representatives of the country's parliament. Because in this case the journalist does not take the trouble to quote other sources, he is in fact taking for granted the authenticity of the official data, in the same way as his predecessor was forced to do under the Soviet dispensation.

The bulk of the second and third paragraphs is built on the journalist's summary of the report's findings, which is clear and easy to understand. The fourth and final paragraph of this 200–300-word story is the author's own opinion of the report's significance. So, what begins as a news report, falls flat because of a lack of named sources and tails off into a mini-editorial-style political commentary on the report.

Though the newspaper gained a large measure of editorial freedom in its final days as a government organ, it was nevertheless obliged even then to function as an official gazette and publish official news. During the August 1991 coup *Izvestiya* was one of the nine newspapers which the State Committee for the State of Emergency permitted to come out. The newspaper reported the committee's decrees and resolutions.[5] After the coup, as an independent newspaper, *Izvestiya* correspondents relished the freedom to report on official news in a critical manner, though their manner of criticism is not generally to give prominence to representatives of anti-government

---

5 *Izvestiya* published two editions on 20 August, the first one reprinting the committee's decrees, the second one siding with Yeltsin (Tolz, 1991c, September, p.24).

groups, as might be expected for a newspaper with pretentions to being a newspaper of record. Rather the reporter reserves the pleasure for him or herself. The enforced self-effacement of reporters (as opposed to commentators, columnists or editors) in the Western tradition is not present to anything like the same degree in the Russian press. This predilection is on the one hand journalists' revenge on politicians whose every word and lie they once had to transmit as gospel. On the other hand the phenomenon of reporters who editorialize is a natural product of a journalistic tradition in which the most respected practitioners graduate to become *publitsisty*, or general philosophers on society. The opinionated reporter is, then, an aspiring *publitsist*.

Another page-one lead story in *Izvestiya* (19 March 1992), again with a banner headline – 'Kiev prepares for meeting of heads of CIS. Military and economic problems are at the centre of attention'[6] – shows similar features to the article on food production and consumption. The language of the headline is neutral and informative. In the following three-sentence explanatory and introductory sub-headline, however, the language of the second two sentences betrays in an obvious way the very subjective opinions of the reporter:

> Kiev awaits the heads of the independent states of the CIS. Banners with greetings on the occasion [of the meeting] have not been hung in the city. The heads of the state and government have been allotted apartments in the former hotel of the administration section of the Central Committee of the Ukrainian communist party, the 'Zhovtneva'.

The structure of the second sentence is odd. It first of all presents details of new information only to conclude by announcing its absence. The new 'information' is entirely inspired by the author's imagination, since what is absent cannot be 'reported'. The 'information' itself is meant to remind the reader of the recent Soviet past, when official banners bedecked the streets on the occasion of important meetings. By bringing in this emotive association with discredited practices of old, the journalist establishes the tenor of the rest of the article. The following sentence, referring to the former party

---

6 '*Kiev gotovitsya k vstreche glav gosudarstv SNG. V tsentre vnimaniya – voennye i khozyastvennye problemy.*'

hotel, makes clear the journalist's desire to compare the new officials with the old party–state élite.

It is already plain from the language of the introductory sub-head-line that the reporter has negative views on members of the delegations. The first paragraph proper hammers home this impression when the author resorts to unsubtle sarcasm:

> As the members of the delegations have had occasion to familiarize themselves with this level of comfort and decor in bygone years, nothing [here] will distract them from the urgent problems of the Commonwealth.

The article continues in this vein to create a text that is at least two important removes away from the neutral news story. First, the language of the article serves as a vehicle to carry the author's own opinions, not those of the politicians he derides nor even of others who might care to deride the politicians for the reporter. Second, instead of dropping the fiction suggested by the headline that what follows is a news report from Kiev, the reporter has chosen to report his personal observations indirectly by means of sarcasm. It is perhaps the pretence that the article is a 'report' that prevents the journalist from making his contention openly, for example, 'I believe that the same people enjoy the same privileges as before ...'. Without factual supporting evi-dence, however, even as an assertion made by a columnist, this statement would, according to Western criteria, sound weak.

It is only in the fourth paragraph of a nine-paragraph story that the journalist refers in comprehensible language to the military problems adverted to in the headline. Only one official, Ukrainian Prime Minister V. Fokin, is quoted in the entire report. Fokin's assertion, that the CIS is not 'eternal', comes in the final paragraph, and is therefore nowhere contested. Rather it serves the function of a telling quotation introduced to win an argument. The article, despite the informative headline, is in fact an opinion piece masquerading as a report.

The 28 January page-one banner headline in *Izvestiya*, 'Flagrant breach of UN sanctions: oil from Ukraine sails to Serbia'[7] is, on the strength of the story, sensationalist and speculative. The 'story' turns

---

7   *'Derzkoe narushenie sanktsii OON: mazut s Ukrainy uplyvaet v Serbiyu.'*

out to be an unconfirmed assertion that appeared in a Reuters' report that a Serbian tug boat and six barges carrying petrol and fuel oil had originated their illegal journey up the Danube to Serbia in the Ukrainian Black Sea port of Reni. It is only in the seventh paragraph of an eight-paragraph story that the reporter, in Moscow, assuming that Ukraine has broken the UN sanctions on Yugoslavia, asks disingenuously whether Ukraine is obliged to obey the UN sanctions on Yugoslavia and, mischievously, whether Ukraine is really in need of (Russian) oil products 'if they are soon to be re-exported'. It is only in the sixth paragraph that the origin of the original claim, a Reuters' report, is made explicit. Rereading the opening paragraph, it is obvious that the *Izvestiya* reporter in Moscow is relying on the information reportedly given by the captain of the Serbian tug boat to Romanian authorities that the cargo had set sail from Reni. The Reuters' reporter, it is clear, has not spoken to the captain of the tug boat. The bulk of the article is taken up with the retelling of the Reuters' report from Romania and a report by the Bulgarian government news agency, BTA, both of which concentrate on the inability of both countries to prevent traffic destined for Serbia sailing on the Danube. What in a Western report would have been the lead paragraph comes in the last paragraph in the *Izvestiya* report, and then after a fashion. The reporter, referring to himself as 'your correspondent', at length informs the reader that the Ukrainian authorities could not respond fully to the allegation but considered it groundless:

> Your correspondent telephoned the information section of the Ministry for Foreign Affairs in Kiev. The section head, V.L. Chyorny, said that unfortunately the Ministry was not yet in possession of the full facts since they originated from different sources. He was therefore unable to answer *Izvestiya*'s questions. However, in his opinion the Reuters' communiqués [sic] were not objective and clearly tendentious. Ukraine strictly adheres to the UN sanctions on Yugoslavia[, he said].

Given the facts as established by the reporter, the sensationalist headline, rather than an accurate summary of the news, is an attempt to implicate Ukraine in the 'major scandal' (*gromkii skandal*) of how a Serbian convoy threatened to set her cargo alight on the Danube when challenged by Romanian frontier guards.

Izvestiya clearly nailed its political colours to the mast in its tendentious coverage of Boris Yeltsin's suspension of the country's parliament in September 1993. In doing so, the newspaper clearly demonstrated that political allegiance (to the Yeltsin 'team') was more important than balanced reporting and comment. Coverage of this event also showed that linguistically it was impossible to maintain the forms of the Western-style objective journalist while writing from the standpoint of a political commentator from the late Soviet era.[8] The lead story of 25 September 1993, 'The last word belongs to us',[9] was an exemplum of biased comment that would not have looked out of place in the press of the Gorbachev period. In many respects, this article, positioned along the left-hand column of the front page, is the reconstructed editorial of the Gorbachev era. The author, Eduard Gonzalez, is enunciating the newspaper's well-known anti-parliamentary stance in non-formal, in places conversational, language. It is immediately clear from the opening paragraph where the newspaper's sympathies lie:

> The judges have ruled that the president has breached the Constitution. But he never tried to hide that fact. In the decree it is stated plainly that any further 'formal following of contradictory norms' is impossible.

The gravity of breaching the Constitution is casually dismissed in the second sentence, which suggests that the breach is not so serious because 'he', President Yeltsin, did not hide the fact. The following paragraph employs a series of rhetorical devices in order to win over the reader to *Izvestiya*'s point of view:

> It is doubtful if anyone will be happy that the head of state was forced to take this step. Because it means that we have reached an impasse. And for that same reason, evidently, there's no point in getting upset. You don't become angry or annoyed at a person who pushes you after running out of a burning house.

The first sentence here assumes that the president was 'forced' to breach the Constitution. So, not only is the deed not so wrong because the president admitted he was breaking the law in his decree, but he

---

8 See above, p.131 passim, on the *Zametki publitsista* (Notes of the Commentator on Public Affairs) and Na temu dnya (On the Theme of the Day).

9 *'Poslednee slovo za nami.'*

had no alternative. The informal flavour of the article, established in the first paragraph with the sentence beginning 'But he never tried to ...', which implies that the author is arguing with the reader, is reinforced in the second paragraph. The sentence beginning 'Because it means ...' is an example of 'parcellation', or a method of imitating the style of conversation in writing by means of adding what appear to be completive afterthoughts to an already stated thought (the first sentence). The impression is thus created of a series of unplanned thoughts coming from the pen of a writer who is more like a conversation partner than a politically compromised journalist who knows exactly what his thoughts are and has thought very carefully about the most effective manner of expressing those thoughts. It is as if *Izvestiya*, unable to legally justify the president's unconstitutional action, has attempted to justify the unjustifiable by employing obviously emotive rhetorical devices in the hope that they will take precedence over reason. The following sentence, 'And for that same reason ...', is also an example of parcellation. The same sentence has recourse to the conversational-sounding parenthetic word[10] 'evidently' (*vidimo*), which, taking as fact the previous contention that the country had reached an impasse, attempts to calm any feelings of incipient panic in the reader by suggesting in a casual way that there is 'evidently' no need to get upset. Nowhere is it stated why or to whom it is 'evident'. The word appears to be there because it itself has a calming effect, creating the illusion that someone all-wise has studied the situation and decided that there is nothing to get worried about. The final sentence of the second paragraph uses a striking image that belongs more properly in the realms of literature than in the main political commentary on the most important political event of the year.

The remainder of the article carries on in the same vein. The villain of the piece is Ruslan Khasbulatov, the parliamentary speaker who had been trying to make *Izvestiya* an organ of the parliament. He is referred to as 'deceitful and sly' (*lzhivy i kovarny*), his 'boorishness and unforgivable impudence' are adverted to. It is as if the author believes he can write in a reckless manner because he has established a familiar register with the reader, with whom he identifies himself.

10 See above, p.139, n.19.

Referring again to Khasbulatov, for example, the author writes:

> We have all observed for many years now how he has built himself a road to
> absolute power, often on the bones of others, and we have kept silence. We have
> all waited to see how things would end up over there [in the parliament]. And
> indeed we are still waiting in hope that the power structures [defence, interior
> and security ministries] are on the president's side. But then the greatest power
> structure of all is us.[11]

The rest of the front-page news concerning the president's political
coup is given over principally to pro-Yeltsin articles. A story on the
reappointment of Yegor Gaidar is headlined 'There will be no new
shock', allaying fears that the population might have to suffer a new
dose of economic shock therapy that might again result in the government suddenly withdrawing certain denominations of banknotes
from circulation. The article reads like a government press release. The
journalist has not spoken to any concerned interest groups and as a
result the article contains no opinions contrary to those expressed by
Gaidar. Another article is headlined: 'Mayor of Moscow appeals to
White House [the Russian parliament] to lay down arms', while a third
reports that the ministry for defence has prepared for a possible armed
attack from the White House. The final article is a small note
headlined 'Afghan veterans condemn A. Rutskoi', intended presumably to suggest to readers that the former vice-president, himself an
Afghan veteran, could not even rely on the support of his former
comrades-in-arms. Nowhere on the front page is there any mention,
favourable or unfavourable, of any opposition to the dissolution of
parliament.

While society is so highly politicized it would be unreasonable to
expect the Russian press to remain above politics. Indeed, during
moments of political drama in Western democracies the press becomes
noticeably partisan in both the manner of actual coverage and the
selection of items that are covered. The British pro-Conservative press

---

11 '*My vse stol'ko let nablyudali, kak chelovek prokladyvaet sebe dorogu k absolyutnoi
vlasti – neredko po kostyam, – i molchali. Vse zhdali, chem tam u nikh konchitsya. Da i
seichas yeshchyo zhdyom v nadezhde chto silovye struktury na storone prezidenta. A
ved' samaya silovaya struktura – my i est'*.' See also other examples in the article of the
first person plural: 'We elected deputies …', 'We, simple mortals, …', 'Yes, we made a
mistake …'.

is one example. Because post-Soviet Russia habitually finds itself either in the midst, or on the brink, of major political crisis, it is not surprising that attempts by the liberal, Western-looking Russian press to imitate the forms of the Western newspaper are so often unsuccessful. For all its claims to being a chronicler of events, the newspaper has always been more a reflection of how a society is run than of the society itself.

Foreign news stories

The article on Ukraine is properly speaking a foreign news story. According to the new, post-Soviet Russian perspective, countries, such as Ukraine, that used to be former Soviet republics now belong to the 'near abroad' group, while other countries are part of the 'far abroad'.[12] News reports from the 'near abroad' tend to be less objective than those emanating from more distant countries which have fewer historical and actual ties with Russia. While *Izvestiya* treats stories from the 'near abroad' as almost domestic news, other foreign stories, in particular the post-Soviet variety of brief foreign items, exemplify how the Western way of treating news has been imported into Russia. These brief foreign news items, which fill a thick column of *Izvestiya* every day, are written in an almost completely Western style. This is because *Izvestiya* now relies predominantly on foreign news agencies to fill the column. Over a 30-day period between December 1992 and January 1993, for example, of 198 such news items, only 48 items (24 per cent) were written by Russian correspondents, the vast majority, 150 (76 per cent), were translations from Reuters, Associated Press and France Presse.

In the 3 February 1993 issue of *Izvestiya*, under the rubric of foreign news stories entitled 'From our correspondents and agencies',[13] all seven stories come from agency reports. As with the brief news reports on domestic news, the headlines for foreign briefs are characterized by informativeness and clarity of language. The headlines for the 3 February issue are a good example:

---

12 *Blizhnee zarubezh'e* and *dal'nee zarubezh'e*.
13 *'Ot nashikh korrespondentov i informatsionnykh agenstv.'*

'Four UN workers killed in Afghanistan' (*Reuters*); 'UN envoy greeted by insults in Haiti' (*Associated Press* and *Reuters*); 'Government troops begin assault of Khmer Rouge positions' (*Associated Press*); 'Capital of Zaire gripped by disturbances' (*France Presse*); 'First group of US troops leave Somalia' (*Associated Press*); 'Chile refuse to extradite Honecker' *(Reuters)*; 'Well known mercenary Bob Denard returns to France' (*France Presse*).

In a *perestroika* issue of *Izvestiya* (11 March 1987), the headlines from a similar, though less prominent, rubric ('From the *Izvestiya* wire-room'[14]), are shorter and, while less informative of the content of the story they advertise, are more informative of the ideological position of the journalist, or sub-editor, who chose the headline:

'Fall in popularity'; 'General strike'; 'Trace of CIA'; 'Yet another candidate'; 'Police tale'.

Though cryptic compared to the 1993 headlines, which are mini-summaries, at least two of the 1987 headlines are clear in their ideological content. Both 'General strike' and 'Trace of CIA' belong to an era when foreign news from capitalist countries concentrated on the plight of workers under capitalism as well as the hidden hand of the CIA behind international intrigue. In the conventionalized world of the cold war, in which both the USSR and the USA viewed the world as divided into two opposing camps, the otherwise connotationally neutral language of these headlines took on a negative nuance. 'General strike' was a signal that the article would report on negative conditions of workers, while any headline with the initials CIA was sure to reflect badly on the USA. Even the seemingly innocuous headline of the lead item, 'Fall in popularity', might be expected to refer to one of the USSR's ideological opponents, and, indeed, the first of the two paragraph item confirms this suspicion:

The majority of Americans think that President Reagan is coping poorly with his duties. This is according to the findings of an opinion poll jointly carried out by the *Washington Post* and the television company *ABC*.

In the post-Soviet era, foreign news briefs now reflect a Western perspective on news events, as well as a Western understanding of

14   '*Iz teletaipnogo zala "Izvestii".*'

what constitutes news. One of the *Izvestiya* items from 3 February 1993, an Associated Press story on US troops leaving Somalia, illustrates this clearly:

> FIRST GROUP OF US TROOPS LEAVES SOMALIA.
>
> 469 US marines have left Somalia for the US on a Boeing 747. In the next few days 2,700 US troops will leave Somalia having completed their mission to distribute and protect food aid destined for the starving population. The UN is moving to place military operations under its own control and install troops in the northern part of the country.. (*Associated Press*).

The first sentence, the headline, is printed in large-sized font bold capitals, the second sentence, a separate paragraph, is printed in lower case, smaller-size bold letters, while the third and fourth sentences, the final paragraph, are printed in a smaller font, also in bold. The font size and form conforms to the importance of the information it is presenting. The order in which the story's details appear is typically Western. In the post-cold war era the mention of US troops is no longer a signal of news that will portray the USA as the ideological arch-enemy. Nowhere in the item is there a hint of criticism of the USA, nor, indeed, would this be expected in an Associated Press report. The US troops are said to be leaving having done their duty of helping the starving. There is no mention of any view that the US departure from Somalia might have been too early. The at times supine attitude now shown to the former enemy is a characteristic of the post-Soviet foreign press. This is a reaction to the particular Soviet sarcastic and superior tone of the 'Gold fever'-type[15] report, filed by *Pravda*'s London correspondent, A. Maslennikov, in 1979:

> These last few days the money markets of the capitalist world find themselves in the grip of yet another 'gold fever'.[16]

It is now only in marginal communist newspapers, such as *Pravda*

---

15 '*Zolotaya likhoradka*'.

16 '*Valyutnye rynki kapitalisticheskogo mira nakhodyatsya v eti dni vo vlasti ocherednoi "zolitoi likhoradki"*' (*Pravda*, 21 September 1979). See also *Pravda*, 4 January 1980, in which an article by G. Vasil'ev carries the same headline and reads 'at the London, New York and Hong Kong stock exchanges [there has been] another attack of "gold fever"...' ('*na birzhakh Londona, N'yu-Iorka, Gonkonga – novy pristup "zolotoi likhoradki"*...'.

or *Sovetskaya Rossiya*, that this model is employed, though now it is likely to be directed not only at foreign enemies, as shown in the page-one *fotoreportazh* from *Pravda*, 1 August 1992:

A DISTANT REGION, BUT NOT YOURS, MADAM JAPAN.[17]

M. Poltoranin has flown to the land of the rising sun to lay preparations for the visit of B. Yeltsin who, it is thought, will exploit the political setting of fifty years [since the islands became Soviet] to hand over two of the Kurile islands to Japan. Knowing the character of our president, it is possible, observers say, that there, in a distant country, he will sign a decree handing over the islands 'for the sake of détente'. In any case there are few who are privy to the thought of the president on this matter.

A more obvious example of how Western values have been imported into the new Russian press is found in a 1992 report from the liberal and pro-Yeltsin *Komsomol'skaya pravda*. The report is a translation of part of a *Financial Times*[18] article written by that paper's Moscow correspondent. Lexically, as we shall see, the piece serves to give prominence to words and expressions untypical of the old Soviet press and emblematic of the Western financial press. Philosophically, it makes assumptions about how economies should be run according to the beliefs underlying the editorial line of the *Financial Times*. Journalistically, the story uses certain clichés which confer authority on the views of certain individuals. Politically, the most remarkable feature of the translation is that it appears at all. The very idea that the former main organ of the Leninist youth organization might publish an article from the *Financial Times* on the 2 January 1992 price rises, the

---

17 *'Krai dalyoky, no ne vashenskii, gospozha Yaponiya'*.
18 The 3 January 1992 *Komsomol'skaya pravda* translation comes from the 2 January 1992 *Financial Times* article, 'Moscow awaits backlash as price control ends', by the newspaper's Moscow correspondent, Leyla Boulton. The original text was: '...But a senior Western financial official said today's rises were primarily a political measure since there was no real monetary, budgetary or privatisation policy in place. The main merit would be to start irreversible change, paving the way for a comprehensive economic reform programme to be agreed with the International Monetary Fund and other experts.' The translation was: *'Po slovam vysokopostavlennogo eksperta, vcherashnee povyshenie tsen nosit v osnovnom politicheskii kharakter, tak kak u pravitel'stva poka eshchyo net chyotkoi valyutnoi, byudzhetnoi i privatizatsionnoi politiki. Osnovnym dostoinstvom etogo shaga yavlyaetsya to, chto on pozvolit nachat' neobratimye izmeneniya v ekonomike i otkroet dorogu pretvoneniyu v zhizn' programmy reform, kotoraya dolzhna byt' soglasovana s MVD i drugimi mezhdunarodnymi organizatsiyami.'*

most important domestic political story of the time, would have been unthinkable even during the early Gorbachev years. The appearance of this story, along with others in the same column on the same subject from a right-wing French newspaper, *Le Figaro*, and the liberal *New York Times*, is a clear illustration of how far the pendulum of the Russian newspaper world has swung from self-imposed isolation from outside sources to enthusiastic acceptance of foreign views. Lexically, philosophically, journalistically and politically this sort of article represents a complete undermining of the foundations of Soviet journalism.

Lexically, for example, the translation refers to concepts borrowed from the current Western capitalist economic jargon, such as the notions of following a 'strict monetary (*valyutnaya*) policy'.[19] The adjective '*valyutnaya*' (monetary, money) is no longer made to carry pejorative overtones as in Maslennikov's 1979 'money markets' (*valyutnye rynki*). Other phrases that come from the same philosophy are 'budgetary' and 'privatization'. As with vocabulary to do with sex and pop-music, none of these words are new to the Russian language. Some, indeed, as '*valyutnaya*' shows, appeared in the press. Rather the acceptance by the liberal press of the Western economic model has placed these words in a new, positive context. 'Monetary policy', 'privatization' and the IMF are implicitly deemed a good thing, just as the capitalist 'money markets' under Brezhnev were considered wicked. Journalistically, the unquestioned views in the piece are attributed to an anonymous 'highly-placed Western financial expert'. In the old *Komsomol'skaya pravda* the legitimizing persona was likely to be a highly-placed party official.

Especially guilty of this form of cliché substitution is *Kommersant*, one of the first Western-style newspapers to appear in the old Soviet Union. On two (tabloid) pages alone of one issue (pp.2–3, 25 November–2 December 1991) the following anonymous sources were adduced:

'Experts from *Kommersant* note...', According to experts...', 'Experts note...', 'Experts from *Kommersant* suggest...', 'According to specialists...'

---

19 The examples are back-translations from the Russian text, which is not a completely accurate translation of the *Financial Times* article. Here, for example, the original read 'real', and not 'tight' or 'clear' ('*chyotkii*'), as in the Russian version.

As with much of the conceptual language of the bolsheviks, much of this new economic idiom is 'foreign' to Russians not versed in the language of Western capitalist economics. Again in common with the language of the bolsheviks, this foreign 'economese' was known only to a small highly educated group with access to Western journals and newspapers, and to Westerners themselves. As was the case with the jargon of bolshevism, the repeated use in the columns of the press of Western economic jargon has made the words familiar to readers without necessarily explaining their meaning. Such is the frequency with which the International Monetary Fund is mentioned in the post-Soviet media that the *Komsomol'skaya pravda* editor feels it unnecessary even to write out what the initials in Russian, *MVF*, stand for.

Sensationalist language

Economics is but one area where previously taboo or in some way stigmatized language has now become legitimate discourse in the press. Another article from *Komsomol'skaya pravda* (3 January 1992) provides an example of how the borrowing of genre forms, rather than new words, has changed the face of the Russian press. The story is a reworking of a Reuters' report on how a love-stricken German youth set himself alight in Czecho-Slovakia because of a row with his girlfriend. The same story was picked up (a day earlier) by a Dublin evening newspaper, the *Evening Press*, and published in much the same manner. The headlines of both newspapers treated the story lightly, 'Lovesick blaze' (*Evening Press*), and 'If to burn, then let it be from love' (*Sgorat', tak ot lyubvi*). Both versions contained approximately the same details of the incident, though the Russian report added 'according to witnesses, before the self-immolation the young man ran through the village half-naked'. Apart from the ironic headlines, the language of both reports is neutral. The report expresses no opinion on the action of the young German. There is no possible moral to be drawn from the story. The incident could not in any way be said to be instructive. It is in fact an example of a story printed with the sole purpose of entertaining the reader. Such 'human interest' stories, essentially sensationalist, were not deemed newsworthy in the Soviet press whose idealized readership would not have been interested in such senationalist fluff.

The translation of foreign reports into Russian is the most direct way in which Western media techniques and models are imported into the country. Another method is for Russian editors to use stories from foreign media as a springboard for their own. This sort of news-generation technique is common practice in the West between different newspapers and magazines. The Russian adoption of the technique, though now in its infancy and not infrequently relying almost exclusively on the foreign report, is an important step in the incorporation of the country's press into the Western media machine. Two examples, one from *Izvestiya* and the other from its sister paper, *Nedelya*, illustrate this new practice. The factual information in the 28 January 1993 front-page *Izvestiya* story 'Money in the presidents' pockets' (*Den'gi v karmanakh prezidentov*) is based on a *Newsweek* report that gave the yearly earnings of the world's leading politicians, including those of President Boris Yeltsin. The Russian addition to the story was a long-winded account of how an *Izvestiya* reporter had contacted the Moscow *Newsweek* bureau to find out, unsuccessfully as it turned out, according to what exchange rate the magazine had worked out Boris Yeltsin's yearly earnings (said to be $1,360). Compared to the non-existent coverage of top politicians in the Soviet era, a journalistic enquiry into Boris Yeltsin's salary represents a new departure for the country's most serious daily. The language in the article is neutral and contains no neologisms. Again, it is the genre – a bottom-of-page-one entertaining story – that is new to the Russian press.

The July 1993 (N° 29) *Nedelya* feature, written by the well-known journalist Melor Sturua, has been 'lifted' almost in its entirety from the 21 June edition of *Time* magazine, five photographs included. The story, headlined 'BORDELLO against the background of [the cathedral of] St Basil the Blessed' (*BORDEL' na fone Vasiliya Blazhennogo*) concerns child prostitution in Moscow. Sturua summarizes the *Time* article, translating the best quotes into Russian. Only in the final two paragraphs of the nine paragraph full-page spread does he add his own moralistic finale:

> We have no business being proud of the destruction of the GULAG if in its place we erect a brothel (*bordel'*).

That the Russian word '*bordel*" appears twice in Sturua's account is an example of how a word that previously existed in Russian, but would not have appeared in the press, is now printed freely. Such was the public prudery in Soviet life in all areas dealing with sex that even the 1977 edition of Ozhegov's standard Russian dictionary did not have an entry for the word. The definition given in the same dictionary for another word appearing in the text related to prostitution, '*sutenyor*' (pimp), is itself an eloquent definition of the Brezhnev-era attitude to this, and other topics: 'In a capitalist society: a person living off the earnings of their lover-prostitute' (Ozhegov, 1977, p.717).

The whole area of sex is now eagerly treated in mainstream (non-pornographic) newspapers. In a 1992 (N° 44) issue of *Nedelya*, for example, one page was devoted to two pseudo-medical feature articles, 'Sex as gymnastics' and 'Sex as medicine'. The articles are replete with words and phrases which, though not new to the Russian language and printed without explanation, would never have appeared on the pages of the old Soviet press. Examples include:

'*mnogo-mnogo lyubvi*' (lots'n'lots o ' love), '*seksolog*' (sexologist), '*seksual'-naya zhizn*'' (sexual life), '*ficheskie uprazhneniya ozhivlyayut seks*' (physical exercise enlivens sex), '*dostizhenie kul'minatsii* (reaching of orgasm), '*polovoi akt*' (sexual act), '*frigidnost*'' (frigidity), '*nochnaya orgiya*' (night-time orgy), '*seksual'nye ogranicheniya*' (sexual limitations), '*seksual'naya blizost*'' (sexual closeness), '*seksual'ny chelovek*' (sexual person), '*seksual'noe obshchenie*' (sexual intercourse), '*eroticheskaya energiya*' (erotic energy), '*tvorcheskii seks*' (creative sex), '*eroticheskii ekstaz*' (erotic ecstasy), '*ispytyvat' orgazm*' (to experience an orgasm), '*seksual'nye otnosheniya*' (sexual relationship), '*neudo-vletvoryonny orgazm*' (unsatisfactory orgasm), '*seksual'noe vozbuzhdenie*' (sexual arousal), '*seksterapiya*' (sex therapy), '*psikhoterapiya seksual'nykh rasstroistv*' (psychotherapy for sexual disorders), '*stimulirovanie erogennykh zon*' (stimulation of erogenous zones), '*spermoterapiya*' (spermotherapy).

The profusion of obvious calques on Western words and phrases points to the Western origin of both articles. The second article, though written by a Russian 'psychotherapist', draws much from American popular psychological books.[20] As well as popularizing and

---

20 The author refers to the American pop-psychology author Eric Berne MD, founder of 'transactional analysis'. An advertisement on the back of another issue of *Nedelya* (N° 46, 1992) offers paid telephone consultations with the 'well-known Australian

legitimizing stylistically neutral but hitherto culturally taboo words, respectable, family-oriented publications, such as *Nedelya*, provide models for Russian journalists of lifestyles, fashion, gossip and health genres that all have recourse to, even demand, the sort of language that was alien to the old Soviet style.

At the other end of the market is the nationalist and conservative press represented by such newspapers as *Pravda, Sovetskaya Rossiya* and, in its most extreme variant, *Den'*. These newspapers are in their own way as sensationalist as the Western-style sensationalism found in the liberal press. The language of the nationalist press, as well as harking back to the Soviet era, can be as shocking as that found in the flourishing pornographic press. Just as, for example, the now liberal *Izvestiya* is no longer obliged to observe the proprieties of being a government organ, and is free to pursue its aspirations to becoming a Western-style newspaper of record, so nationalist and Soviet newspapers such as *Pravda* and *Sovetskaya Rossiya*, stripped of their former power and responsibilities, are free to follow to the extreme the Leninist ideas of principled journalism. Rather than affecting to adopt an objective pose in the Western manner, the nationalist journalist has a clearly expressed point of view, expressed in the most direct language.

The language is marked by a sense of seething anger directed against the Yeltsin cabinet, blamed for the destruction of the country's economic and social fabric. These concerns, and the language in which they are articulated, are well illustrated by the following extract from a typical front-page letter, serving as lead story, that appeared in *Sovetskaya Rossiya* (1 August 1992). Unhappy that the Russian 'democrats' proposed declaring a public holiday in August to commemorate the defeat of the 1991 coup, Vladimir Palashin wrote:

The collapse and destruction of the country, the impoverishment of the people, speculation and crime on the rampage, thieving prices and a market, economy, legal system and morality that has run riot, the loss of all social guarantees and rights, a deterioration in the standard of living of ordinary people and the enrichment at the people's expense of new millionaires, unemployment and civil war on the territory of the USSR, the smothering of other points of view and freedom

---

sexologist, Nancy Williams...on the subject of female orgasm, oral sex and self-satisfaction'.

of speech .... On the basis of these stones is laid the foundation of the 'triumphs' of the 'democrats' on the occasion of the so-called 'victory' of 19–21 August.

The use of inverted commas to signify irony is a typical feature of the nationalist press. The uncritical acceptance by the liberal press of the necessity for Western intervention to cure Russia's ills is replaced in the nationalist press by a xenophobia supported by a nostalgia for the Soviet era. Continuing the tone of irony, the letter suggests that the fireworks for the August holiday will be set off in honour of

the impoverishment and successful deceit of the ordinary people, the collapse of the state and in honour of the successful fulfilment of the plans of the USA and the IMF to destroy the Soviet socialist state and dismember the unitary Union.

For *Sovetskaya Rossiya*, unlike *Komsomol'skaya pravda*, the IMF is an enemy. For *Sovetskaya Rossiya*, which declares itself an 'independent popular (*narodnaya*) newspaper', the victims of the 'anti-popular policies (*antinarodny kurs*) of the Yeltsin–Gaidar team' are the 'ordinary people' (*prostoi narod*). The ultranationalist *Den'* does not recognize the legitimacy of the Yeltsin government, routinely referring to the president as the 'ring-leader' (*glavar'*) of the 'provisional government of occupation' (*vremennoe okkupatsionnoe pravitel'-stvo*).[21] *Pravda* and *Sovetskaya Rossiya* give prominence to letters and communications from those who do not recognize that the USSR has come to an end. The writer of the front-page letter to *Sovetskaya Rossiya*, for example, is angry that there is 'unemployment and civil war on the territory of the USSR', while a quarter-page message 'from grateful Canadians', that appeared in *Pravda* (2 February 1993) on the occasion of the fiftieth anniversary of the battle of Stalingrad, commiserates with the current tribulations of 'our Soviet friends'. The message also refers to Joseph Stalin as a 'great leader' and reminds readers that he was named 'Man of the Year' by *Time* magazine in 1943. For the nationalist press the 'Yeltsin–Gaidar' team is the focus for all that is wrong and evil in post-Soviet Russia, in particular the '*gaidarizatsiya*'[22] (Gaidarization) of the country's economy. The most

21 See, for example, *Den'* 26 June–1 July 1992, 2–8 August 1992 or 12–18 August 1992.
22 *Pravda*, 2 February 1992, p.1, '*Trudno? Eshchyo budet trudnee, tak schitaet V.Chernomyrdin.*'

vicious and personalized attacks on all members of Yeltsin's cabinet who favour his course of economic reform appear in *Den'*, which defines itself as the paper of the 'spiritual opposition'. Its daily front-page rubric '*Den'* agency', a bizarre collection of quasi-sententiae on the state of the country, insults both the Yeltsin regime and the old Gorbachev-led government, under which the rot set in:

'Gaidar plucks his eyebrows and uses lipstick' (26 July–1 August 1992); 'Everything that the travelling Gorbachev did not give away is being handed over by the wandering Yeltsin',[23] 'Thatcher and Gorbachev are waltzing on the ruins of the USSR' (both 2–8 February 1992); 'It has transpired, in Moscow, that apart from the two Yakovlevs,[24] there are also several other freemasons', 'The Soviet Union is the former CIS' (both 12–18 July 1992).

As well as using heavy irony and plain insulting language to refer to their enemies, the arsenal of the nationalist press also makes use of some of the methods associated with the Westernizing press. Though the xenophobic nationalist press devotes few column inches to news reports written by foreigners, it occasionally uses foreign copy as a club with which to beat the government. A front-page *Pravda* headline in a rubric devoted to the 1993 Russian referendum, 'Washington has already cast its vote' (7 April 1993), read:

'We have absolute confidence in president Yeltsin. At the present time there is no one who could in reality replace him', declared the US Secretary of State W. Christopher referring to the forthcoming Russian referendum in an interview given to the television station *ABC*.

Inside the same issue, a page-three article headlined, 'A country of bureaucrats and a "black market"', was an edited version of a damning report on the state of Russia that appeared in the *US News and World Report* newspaper. The report, written under headings of 'Corruption', 'Flight of capital', 'Earnings of government officials', 'Cul de sac',

23 '*Vsyo, chto ne razdal puteshestvuyushchii Gorbachev, dodaryvaet stranstvuyushchii El'tsin*'

24 An anti-semitic reference to Gorbachev's former ally, the liberal Alexander Yakovlev ('Jacobson') and former *Moskovskie novosti* editor, Yegor Yakovlev, both perceived as key figures in the destruction of the Soviet Union and, in the case of Yegor Yakovlev, at the time director of the Russian national television service, a continuing baneful presence in the political life of Russia.

'Aid misdirected' and 'Political consequences', painted a dismal though far from unrecognizable picture of the country. Paradoxically, given the xenophobia of *Pravda*, the report carried more force because it was written by the enemy who had no longer any vested interest in exaggerating the country's ills.

6. Soviet Journalists Speak

1. Sergei Grigoryants

Transcript and translation of taped interview with Sergei Grigoryants, editor and founder of *Glasnost'*, on 27 July 1987 in Moscow.

John Murray: When was the first issue of *Glasnost'*?

Sergei Grigoryants: The first issue came out on 3 July 1987.

JM: What is your circulation?

SG: It's very difficult to determine the circulation. At the moment we're printing from a hundred to a hundred and fifty copies, but we do print more according to demand. On the other hand, there are a lot of foreign issues of the magazine: in English in New York, in French in Paris, as well as in Russian and, apparently, there's going to be a collection of articles from *Glasnost'* printed in Norwegian in December, afterwards in Swedish. But the most important thing is that in many cities in the Soviet Union, *Glasnost'* is retyped. This is happening in Sverdlovsk, in Kiev, in Lvov, in Minsk and a lot of other cities. In Armenia *Glasnost'* comes out in Armenian in a slightly different version and there it has a print run of about three thousand. What's more, this Armenian edition will be republished, and type-set, in Armenian by the Armenian colony in Los Angeles. There's also an edition being prepared in Georgia and in Leningrad. In other words it's very difficult to determine the exact circulation figures for the magazine, we can't even say ourselves.

JM: It comes out three times a month ...

SG: Unfortunately we haven't been able to keep any fixed dates for publication. We publish three issues a month, but we don't manage to publish one issue every ten days. At the moment, unfortunately, more often than not all three issues come out towards the end of the month. But we hope in the future the magazine will come out on a regular basis. Also the latest issues – 7, 8 and 9 – have been almost twice as large as the first issue.

JM: The magazine isn't sold in newspaper kiosks ...

SG: No, though, so we're told anyway, people are asking for it now in the kiosks. And we've been told by post-office workers that people are trying to subscribe to it at the post offices. But I'm afraid that it will be a long time before people can buy *Glasnost'* at kiosks or subscribe to it.

JM: How many journalists are there on your staff?

SG: It's difficult to say because there's a comparatively small number of people who can afford to devote all their time to the magazine. It would be somewhere in the region of five to six people. Added to that, several dozen people give as much time to the magazine as they can afford to, anything from a few hours a day to a few hours a week.

JM: How many different departments are there in the magazine?

SG: The question of departments is a little difficult. Our present aim is that each issue, while not being dedicated to one theme only, contains a selection of articles on one particular topic. So, for instance, in the eighth issue we had a large number of articles on the national question in the Soviet Union, the ninth was mainly about issues in religion and the tenth will deal mainly with environmental questions. The eleventh, what we call the provincial issue, will concentrate on the large number of monstrous things happening mainly on the periphery of the country. We'll be talking about how the inhabitant on the periphery is absolutely powerless before the powers-that-be. The twelfth issue will be given over to the seventieth anniversary of the October revolution.

JM: What is the favoured genre in *Glasnost'*?

SG: The character of the articles is changing. At first we thought it would be purely an information bulletin. In time it transpired that information had far less meaning and value than two or three years ago when it was harder to come by and was diffused by far fewer channels. And what's more, because of the large number of periodical publications in the country, the information we received, whether it was current or whether it was out of date, was received by numerous other journalists at the same time who were in a position to use it earlier than us. For that reason and because the readers much prefer it, or so it seems to us, we print analytical articles on the present state of the country and its hopes for the future. And this type of analytical article is occupying more and more space in the magazine. The increase is paralleled by the increase in the size of the bulletin itself, which over time has to all intents and purposes become a magazine (*zhurnal*) and accordingly the character of the articles is changing.

JM: Do you print an editorial?

SG: No, we don't have a regular editorial. Sometimes we have them, sometimes we have generalizing articles connected with the central topic of the issue. But, no, we don't as a rule have editorials.

JM: Does the editorial board adhere to any particular political line?

SG: No. For us it's more important to stress pluralism in public affairs and in ideology. We're convinced that any further development of the country can only take place on the basis of free choice made by the citizens of the country and by making a realistic analysis of the current situation and possibilities of the country. We do not want to impose our opinion, whatever it may be, on anybody. What's more, different people working for the magazine can have different points of view. We feel that Russia has suffered enough over the last seventy years from the imposition of only one view of the historical process.

JM: Do you read official Soviet newspapers?

SG: Very little, unfortunately. Though I do read some things, none the less.

JM: Whatever chances to come your way ...

SG: No, I read what, as they say, are the most interesting articles.

JM: Do you think *glasnost'* is present in official Soviet publications?

SG: Yes, of course I do. The change has been especially noticeable in the national newspapers. Naturally *glasnost'* is apparent; it has been for two years now.

JM: And has the content changed in any particular direction?

SG: Both the content and the presentation, as well as the variety of topics covered by the Soviet press have expanded greatly. And the tone in which things are discussed has changed and become freer. The Soviet Union has never known such a degree of freedom of the press, especially the literary journals and several national papers. At the same time it would be wrong to exaggerate the changes. This official *glasnost'* has strict limitations. Some topics are forbidden the same as previously while others can only be covered in a particular manner and from a particular point of view. If this weren't the case there would be no need for publications like our own.

JM: Would you say the limitations of *glasnost'* are constant or moving?

SG: Difficult to say. There are changes sometimes, changes from month to month, but over the last year and a half, well, let's say from the time the present situation was firmly established, there probably haven't been any genuine changes. Some months have produced more interesting material than others, but these variations are not significant at a profound level.

JM: In yesterday's edition of *Pravda*, Gorbachev in his speech to the French communist party delegation said, on the one hand, that *perestroika* without democracy and *glasnost'* was doomed to failure, and, on the other, that a 'struggle would be waged against those who do not like socialism'. Do you see a contradiction in this?

SG: In the first place, I see here a straight contradiction between what Gorbachev himself said two months ago at a meeting with the representatives of the press. There he said that while we undoubtedly cannot agree with the opponents of socialism, we will argue with them, while preserving the conditions of democratization and *glasnost'*. Now he speaks not of 'arguments' but of 'struggles'. This is a return to the pre-Gorbachev situation ... at least in terminology. We shall see how things turn out later on. That it represents a threat and a u-turn from the previous policy is beyond doubt.

2. Igor' Karpenko

Transcript and translation of taped interview with Igor' Karpenko, senior editor in *Izvestiya*, on 12 April 1988 in Moscow.

Igor' Karpenko: The first thing I should tell you is that over the last year our circulation has gone up by over 2,500,000. We've now

got 10 million subscribers to *Izvestiya* ... and we've overtaken
Pravda. There's never been such a large jump in the circulation
figures of any Soviet newspaper over such a short space of time.
It's a record. This month alone we've got over 100,000 new
subscribers.

John Murray: And where have all these new readers come from?

IK: We've taken one and a half million readers from *Trud* [the trade
union paper] and a million copies from *Pravda* [party paper].

JM: How many copies will now be sold daily at the newspaper stalls?

IK: Only half-a-million or so. Last year we were given paper enough
for a million but because of the increase in subscriptions and the
paper shortage we've had to cut our retail circulation figure.

JM: I notice that brief reports on economic achievements have all but
gone from page one, if not altogether ...

IK: Yes. Our front page has changed dramatically. Before, I don't
know if you noticed, people would turn to the back page first. That
was where all the interesting news was. One of our priorities was
to restructure the front page in such a way as to return to it its lost
prestige.

JM: You've recently introduced a page-one column: 'From last week's
mail'. Does this mean you're giving more attention to readers'
views?

IK: Yes. The number of letters we receive daily has more than tripled
over the last year. We used to get about 3,000 a day. Now we're
literally inundated: we get on average 10,000 letters a day. We've
had to expand our letter department. We've been allowed to take
on extra staff to handle the influx.

JM: What sort of letters do you print?

IK: Take for example the letter on the front page of today's edition,
it's a fairly typical example. The deputies from Solyanka wrote in
to complain about the closing down of a level-crossing by the
railway company, thus forcing the local farmers to make a 15-km.
detour down the line to the next nearest level crossing in order to
move their state-owned cattle to grazing land. What's the problem
here? Well, the railway company has gone over to a system of
cost-accounting and is trying to cut costs wherever it can. Now,
while the desire to economize and become more efficient is

laudable, the deputies, we think, are right to complain. We are against cost-accounting at someone else's cost. The railway company shouldn't be allowed to get away with riding roughshod over the opinions of the local soviets [councils]. On a broader level the letter points up the conflict between large state concerns, such as the railway, and the centres of regional, local power. As the organ of the soviets, we support and encourage the return of real power to the soviets.

JM: Would you say *Izvestiya* now reflects the views of its readers more than before?

IK: What I can say is that we have concluded an agreement with a sociological institute who will conduct regular opinion polls of what our readers think about what we write. We now regularly send questionnaires to from 3,000 to 5,000 readers after the publication of an important story. We are very interested in what our readers think.

JM: Are there now fewer pieces from *TASS* [the Government news agency] appearing in your paper?

IK: Unfortunately, the stream of *TASS* news is still flowing. Well, there are some *TASS* stories we ourselves eagerly await, like the Reagan–Gorbachev summit, that's big news in itself. But as a rule we in *Izvestiya* try to cover as much as possible with our own reporters. *TASS* coverage isn't up to the *Izvestiya* standard: too much officialese language. Now we're doing stories only *TASS* would have covered previously. For example, we covered Gorbachev's visit to Leningrad last year. It was a risk, but we got away with it. Nothing was said. A couple of years ago *TASS* would automatically cover any visit of the general secretary anywhere. There was no law preventing other papers from covering the story, but there were no precedents either.

JM: Soviet papers carry a lot of official news. Do you think they might start carrying less in the future?

IK: There are a few things here. Before, it was accepted that all more or less official speeches, announcements, communiqués, and so on, should be printed, usually verbatim, by all newspapers. And that's the way it works at the moment. This may soon change. I was recently invited to submit my views to the central committee on the whole question of the place of 'official' news in the Soviet newspaper. I can let you know that the view is that it might be more rational to divide up official news among the appropriate papers. For example, let *Pravda* cover all party official news.

JM: And *Izvestiya* all government news?

IK: Yes. I can also tell you that there is a desire that the length of political speeches, et cetera, be cut, because we realize that they're often just too long and people don't read them.

JM: Izvestiya is often referred to as the government paper. Is that a definition you would endorse?

IK: Yes. We're the paper of the [pointing to the masthead of one of the newspapers on his desk] look: 'News [*Izvestiya*] of the soviets of the people's deputies of the USSR'.

JM: Does that mean you can't criticize the government?

IK: It means we don't and, to my knowledge, never have criticized the praesidium of the Supreme Soviet. We can and have criticized committees made up of individual deputies. But it's an interesting question ... there's no law against it.

JM: Can anyone criticize the government?

IK: Pravda can and has done.

JM: So *Pravda* occupies a special place among newspapers?

IK: The general understanding among newspapers is that *Pravda* is, if you like, above everybody else. Nobody can criticize *Pravda*. Though last year, *Izvestiya*, while not criticizing *Pravda*, on a couple of occasions took issue with it.

JM: Do you think *Izvestiya* will open its pages to advertising?

IK: There's hardly much point in advertising when there's a shortage of practically everything. Hopefully, that state of affairs won't last forever.[1] I think we will probably carry advertisements eventually.

1 By 1990 *Izvestiya* was regularly displaying advertisements. See also Weasel, 1990, p.10, on *Pravda* opening up its pages to advertising: '*Pravda* is now in search of new shackles – capitalist ones this time. As has been reported, *Pravda* is not only soliciting advertising for the first time in its history but it is making advertisers the most extraordinary offer: "We give you a chance to advertise in *Pravda* a journalistic story about your corporation including your own interview, your ad, and photographs of your products," it says.

'This is something which no respectable newspaper in the West, particularly in the United States, would dream of doing. Editors would man barricades rather than submit

At the moment *Nedelya* [The Week], our weekend supplement, does carry a few advertisements. That's because space isn't so much at a premium as in *Izvestiya*. We might try to promote one brand of fridge over another which we knew to be badly made. *Moskovskie novosti* had an ad. a couple of editions ago with a picture of Gorbachev and Reagan signing the agreement in Washington, each holding a pen. Above them was written: 'The Pen is Mightier than the Sword', below a picture of a Parker pen.

JM: But you can't buy Parkers here, can you?

IK: No. But *Moskovskie novosti* is sold not only to Russians ...

3. Vitaly Korotich

Transcript and translation of taped interview with Vitaly Korotich, editor of *Ogonyok,* on 28 September 1988 in Dublin.

John Murray: Last year the number of subscribers to *Ogonyok* rose by over half a million. This means you now have around one and a half million subscribers. How do you account for this impressive leap in circulation?

Vitaly Korotich: Our circulation has in fact risen by 800,000. The main reason for this is that we've become interesting for our readers. Previously, *Ogonyok* was simply uninteresting, nobody believed what was written in it. Now, people believe us and that's the way we intend to keep it.

JM: Who is the average reader of *Ogonyok*?

VK: The average reader? I don't know. We're trying to find out for ourselves. The problem is that at the moment there is practically no way to gauge public opinion in the Soviet Union. This is one of the tragedies not only for *Ogonyok* but also for the newspapers and television. We simply don't know who we're writing for. I try to write for the fairly well-educated reader with an interest in contemporary life. At the moment we rely on letters we receive to tell us who our public is ... we get a lot of mail.

---

to such a request. It is somewhat disturbing to discover how little the Russians know about such principles.'

JM: *Ogonyok*'s letters' column, 'The Readers' Word', is one of the most popular in the magazine. How do you decide which letters to print?

VK: Well, we have two aims: first of all we make a point of publishing purely controversial, problematic letters; secondly, we print letters from Stalinists, from people whom we consider dangerous.

JM: Has there been an increase in the number of letters you've been printing?

VK: It's going up all the time. In 1984–85 we got somewhere in the region of 20 to 30 letters a day. Now we're getting around 400.

JM: A day?

VK: A day.

JM: One important component of *glasnost'* is a reappraisal of post-revolutionary events, often involving the rehabilitation of those who suffered under Stalin. What was the reaction of your readers to the publication of such sensational stories as those on Bukharin, Raskol'nikov and many others?

VK: We get enormous public support when we write articles dealing with this period of our history. There is a great yearning for justice among the people. And we intend to go on publishing stories like these, only at the moment we don't have enough documentary material at our disposal.

JM: But these documents exist …

VK: Of course, they're somewhere in the party archives. We just have to be given access to them.

JM: In a sense the reappraisal of the events that took place under Stalin is a continuation of what was begun by Khrushchev and stopped by Brezhnev. Would you agree with that point of view?

VK: Naturally, I agree. But the important point here is that the process was only begun by Khrushchev, and because of his limitations and our situation at the time, there were no grounds for any great hopes then. Now we intend once and for all to have done with the discussion on Stalin and Stalinism.

JM: Is there any guarantee that *glasnost'* in the media is irreversible?

VK: What do you mean 'guarantee'? There's no definite guarantee, the guarantee lies within ourselves. But the situation has changed.

There's widespread enthusiasm for critical material to be published and a deep desire to understand what is really happening in the country. The bureaucrats are profoundly worried by all this. These bureaucrats are revolutionaries turned to stone, like the Ayatollah's entourage in Iran. They're the people who oppose Gorbachev, the usual 'fat cats', people with no idealism, people who believe in nothing.

JM: Would you go along with those who say that criticism ought to be 'creative and positive' and not 'slanderous'? Surely it is no coincidence that those who make those statements are the very people you referred to as the dinosaurs of Soviet political life.[2]

VK: I detest the word 'slander'. You see, there are people who make pronouncements to the effect that if we denounce and expose Stalin and Stalinism we are destroying our ideals. If you follow this line of logic, then in order to strengthen our ideals we shall have to resort to repression. That I am categorically against. I don't think there's any such thing as slander, as long as you get your facts right.

JM: As a party member you must acknowledge the subordinate position of your magazine to the goals of the party ...

VK: What can I say to you? ... at the moment the aims of the party, of the party leadership and of Gorbachev himself are the most revolutionary in our society. Therefore to subordinate ourselves to their rules is good. When the magazine was subordinate to Brezhnev's party, the results were dreadful.

JM: Does your dependence on the party not in fact mean, willy-nilly, that your fate and the fate of *glasnost'* ultimately rest in the hands of those members of the politburo and the central committee who support the politics behind *glasnost'*?

VK: I think that the party is playing a very positive role at the moment; Gorbachev supporters have in reality become that very vanguard which the party called itself under Brezhnev and Chernenko. Today, it is the party that sets the tone. And we are not obliged to obey the party since Gorbachev demands no such obedience.

---

2   In his speech to the writers' conference.

JM: What are the forbidden topics that still remain for the journalist in the Soviet Union?

VK: So far I haven't come across any.

JM: At present your own journal, *Ogonyok*, and the newspaper *Moskovskie novosti* are considered to be the most progressive publications in the country. How, in your view, does the editorial policy of the conservative newspapers and magazines, such as *Moskva* or *Molodaya Gvardiya*, differ from yours?

VK: We are in constant contact with the magazines that take a conservative and chauvinistic stance and that are opposed to ... *glasnost'*. What I can tell you is that today, for the first time ever, the conservatives are on the defensive. They are in the minority and this is very significant.

JM: You mean they are in a minority among the editors of the main magazines and newspapers?

VK: Yes. They've never been able to defend themselves. We, the liberals, have been defending ourselves all our lives; they've never had to defend themselves, all their lives they've spent screaming and shouting and attacking. Today, they're not in such a position.

JM: But they still enjoy support ...

VK: They do indeed enjoy enormous support from part of the leadership who are simply in love with them. But among the people, they're becoming more and more unpopular.

JM: Has the official line changed towards up until very recently semi-banned authors such as Pasternak, Mandelshtam, Akhmatova, and so forth?

VK: Policy has changed in that we are now publishing these authors. However, there is fierce hostility to the new policy from, of all places, the writers' union, from the court poets. These people get very angry when we publish the work of previously maligned authors, as for example did the historical novelist Pikul' when *Ogonyok* took the decision to serialize a forgotten novel on the war by Grossman.[3]

JM: In Selyunin's article in the May [1988] edition of *Novy mir*, 'Sources', the author, probably for the first time in the official press, convincingly argues that the deep roots of many of the

3 Vasily Grossman's novel, *Life and Fate*.

difficulties the country has gone through originate in the immediate post-revolutionary period and early twenties, that is, before Stalin. In particular, he shows how the political decisions made by Lenin himself paved the way for Stalin's crimes. Is this the first step towards the decanonization of Lenin as well as towards a more objective analysis of Soviet history in general?

VK: First of all regarding Selyunin's article. I think we can return to Lenin, but I am against any destruction of the whole mythology. What for me is vitally important is to get to grips with the period beginning with Stalin and ending with Brezhnev. It would, I think, be wrong to equate Lenin and his mistakes with those of Stalin, Brezhnev and Chernenko. At the very least, Lenin for us remains an ideal towards which we must strive ... the Church never criticizes the figure of Christ ...

JM: But would you not earn the respect of your readers if you adopted a more critical attitude towards Lenin?

VK: We would, yes, that's absolutely true ... but I ... we're doing that at the moment in Shatrov's plays. But I'm against Lenin being ... you see, the people who want to save Stalin will begin to equate Lenin with Stalin and the difference is that while Lenin made mistakes, Stalin and Brezhnev committed crimes. And if we begin criticizing Lenin, then we'll end up destroying the whole temple, beginning with the foundations. I believe we have to leave the foundations intact. It's a purely tactical move. That's my opinion, anyway.

JM: Recently Sergei Grigoryants, editor of the independent, unofficial magazine *Glasnost'*, was arrested in connection with his part in the formation of a new, second political party within the Soviet Union. What is your opinion of the magazine and how do you react to his arrest?

VK: As for Grigoryants, his mistake is that he has resolutely refused to look for support among people within the country. I've only seen his journal once, it was given to me by the Moscow correspondent of the *New York Times*, but he has never approached us at *Ogonyok* or *Moskovskie novosti*, that is, even the most progressive publications.

JM: But Grigoryants has said he would like his magazine to be sold, like yours, at newspaper stalls or by subscription, but is prevented from doing this ... [4]

VK: That's all well and good, but he has communicated this thought primarily to Western journalists and has steadfastly refused to go to the people within the country.

JM: Because he is denied the possibility of doing so ...

VK: What do you mean 'denied the possibility'. Listen, let him come to me, let him approach other newspapers and magazines. But he should stop behaving as if he were supported by the Western media.

JM: But the Western media support you, too, they support the principle ...

VK: Yes, yes, we too support the principle. I don't believe that any changes that take place in Ireland can be effected from outside the country ...

JM: Of course ...

VK: In order to change life in the Soviet Union we must act from within the country. Grigoryants appeals to those outside the country and does not circulate his magazine.

JM: Because, surely, he is not permitted to ...

VK: Well let him search for an outlet. Let him come to me and say: 'Hello, I'm Grigoryants'. Whatever my response, it will be of benefit to him. If I say no, then, alright, I'm scum, a swine, a dogmatist. If I say yes, then he'll have opened up new channels for himself. But he refuses to get in touch with even, well, the liberal publications.

JM: What do you think of the other independent magazines, like *Merkury* in Leningrad?

VK: I disagree with the entire principle of unofficial publications. Instead of creating a new writers' union, we must fight within the existing one. These unofficial writers ought to try and get published in the existing organs of the press. Soon all these independent publications will no longer exist. And anyway, they can only produce about fifty copies since they use typewriters and carbon paper.

JM: But if they were permitted to have the means ...

4 See above, p.170.

VK: Maybe. But for the present, they won't be given any such means.
Let them bring their articles to me.

JM: But perhaps they feel you would not publish their material ...

VK: Well let them at least ask. That, you see, was Solzhenitsyn's
mistake, he began to look for publishers outside the country ...

4. Boris Shestakov

Transcript and translation of taped interview with Boris Shestakov,
director of Moscow bureau of *TASS* (*MosTASS*), on 17 May 1990 in
Dublin.

John Murray: Could you say a little about what exactly your job is?

Boris Shestakov: I'm the head of the Moscow bureau of *TASS*, which
exists in Moscow in parallel with the central apparatus of *TASS*.
There is the general director of *TASS* in Moscow, and myself,
the head of the Moscow bureau. *TASS* has a bureau in Leningrad, Vladivostok and Khabarovsk, everywhere else *TASS* only
has one correspondent. There are a lot of people working out of
a bureau. We're often confused with the central apparatus,
because it too has its headquarters in Moscow. We cover local
affairs.

JM: And do you provide a service for other newspapers in the country
about events that occur in Moscow?

BSh: Yes, we are concerned with events of local significance, because
what, for instance, Gorbachev does, or what happens in the parliament or in the council of ministers, that is covered by the central
apparatus [of *TASS*]. But we also have what you might call a team,
made up of the heads of various editorial departments, which also
covers events of national significance. I, for example, cover
parliamentary affairs, I work with Gorbachev when, for example,
he makes a speech somewhere or receives someone.

JM: What is the precise official status of *TASS*?

BSh: Its official title reads: the Telegraphic Agency of the Soviet
Union subordinate to the council of ministers of the Soviet Union.
We must reflect the official opinion of this body in official

communiqués or reports, though in unofficial reports we are able to go as far as to criticize it.

JM: And do you in fact criticize it?

BSh: Yes, we do. Now, we criticize it, before we didn't [laughs].

JM: How do you explain your scant coverage of the [1990] 1 May parade on Red Square when Gorbachev and the politburo were jeered off the platform by protesters. This received front-page prominence in the Western media, but only a few lines in the *TASS* report.

BSh: Yes. I was in charge of the brigade [of journalists] that covered the 1 May parade. The thing is, well, you must look at things in accordance with their real significance. There were two parts to the crowd. In one, there were 70,000 people, in the other, 20,000. I think that that part of the crowd, the 70,000, who did not take part in the protest deserved no less coverage than the 20,000 who did protest.

JM: But from a journalist's point of view, surely the 'news', the novelty of the event was that 20,000 people for the first time on Red Square protested against the party leadership?

BSh: You think that. I think, on the contrary, that this was a peripheral event. Listen, if you like I could scour Dublin and find 20,000 Stalinists, and I have reason to believe this could be done, I think I could find that number ...

JM: In Dublin?

BSh: Yes. But if I then leave here and write that Dublin is full of Stalinists, would that be the truth?

JM: No, it wouldn't. So, you believe that those 20,000 demonstrators were not typical.

BSh: Yes, they were not typical. That is my opinion as a journalist. You can agree or disagree with it. But I simply know, there's a word for it, I'm a very blunt person, I call them depraved [*urody*].

JM: That's a very strong term to use.

BSh: Yes, it is.

JM: But would you not say that what happened to some extent is a reflection of the unpopularity of the leadership at the present moment?

BSh: Yes, I agree with you. But these people are using the very real difficulties of the country for their own political games. That's my opinion.

JM: A photograph published recently in *Ogonyok* showed a protester carrying a banner that read 'We are not "elements", we are the people!'. Would you not say that *TASS* is largely responsible for branding people who protest against the regime as 'isolated elements', 'hooligans' or, in your own words, 'depraved'?

BSh: Let me explain. Among the 20,000 protestors on Red Square three portraits were visible in the crowd, those of Nicholas II, Stalin and Yeltsin. That's the answer to your question. How could people who are in one crowd bearing portraits of Nicholas II, Stalin and Yeltsin possibly be called normal? For me they cannot be called normal.

JM: Fine. Now let me turn to …

BSh: But I'm quite prepared to argue with you. Ask me more questions …

JM: No, thank you, I've understood what you're saying.

BSh: I expressed my opinion about the march in three newspapers, it's not that I'm forcing my views on to you, or telling you something in confidence. I've written about this openly in *Vechernyaya Moskva*, in *Literaturnaya gazeta* and, what was it now, ah yes, in *Sovetskaya Rossiya*. This was after the 1 May parade, somewhere around 6 or 7 May. Of course, I understand, *Sovetskaya Rossiya* is not the best place to put forward anti-democratic views, I'm very much afraid of being seen to belong to the conservative wing. I'm not a representative of the conservative wing, I'm categorically against the conservative wing.

JM: But as a *TASS* journalist do you have a choice?

BSh: I can have, am entitled to, my own point of view!

JM: Your personal point of view?

BSh: Even my personal point of view! In none of the three pieces I wrote did I say I was a representative of *TASS*. They were signed simply 'Boris Shestakov'. I do not want to be in the same group as, say, Ligachev. That is not the type of company I want to be associated with. But I also don't want to be associated with the group who demonstrated on Red Square on 1 May because I think that, objectively speaking, they are detrimental to the democratic movement in Russia.

JM: Although from a Western journalist's point of view, excuse my directness, surely your personal moral position should not interfere in your coverage of a story.

BSh: Why not? I covered the 1 May parade for *TASS* and signed the report 'Boris Shestakov, *TASS*', and that was that, my official duty. After that I am writing as a private individual who attended the 1 May parade. For that reason I didn't write *TASS*. In this case, I was there, I saw what happened and I think that these people are, by their actions, preparing a right-wing coup. Right-wing, mind you.

JM: Though there were left-wing groups among the demonstrators ...

BSh: Yes, but ultra-left-wingers are always alongside right-wingers. As I wrote in *Vechernyaya Moskva*, 1 May showed me that the Black Hundreds can be coloured white. Extremists today are the most terrible, the most damaging thing possible to *perestroika*, which I sincerely support.

JM: Has *TASS* managed to restructure itself or is it still a victim of the years of stagnation?

BSh: For the moment yes, it is still a victim. *TASS* has not succeeded in fully restructuring itself.

JM: In what particular areas has it not succeeded?

BSh: Well, if you like, our relationship with the council of ministers keeps a tight hold on us [pointing to throat in gesture of strangulation] ... we cannot ... we are subordinate to the council of ministers.

JM: What does this mean in practice?

BSh: It means that the general director of *TASS* is appointed by the chairperson of the council of ministers and is practically a minister ...

JM: He holds ministerial rank ...

BSh: Yes, ministerial rank, and as a minister, he is obliged to defend the decisions of the government. I personally am not always in favour of these decisions ...

JM: The general director of *TASS* is not always necessarily a trained journalist ...

BSh: In the present instance, he is. Leonid Kravchenko, the director, is a people's deputy of the USSR from the union of journalists, and has spent all his life as a journalist. As indeed was the previous director, the late Sergei Losev, of whom I was very fond, and therefore have taken a fighting stance in relation to the present director. We've just had elections to the party congress [to be held in July 1990] and Kravchenko was one of the candidates to be sent as a delegate to the congress and I proposed that he not be selected and he wasn't selected! So, it may be a small thing, but I'm proud that I said my piece. In my opinion he is a person, to a certain degree, of a conservative cast of mind.

JM: Perhaps it is for this reason that, for example, the present crises in the Baltic republics are reported from an almost exclusively pro-Russian point of view.

BSh: That is not true, believe me. Do you mean the *TASS* coverage?

JM: Yes.

BSh: No, here it would be more accurate to say that events are covered from the point of view of the conservative wing of the party, from, let's say, Ligachev's position.

JM: And this is reflected in your reports?

BSh: Well, I hope not in my personal reports, but, in principle, in *TASS* reports in general, yes.

JM: And what has Ligachev to do with *TASS*? How does he bring his influence to bear?

BSh: He represents the other half of the party.

JM: And the Director of *TASS*, Kravchenko, is selected from the *nomenklatura* lists of the central committee ...

BSh: Yes. Let's say he is closer in his political convictions to Ligachev than to, say, [Alexander] Yakovlev.

JM: And does *TASS* not have any connection with [Vadim] Medvedev?

BSh: Formally, Medvedev is in charge of ideology and newspapers, too. But, thank God, I know Medvedev well. I know Medvedev because I studied in the Academy of Social Sciences when he was rector. I think that as an ideologue, he's, unfortunately, not very impressive. I'm not sure how appropriate it is here to give an assessment of him, it's, well, it's their problem. I think that *TASS* today is to a certain degree in alliance with *Sovetskaya*

Rossiya, which is very, eh ...

JM: Of which the editor is Chikin ...

BSh: Yes, Chikin, and this fact is cause for concern. It's a very conservative newspaper. It was no accident that it published the Nina
Andreeva letter and several similar pieces.

JM: What about *Moskovskaya pravda*?

BSh: *Moskovskaya pravda* is different. It is simply the organ of the
party city committee and, well, you don't bite the hand that feeds
you. The same, incidentally, goes for *TASS* and the council of
ministers. We can't 'bite' the council of ministers. I think that
TASS should not be attached to the council of ministers. *TASS*
should be independent. That's my opinion and you can print it,
I've already expressed it more than once. All the more so since in
a multi-party system it'd be very strange if *TASS* were to reflect
the point of view of one among several parties.

JM: And is there a chance that *TASS* will become an independent news
agency?

BSh: Under the present director, no.

JM: Does the future of *TASS* depend on him?

BSh: Of course. The ship's course depends on the captain, does it not?
He commands the direction which the ship will take. You see what
worries me is not so much the political situation today, rather the
economic one. The struggle on the surface seems to be political,
whereas it is really a struggle between economic systems, the
private sector, the state sector, the cooperative sector. I believe
that there should be no monopoly in any sphere, be it economic or
political. What is necessary is a variety of economic systems. The
cooperative system is necessary as is the private economy. Our
economy can only be saved by the introduction of market
relations.

JM: In the media also?

BSh: Yes, in the media, too.

JM: What is your view on the draft law on the press? What do you
think ought to be the main articles in a law on the press?

BSh: People are now arguing on two articles in the draft. Apart from
these two articles, everything else seems to have been approved.
The first one is the question of whether anyone, say me, can come

along and set up a newspaper. A group of people can set up a newspaper, but one person cannot. I think the proposed restriction is stupid. If I want to set up a paper, I get my wife and my son – you see, there's no real difference – and there you have a group, in other words it would be impossible to prevent a person from setting up a newspaper. Either people can set up a newspaper, or they can't. That's the first point. The second contentious point is the question of whether a journalist is entitled to refuse to write about something if it is contrary to his convictions. This is a very contentious question. Nowhere on the planet, not in France, nor in America or Ireland is a journalist allowed this right. I have asked my colleagues.

JM: According to the Code of Professional Conduct of the NUJ, a journalist has the right to refuse to do work 'incompatible with professional honour'.

BSh: According to the Code, yes, but in practice, never. Methods will be found to get rid of you [if you refuse]. To go back to the first contentious issue in the debate on the press law, I think the proposed restriction is stupid and any individual ought to be allowed to set up a newspaper.

JM: And what are the authorities worried about?

BSh: I'll tell you what they're afraid of, I'll explain. It's no secret that in the Soviet Union there are underground millionaires, they're practically operating in the open now, people who've made money by buying and selling computers, et cetera. They are afraid that these people will begin to buy the press. And, you see, the press is a dangerous weapon, and they're afraid that the entire press will end up in the hands of the black economy. That is what they're afraid of. I say: what's the difference? Let's say one of these millionaires, or even three of them together, as a group, set up a newspaper. It will be impossible to prevent this from happening. A millionaire can set up a newspaper, but he can't make it interesting. In a market system, only a good newspaper will survive. That's why I think there's nothing to be afraid of. As regards the second issue, whether or not a journalist has the right to refuse to do work against his conscience, it's more complex. I know from personal experience. Twice I refused when I was asked, or rather entrusted, to write a critical article about Sakharov. Twice I said 'no', simply 'no', and that was that. And as a result, I had certain problems.

JM: Could you not have said 'this is not my field'?

BSh: Unfortunately in the Moscow bureau it would have been impossible to say 'not in my field', it was impossible to say this. If, say, my speciality had been agriculture, then I could have said 'this is not my field', but Moscow is Moscow, and he was a Muscovite. Things are more complex here ...

JM: So, as things stand, you are restricted to writing about what is permitted by the limitations imposed on you by the authorities.

BSh: It's not a question of journalism, but of *TASS*. Let me explain. When I want to write about something which is contrary to the official *TASS* line, I write outside of *TASS*, as a private journalist, for *Literaturnaya gazeta*, *Vechernyaya Moskva*, where my articles are signed simply 'B. Shestakov', whereas normally I sign my articles 'B. Shestakov, *TASS* correspondent'. As long as the word '*TASS*' is not there, I can say what I like.

JM: *TASS* does not only issue news reports on events, but also writes commentaries to these events ...

BSh: Yes, of course. *TASS* has its line, and it publishes not only communiqués and news stories, but commentaries and even long analytical articles. But, if you'll allow me, I'd like to say that just as I don't obey my general director, so I can have disagreements with my staff. One of my staff disagrees with my point of view and writes about how the cooperative owners are scoundrels, thieves and swine. I refuse to publish her pieces, even though her opinion coincides with the opinion above me, I mean that of the general director of *TASS* who holds the same point of view as she does. But I say that as long as I'm in charge of my bureau, no such pieces will be issued from there. She is left with the option of going over my head to my superiors to get permission to have her work published, we have that system, which means, for example, that if I sign a piece 'B. Sh', I have read it and given my approval to it.

JM: What about the question of censorship in general? Have you had many dealings lately with *Glavlit*?

BSh: I occasionally see them in the corridor, but haven't spoken to them for, it must be, three or four months now. Really, they're just not there any more. But what is more frightening is the presence of the internal censor, which is present, in me it is present, because while I work for *TASS* and am obliged to reflect the point of view of the Council of Ministers, I am obliged to censor my own material, not *Glavlit*, but me. But then, for example, someone could write an ultra-left piece, and here my own political censor would come into play, or, one could write, like my colleague, about how the cooperatives are thieves and swindlers, and I don't agree with this. I think the cooperative owners are victims of our command–administrative economy, conditions are made impossible for them to work in. That is why I struggle [on their behalf] as much as I can, I wouldn't like to exaggerate my services, but what I set out to do, I more or less achieve.

JM: Do you feel that you as a journalist have a duty, that you should be working for the success of *perestroika*?

BSh: My duty is to my two children. Big words are not necessary here. I want my children to grow up in a country that is democratic, normal, rich and good.

JM: And what is your view on Lenin's prescription for the press to be the 'collective propagandist, agitator and organizer'?

BSh: Well, you can't put it better than the English expression 'forget it'! [laughs]. I don't agree with those who now criticize Lenin as assiduously and zealously as they praised him five years ago. I always had my doubts that Lenin could be applied directly to the problems of today. We must not look to Lenin for specific prescriptions, they simply don't work in today's world. We must look to Lenin in order to learn how to acquire the ability to work out specific solutions to specific problems. I am convinced of this. And Lenin for me is great because once, at the beginning of the century, he found some specific recipes for specific situations. Unfortunately, his legacy was placed in very bad hands. You know that now we have an argument about who's responsible: Lenin or Stalin. Did Stalin distort Lenin, or were all the perversions already inherent in the system before Stalin. My own view is that Stalin distorted things. The fundamentals were pure under

Lenin, and capitalism today has a human face because it was socialism under Lenin, do you see? The Swedish model is nothing more than a symbiosis of Marxist capitalism and Leninist socialism, and, as a result, we have a very interesting variety of capitalism, with a socialist face. You see, we have always had a problem with distribution, with just distribution. My difficulties with Yeltsin are, well, Yeltsin talks about the injustices of our distribution system, about special hospitals and shops for the leadership; that's all very well, but our special hospitals and shops for the leadership are worse than any hospital or shop you have here in Dublin. So, what we must do is take radical measures about production, and not about distribution. You can only distribute what you produce. And here, Yeltsin has nothing to say, because here unpopular decisions have to be taken, here we have to introduce the market economy that everybody's afraid of. For 72 years we've been told of the horrors of capitalism, about unemployment, hunger, poverty, and then, all of a sudden, today we seem to be taking this system ourselves, and the people are terrified; the people, it turns out, have been turned into idiots, they believed all these fairy tales. That's the tragedy, and the reason I hate Yeltsin is that he is a swine who is trying yet again to make idiots out of the people. He talks about fair distribution, but never says that the people will have to work very, very hard in order to have something, and that five years will pass before we will reap any fruits. There is no other way, and he never says this. He has been asked directly several times: are you for or against the market economy? He always avoids giving a straight answer, goes around in circles. This is dishonest.

JM: Is is true that *TASS* issued a communiqué about the 1986 Chernobyl accident only after the effects had been felt abroad?

BSh: Yes, that's true. I can talk about, not the, so to speak, radiation effects of Chernobyl, but its propaganda effects on *TASS*. It was our first shock and we didn't know, the leadership didn't know, what to do or how to react to it. Were we to report or not to report? Before we wouldn't have written anything, there was no problem. But now, we thought, things are different.

JM: And did you and your colleagues know about the accident?

BSh: Of course, yes, we knew what had happened.

JM: And what would happen if a similar accident were to happen today?

BSh: There would be no question of not writing about it. Chernobyl was a hard lesson for us.

JM: And, if I may, a few questions on your private life. Can you tell me a little of your personal background?

BSh: Well, I was born in the small city, well, a large city by Irish standards, of Ufa, in 1948, so I'm 42 years old. I went to school there and then went to Moscow University. There I studied for two years at the Faculty of Journalism, then I was sent to study in Hungary. I got a degree from Hungary from the day faculty, and from Moscow, by correspondence. In Hungary I studied Hungarian and English philology. That was twenty years ago, so you'll have to excuse my English which I've almost forgotten, but my Hungarian, well, people take me for a Hungarian when I speak it. I got my degree in Hungary and immediately began working as *TASS* correspondent there. And there I worked until 1980, from 1974 to 1980, that is. Well, there's a small detail here. I began working for *TASS* in 1973 in the last year of my studies because *TASS* had no correspondent there and they, so to speak, asked me. I worked there till 1980, then I returned to Moscow and entered the Faculty of Social Sciences, where, I told you, Medvedev was my rector, and studied there from 1980 to 1983, when I became a Candidate of historical sciences. My dissertation was about the Hungarian press, and I also had a book published. Then, for the next four years, I worked as a *TASS* commentator on foreign military–political questions. All about disarmament, the arms race, NATO, the Warsaw Pact. And, finally, for the last two and a half years I've worked as head of the Moscow *TASS* bureau.

JM: Do you like your present job?

BSh: Yes, I do like it. It's completely different from my other jobs. We have a saying that goes: better to be the best lad in the village, in other words, better to be the number one in the Moscow *TASS* bureau than seventeen in the central apparatus of *TASS*. I really enjoy my job. The city is amazingly complex. Imagine, in Ireland you have a population of three and a half million, in Moscow we have eight and a half million, plus four million visitors every day. There are literally millions of problems, the city is ungovernable. We cover all sorts of things that happen in the city, for example, just before I left for Ireland, I got seven reporters to go out and check whether the *kvas* and gas mineral water that are sold on the streets were drinkable; in other words, we're seeing how ready Moscow is for the summer months, or, for example, we write a lot about the problems of the Moscow city council. ... By the way, tomorrow we are going to meet the deputy Lord Mayor of Dublin ...

JM: Did you know that our Lord Mayor is the son of our Prime Minister?

BSh: Oh, so you have dynasties here, too. We also had dynasties under Brezhnev, all his relations were fixed up in good jobs. Yes, that phenomenon is a familiar one.

JM: Do you travel abroad a lot?

BSh: Yes, I have a lot of friends. Well, how can I put it? When I worked in Hungary, I covered the socialist countries, though that concept no longer exists ...

JM: Does the fact that the concept of 'socialist countries' no longer exists cause any problems for *TASS*?

BSh: I have a colleague who is in charge of the *TASS* section that deals with the socialist countries ...

JM: And what does he do now?

BSh: Well, the countries still exist, only the name of the section is inappropriate. Anyway, I often see him, he's a friend, and ask him, or suggest that, instead of calling himself head of the *GRSS* [*glavnaya redaktsiya sotsialisticheskikh stran*, 'main editorial section for socialist countries'], he should call himself head of the *GRBSS* [*glavnaya redaktsiya byvshikh sotsialisticheskikh stran*, 'main editorial section for former socialist countries']. This is in jest, of course. But to get back to your question, I do travel a lot, though mainly to the socialist countries, though I have been to some capitalist countries. This is my first visit to an English-speaking country.

JM: And do you like Ireland?

BSh: I am in ecstasy over the country. I intend to write a lot about the country when I get back. I'll write a series of articles on Ireland for the *TASS* magazine, *Ekho Planety*, which specializes in foreign affairs, though in the present environment you can't really separate foreign and home news. Everything I write about Ireland will have a direct relationship to what is happening in the Soviet Union at the moment.

5. Igor' Zakharov

Transcript and translation of taped interview with Igor' Zakharov, deputy editor of *Nezavisimaya gazeta*, on 20 October 1990 in Moscow.

John Murray: What sort of paper will *Nezavisimaya gazeta* be?

Igor' Zakharov: It's a newspaper that will come out at the end of 1990, there'll be a few dummy runs at the end of December, at Christmas, so that from 2, or at the most, 3 January, it will be able to come out regularly. It'll be broadsheet, political and independent; a daily, a large newspaper, and first and foremost a news-carrying newspaper, only after that a newspaper carrying comment, although the divisions are sometimes hard to distinguish. There is no such paper at the moment in the whole country, because the best paper is, of course, *Izvestiya*, but *Izvestiya* is the organ of the Supreme Soviet, it has a lot of intrinsic limitations as a newspaper, it can't be critical of its publisher, the Supreme Soviet, it can't be sharply critical of the central authorities, because it is their mouthpiece, and *Izvestiya* has a long history and rigid stereotypes about what can and what can't be done. It is sometimes too deferential, too reserved, it sometimes doesn't go the whole way in telling a story, because for *Izvestiya* there are names and institutions that are taboo. It can't criticize the president because he's the president, and not because what he's doing is good or bad. That's to begin with. The second best newspaper is probably *Komsomol'skaya pravda*, or if we're talking about city newspapers, then *Moskovskii komsomolets*, but that is, in the first place, a youth paper, and second, it is after all

a newspaper of a sensational character. They write about something if it is a real sensation. And I, as a reader, and not only me,
want to know above all what happened yesterday in this country.
A fairly full picture of what happened yesterday. But to find out
that now I have to read *Izvestiya*, *Komsomol'skaya pravda*,
Moskovskii komsomolets, *Sovetskaya Rossiya*, plus three more
newspapers, and watch the television, and listen to radio *Svoboda*
[Freedom], the *BBC*, and discuss the news with acquaintances,
and only then will I have a picture of what happened. But all that
should be in one newspaper. So that, in the first place, it should
be a large newspaper, and, second, it should be a news-
carrying paper and thirdly, it should be political. It will naturally
also cover culture, science and sport, which doesn't interest me in
the slightest, but you can't have a daily without sport, so there
should be sport. That's the main reason why it's being created.
And the Moscow city council [*Mossovet*] is the founder of the
newspaper.

JM: And what does that mean?

IZ: I'll try to explain. When it became clear this summer that the
Moscow city council did not have its own newspaper, because
Moskovskaya pravda remained a party paper, and *Vechernyaya
Moskva* didn't want to become the organ of the council, and
wished to stay completely independent and in receipt of money
from the Moscow party organization, it then emerged that there
was no newspaper in Moscow which was not a party newspaper.
And then the Moscow city council founded two newspapers, one,
Kuranty, is a genuine city newspaper, it deals with questions such
as what was discussed at the council meetings, why a street hasn't
been repaired, why salami wasn't delivered to shop N° 16 and
what's on, where, and in what cinemas. It's a proper city newspaper, it's a good newspaper and it's the organ of the council, their
official organ. The second newspaper, founded on the same day,
Nezavisimaya gazeta, what we're talking about now, is independent not only because of its title, but because it is not an organ
for some organization. The Moscow city council founded the
newspaper, which means it gave money, that is, it loaned money.
We have to return this money by the end of next year; it helped us

find premises to rent, we're paying for them; it helped us, it's helping us now, with telephones, tables, typewriters, but that's also done on a commercial basis. But we are not an organ and have no political or financial leadership from Moscow city council. So they gave us money, on the basis of the reputation of Tretyakov, the editor of the newspaper, on the basis of the concept of the newspaper, but after that, boys, you do as you please, that's your worry; you're not our organ, we do not answer for you either financially or politically. That's the main difference.

JM: In your view, is the new Law on the Press a good law?

IZ: It's a good law in as much as laws can be good in a state where as a rule the laws are wonderful, but far from all of them work, and if you take the constitution, even the Stalin constitution, it's a wonderful document, there are wonderful things written in it. The only thing is they're not very real in practical life. As regards the law on the press, then, if I were to give it a mark, I would award it a four and a half [B+], even a five minus [A–]. It has all the essentials for what is essential for the existence of normal periodical publications not bound or subservient to any party or state structures. It's a good law.

JM: What about the new censorship agency, *GUOT*,[5] which has taken the place of *Glavlit*.

IZ: Oh yes, I know what you mean, I just hadn't got around to remembering that abbreviation...

JM: It's the new censorship agency.

IZ: Yes, it's censorship, it doesn't matter what name you give it.

JM: Well, my understanding is that they now operate as consultants to newspapers, whereby editors can ask them to examine material to see whether it contains prohibited matter. But only they have the official list of themes that are forbidden.

IZ: No, that's not the way it works, it's not only they who know. Even in the years of stagnation ... for twenty years I worked as a journalist for different organizations, mainly for the APN [*Novosti* News Agency], regularly, two or three times a year, the

---

5   *Glavnoe upravlenie po okhrane gosudarstvennykh tain* (Main directorate for the preservation of state secrets).

censor, the official censor, would come and arrange a meeting with the administrators, the middle management, the duty editor, department heads, the editor, the editorial board; in a newspaper the same thing would happen. So, the censor would say: 'Comrades, there has been a slight change. Now, we bring to your attention that the following things are now under our control', for example, all statistical data on gold, oil and diamonds, or the distribution of military units larger than a regiment, or, on the contrary, the specific location of military units smaller than a division. So that there was a list that was quite clear, and after working in a paper or a magazine for about a year, nearly every employee had enough experience to know, or their immediate boss would know, from listening regularly to those meetings, what was on the censor's list, because in principle all they're interested in is state secrets. So that the fact that the president has three lovers, what their names are and how much money he spends on them, that is not a state secret, and if, before, that sort of material found its way on to the censor's desk, then the censor did not have the right to cross it out. The censor was obliged to carry out what, according to the terminology, is called an ideological intervention. So that if in the article it said that in Yakutiya 360 kilogrammes of diamonds were mined, he crossed it out straight away. But, regarding the lovers, he would pick up the telephone and make a call to the director, to the editor or the deputy editor, and would say: Ivan Fyodorovich, strange things are being written in your newspaper. Sort things out, would you? As a rule, that sort of interference meant that it was necessary to take out the passage, and also necessary to punish somebody for it. But, formally, the editor could say: Leave me alone, that is my concern, and then, taking the responsibility himself, do what he wanted. The list of what the editor could sanction, the number of articles on different themes, that didn't fall into the censor's list. They simply came and said 'We are not going to read articles on foreign policy, on ideology'. They were shrinking all the time. One year ago they hardly read anything. If I as an editor thought, now look, here's an article with a lot of discussion on diamonds, or the movements of military units, I'd better show it to the censor. That's consultation as well.

JM: Do you think the decree against denigrating the president's name is a form of censorship?

IZ: No, no, no, no, I think this is because for various reasons in this country there is not enough civilized behaviour, you can't expect identical good and noble behaviour from everyone, and, because they were afraid of insults to the president, a special decree was issued concerning the preservation of the president's honour. Even though there already exists in the legal code a law protecting the honour of any citizen, because people will say fewer nasty things about me than about the president, that's the only reason why.

JM: And why can't nasty things be said about the president?

IZ: Because this is a country with a paternal, patriarchal ideology. The president is the father, he's the boss, you can't speak badly about the father. It's unavoidable, it's a psychological question, not a political one.

JM: So you agree with the decree protecting the honour of the president?

IZ: No, I'm trying to explain why the decree came into being. Because, listen, if you take the case five years ago, you were not only not allowed to say anything bad, but everything you said about the head of state had to be phrased in the superlative degree. And then suddenly a drastic change in the state, suddenly you can say he's a fool, that he's this and that. That's psychologically unacceptable. No, he says, I can't put up with that, no, not that. And his camarilla, his aides, they try to make him secure against insults. But, as you saw with the Novodvorskaya episode, she said everything she wanted to, and she's at liberty. It's just another decree that doesn't work.

JM: What about the decree against the vandalizing of monuments connected with the revolution?

IZ: That's an attempt to slow down the changes, so that they don't happen so quickly. So that psychologically one can prepare oneself for them. Because today we're worshipping Lenin, and tomorrow we're covering him with dirt. And this is all happening so quickly, that for a lot of people it's not acceptable. So that I think it's a psychological question. Slow down a bit, he's saying, good, everything's fine, just a little slower, not so quickly.

JM: You said you worked for APN before.

IZ: Yes, APN. For all these years I worked producing propaganda for foreign consumption. For 13 years I was the editor-in-chief of newspapers and magazines that the Soviet Union produced for foreign consumption. *Soviet Weekly, Études soviétiques, Fakten von der Sowjet Union,* from England to Portugal, so that my propaganda – well, I consoled myself with the thought that maybe I wasn't telling the entire truth, or always telling the truth, about the country, but that it was for foreigners, and that foreigners had a choice of information. They had other sources of information apart from *Soviet Weekly,* and if they still, in spite of the choice, had only read *Soviet Weekly,* then that was their own personal affair, they were idiots themselves. If I had been taking people in in that way inside the country, I'd be a lot more ashamed of myself, because there was no freedom of choice here. And, incidentally, the paper we're going to bring out is also there to increase the possibility of choice, so that there's not only *Pravda* or only *Izvestiya,* that is its ultimate use.

JM: So, you're now employing staff for the paper. A lot of reporters from other newspapers are waiting to see how the paper will turn out before committing themselves to you.[6]

IZ: Yes, they are waiting to see, because there's still two months before the newspaper comes out, and there's nothing for reporters to do. So we have signed agreements with a lot of staff, and they'll join the paper in November, or even from 1 December. For the moment we have more administrative staff working. But, in *Izvestiya* they have a staff of 300, in the English *Independent,* they have a staff of 250, here, at least up to the new year, we'll have a staff of 70, maybe 100, maybe even 150, including typists, test readers (copy testers), couriers, drivers. We'll have 70 doing creative work, I mean editors, reporters, commenta-

---

6   For example, one reporter from *Moskovsky komsomolets,* another from *Kommersant* were at the time of the interview considering offers made to them by the paper.

tors. After, there'll probably be more added, when the paper gets bigger.

JM: How many pages will be in it?

IZ: We'll start with eight, broadsheet, pages. but towards the end of the year, or even before that, it should have 16 pages. And even if you say that for an Irish or English publication 16 pages is very little, I insisted when I was registering the paper that the number of pages given over to advertisements would not be included in the 16 pages. If there are more pages, then so be it, because when *Izvestiya* or *Moskovskii komsomolets* ... they only have four pages, and sometimes they have half a page, or even a whole page, given over to an advertisement, and the sort of advertisement they have is of no use to me, I don't get any money for it, I want to have information in that space, because there you have advertisements of a very narrow type, it's not the sort of advertisement that says there'll be sales in the largest department stores, that sort of advertisement interests everyone. But when it's about the sale of some machine tool in some factory to be paid for without a cash transfer, that's not advertising for the broad public. For that reason it shouldn't take up space in the newspaper in place of news from a reporter.

JM: But surely if the advertisers can afford to put the advertisement in the paper, then the paper doesn't mind what is being advertised.

IZ: Yes, I know that once a week *Moskovskii komsomolets* could publish not four, but six pages, and print all the advertisements on the extra pages. But, ask me why they don't do that.

JM: Is there a problem with the price of paper? The price, I understand, is set to rise threefold.

IZ: Because the subscription price has increased on papers sold after January [1991], all the circulation figures will fall two- or threefold. It's a psychological barrier, if I myself spent 300 roubles on subscriptions, I'm not going to spend 1,000 roubles on subscriptions. And for a lot of other people, all the more so. So that if now, at the moment, there's a 30 per cent shortage of paper, this means that a lot of journals are published only with huge delays. *Novy mir*'s fifth issue [May] hasn't appeared yet, for example, but the absolute record for delayed appearance is held by the journal *Literaturnaya Armeniya*. They have a lot of problems, with paper, the earthquake, Azerbaijan, Karabakh, lots of difficulties, but they hold the record. I still haven't received last year's eleventh [November 1989] issue. Other journals are issuing their third and fourth numbers now, there is a shortage of paper. But if circulation figures fall two- or threefold, then one result will be that there will be an excess of paper. It's a psychological thing. The price, naturally, won't remain as low as it is now. It's the deficit psychology. But there will be paper itself. The price will be a little higher, that's another thing, but the goods will be there.

JM: So, you don't foresee any technical problems with the launch?

IZ: At the moment I don't see any. And aside from that, I occasionally remember that we were founded by Moscow city council, so that when I go to *Gosplan* of the USSR [the state planning agency], I won't be saying that we are merely an independent newspaper, I'll be saying we're an independent newspaper founded by the Moscow city council, I need paper. And then I receive a certain amount of paper at state prices, which will allow us to have a reasonable circulation when we start up. After that, I'll go and buy paper, and the money we've got from the Moscow city council won't be enough, so we'll have to pay for the paper with our own money, but it's all the same.

JM: And what will your circulation be?

IZ: The minimal print run, at the beginning, will be 200,000, and that'll be 200,000 that will go on sale. At the start in Moscow and Moscow region [*oblast'*], after that, in Leningrad and the North-West, including the Baltic republics, next, in the Donbass, that's in the Eastern Ukraine, the miners, the fourth place is probably Western Siberia. It'll work in a political way, wherever you have more democracy, there you'll have a greater number of *Nezavisimaya gazeta* papers being sold.

JM: Do you have a link with the English *Independent*?

IZ: Yes, we did meet them, of course, we have the same name as they do, and I think that sooner or later, quite soon, we'll conclude some sort of agreement with several other leading newspapers on exchange of information, or perhaps other forms [of cooperation], organizationally, perhaps. And we could be useful to them, even now, because three-quarters of the country is closed to foreign journalists, and, well, for example, Masha Slonim from the BBC Russian service, could ask: Have you got somebody in Sakhalin? I'm interested in Sakhalin, but we can't go there. Because it's too far to go, simply. We do have somebody in Sakhalin. So that from that point of view it could be mutually beneficial.

JM: And did you know that three weeks ago a *Novosti* bureau opened in Dublin?

IZ: I even know who's in charge of it ...

JM: Boris Korolyov.

IZ: Korolyov.

JM: Did you work with him before?

IZ: Yes, I know him quite well. Last year Korolyov and I flew to London with Gorbachev.

JM: They would be offering the same news services as you, they say: We have our own correspondents not only in the Soviet Union, but all over the world, for example, our paper [the *Sunday Tribune*] bought an article from one of their correspondents in Baghdad. Won't they be in competition with you? What sort of news agency is *Novosti*?

IZ: Oh, *Novosti* is a very traditional type of news agency, before it was subservient to the central committee of the CPSU, now it's subservient to the president, which means it's a state structure. On the one hand they are our competitors, because they also have their correspondents in Sakhalin. But everything depends on what the correspondent can permit himself to write, first of all what he's capable of as a creative writer, but second, it depends on who he works for. Is *Nezavisimaya gazeta* a competitor with *Izvestiya*? Yes, it is. But, on the other hand, some people want to read *Izvestiya*, others want to read *Pravda*, and some *Nezavisimaya gazeta*. That's a normal situation.

JM: So, your paper won't have transcripts of lengthy official reports.

IZ: No. I have a ready answer. The question has already arisen on a couple of occasions, I'll say 'We sell advertising space', and if the president buys space, and wants to publish the entire text of his speech, we will of course publish it, but he will have to pay for it ... maybe in hard currency ... everyone now asks for hard currency. But we will speak about the president's speech as a news story, and we'll mention whatever our journalists consider worth mentioning.

JM: Reading *Moskovskii komsomolets* yesterday, there was an article headlined 'Who is Manipulating the Democrats?'. In it there were a lot of things left unsaid, as if understood ...

IZ: That is something I hate ...

JM: ... they all but said that Lev Ponomaryov[7] was a KGB agent, then said there was no basis for this, and after that nothing more was said.

IZ: Yes, that is terrible. That's like if you're walking down the street, someone stops you and says 'John Murray. Ah! You're an idiot.' You ask 'Why do you say that?' The person says, 'You're an idiot, and that's it.' To do that is stupid, it's unprofessional. You should ask Ponomaryov, ask the KGB, they should have asked his colleagues, his acquaintances, in short, you should be a reporter, and clarify the situation. You may come to a conclusion, you may not, but you can say in this person's opinion, in that person's opinion, otherwise it's not professional, it's stupid. And we won't be having any of that in our paper. I'm not interested in commentary. If you cut out all the commentaries from *Moskovskii komsomolets*, in other words what in Russian they call philosophizing (*razmyshlizm*), or from *Moskovskie novosti*, an excellent newspaper ... but the journalists there themselves say it has very little news, it has a large amount of philosophizing. You cut out everything from the paper that is philosophizing, and what do you have left? You're left with a quarter of one page. That is not a newspaper, it is not a newspaper.

---

7 A deputy in the Russian parliament and fairly prominent figure in the democratic movement at that time.

6. Alexander Pumpyanskii

Transcript and translation of taped interview with Alexander Pumpyanskii, editor of *Novoe vremya* (*New Times*), on 20 October 1990 in
Moscow.

John Murray: What was the beginning of *glasnost'* in your view?

Alexander Pumpyanskii: If we're talking about the press, then in the
   early stage of *glasnost'* genuinely new voices emerged, such as
   Moskovskie novosti, et cetera, but this was all still a very limited
   sort of freedom, because in some way these were testing voices.
   And, moreover, there were different reactions to the early manifestations of *glasnost'*. The party apparatus, for instance, was
   also, along with journalists themselves, surprised by the new
   press, and, to a certain extent, surprised at its own liberalism,
   'Look how much we can tolerate!' And the reaction of the party
   apparatus, of which the most prominent figure was Ligachev, was
   of a particular nature. From time to time they shouted and
   banged their fists, demanded that people answer for publishing
   certain things. And it must be said that they didn't receive a
   proper rebuff, because Gorbachev or Yakovlev, well, maybe
   Yakovlev was in a position to give a hint that he held a different
   position, but none the less, the actual support they received was
   varied. For example, party conservatives got upset by different
   manifestations of *glasnost'* in the press and in literature, but
   nothing happened as a result. The heads of editors did not fly, they
   weren't chopped off. So, it turned out that Yakovlev and Gorbachev had been supporting the press in a quiet way, not allowing
   the conservatives to translate their anger into practical action.
   However, on the verbal level, it still looked like the situation was
   being controlled by the conservatives, in any event they could
   stamp their feet and bang their fists as much as they wanted. And
   it seemed that it was they who were controlling the situation,
   whereas in fact that was no longer the case. But this only became
   clear later, in time, when these voices grew stronger. In what
   might be called the second phase of *glasnost'*, I think the
   newspapers that had become very avant-garde, such as *Moskovskie
   novosti* or *Ogonyok*, when all of a sudden, they had got stronger,

and it emerged that they already existed, and it wasn't like during the first phase when every issue was a surprise, in the second phase, this became the norm. Everybody came to understand that these magazines and papers would be the same, and that each issue would not be the last one. During the first phase, it seemed that each issue might be the last one and that tomorrow's issue would be changed, or that the editor would be replaced, or the character of the paper would be changed. In the second phase, nothing of the sort. I think that now [October 1990] the third phase has begun. First of all some of the big publications have joined the avant-garde newspapers. *Izvestiya* has become very radicalized over the last year, *Argumenty i fakty* ... in fact the battle around *Argumenty i fakty* is an important indicator, there was a direct attempt to remove its editor, Starkov,[8] though nothing came of it. This was also an indicator. After that, perhaps that is one of the watermarks, of course it is ... after this, newspapers began to be conscious of their strength, the left, free newspapers began to be conscious of their strength. And, I repeat, they were joined by the bigger newspapers, like *Izvestiya*, *Komsomol'ka* [*Komsomol'skaya pravda*] is an excellent newspaper, free to write what it wants, and with a large circulation, *Argumenty i fakty* has an enormous circulation, and is also free to write what it likes, et cetera, plus the law on the press came out, censorship was made illegal. Parallel to this it emerged that the party apparatus was disintegrating, Ligachev was no longer there, it was no longer at all clear what the ideological department of the party was doing, whatever they might have been doing, it bore no relationship to everyday life of newspapers and magazines, maybe it bore some relationship to party newspapers, but they are the very worst section of the press and the one losing all popularity. So that, and you may not have noticed this, during this third phase, we have normal freedom of the press, or something approaching it, or, at the very least, we have put one foot into that situation. Nobody, or in any event the majority, is keeping an eye out for the leadership, nobody is afraid any more of reproaches, and if there are worries, they are completely new ones. Now our worries are about existing in the

8 See Murray, 1991a, p.15, for an account of the Starkov affair.

marketplace, about the price and availability of paper, money, finance, competition and becoming commercially viable, because, naturally, one has to make money, and think of producing a quality product. Our worries are on a completely new level.

JM: How has foreign coverage changed?

AP: Foreign coverage has also changed considerably. First of all it has changed in the context of the new, general freedom in the press. Secondly, there has been a differentiation in society itself on the political spectrum. Because it has emerged all of a sudden that there is no longer a monolith, which was there before, apparently. Different circles and professions have completely different interests, we can even judge by the battles in parliament. There is the military faction, which follows its own line, it is in opposition in a certain sense of the word; then you have the foreign ministry position, which is very progressive, in the sense that it is personified by Shevardnadze and his close associates, and the press also reacts to this, in the press we also see this. And in fact in journalism, if we're talking about foreign coverage, then in a certain sense it was the most conservative type of coverage in the media. Here least of all did you find different points of view and so on, and here also there have emerged, we, at least, try ... if before it was out of the question to think of writing anything against, I don't know, say Cuba, or North Korea, or, on the contrary, write something positive about South Korea, or about South Africa, now we publish all those sorts of articles, or about the four islands, the situation concerning the [Kurile] islands.

JM: What about coverage now of Northern Ireland?

AP: I wouldn't like to say, I'm not sure, and it's a good question. What has, I think, happened, is that Soviet society has turned in on itself, it has moved away from external politics, society is interested in itself, and is interested in what happens abroad only to the extent that it has a bearing on what happens at home. The relations between us and the countries of the Warsaw Pact or Eastern Europe, yes, that is of interest, but only to the extent that it concerns us. We have, for instance, soldiers returning from there. Or we're interested in the Third World, in whether they'll pay us back what we loaned to them or not, or whether we're going to support any particular country in the Third World or not, and with what, with money or arms, in this sense we're interested. In that sense, Northern Ireland is a little distant from our worries. Previously the attention of the Soviet press on Northern Ireland was a little, so to speak, hypertrophied, because it was, or appeared to be, a typical model ... there you had a small political arena where you were able, or appeared to be able, to make wonderful criticisms of imperialism, British imperialism in the given situation, or colonialism, or whatever you wanted. In so far as now the spectrum has widened, we can now approach England and the West in general in a more objective manner, then that earlier function seems to have diminished a little. But, something else has appeared. Again in so far as it has a bearing on what happens here. Ulster has become something of a symbol, so that Karabakh is compared with Ulster, let's say, we find our own Ulsters here, in our own country, and in this way, as a reflection, or a comparison, it is of interest.

JM: How do you account for the lack of coverage in the Soviet press compared to the Western press on Gorbachev being awarded the Nobel prize?

AP: The same reasons. In my view the lack of coverage is a very unjust and incorrect position to take, but it has its explanation. We made it our lead story. The most progressive part of society genuinely welcomes this award, because it is a major event, the part the Soviet Union is playing in the process of world civilization. But our society is now so annoyed and angry, and so enmeshed has it become in its own illness and problems, that it doesn't even notice this award. A lot of people inside the country do not give enough credit to our successes in foreign policy, because the empty shelves and the internal problems in the country distract them from everything that happens abroad, and it may be a sort of law of human psychology, which sometimes is aggravating, 'Ah, him! He shouldn't be doing this, he should be sorting things out inside the country!'. That, alas, is the type of psychology that exists.

JM: Is there any significance attached to the painting of Lenin hanging over your desk?

AP: No, none whatsoever. That's a painting by a good artist, Rudol'f Khachatrian, some years ago he painted it, on the occasion of some Lenin jubilee. He painted the picture of Lenin, we published it in the magazine, and he gave us the painting as a gift, so that, because he's our friend, the painting hangs here not because it's Lenin, but because it's Khachatrian. Although, our magazine is in no way, we've taken Lenin out of the ideological ... in the sense that we don't have a dependency on communist ideology, that's what I mean. We are not a magazine that supports communist ideology. We are not a propagandist of one particular ideology, or one party. That's our principle, and that's what we try to do. We provide political analyisis. In the next issue of the magazine you'll see, it comes out today, the most varied ... look, in this issue we published something by Zhelyu Zhelev [Bulgarian president], whose thoughts are that communism and fascism are two phases of a totalitarian system, and, what's more, he says that communism is a more perfect, and therefore more dangerous, form of fascism. We don't feel solidarity with his viewpoint, but we give these views, we cover the most diverse views. And, naturally, the crisis in communism, in socialism, in the ideology of communism, the crisis of the Communist Party, and of party power, et cetera, in this country, in Eastern Europe, in the world, all these things are objects of investigation for us, we write about all this and try to follow it as deeply as we can. At the same time, our strength is our ability to write serious analysis, serious journalism. We don't lower ourselves to vulgarity, to bad taste and so forth, which appears now and then.

JM: Some of the Western left intelligentsia consider that the Soviet Union has in its foreign policy become a little too uncritical towards, for instance, the USA. In other words, the USA is in fact an imperialist power, but while before you criticized this, now you go out of your way to avoid criticism.

AP: That undoubtedly deserves a sober analysis. I don't exclude the possibility that this exists as a tendency among professional foreign affairs journalists, because when the path is changed, then people go along this path and do not look to either side of it. There is an element of this, you have the saying, if you force an idiot to pray, he'll smash his head open, but at the same time, what was called at the time criticism of American imperialism was to a great extent nothing of the sort. It was the confrontational existence of two systems, when *a priori* everything that was from the other side was rejected. This was done on both sides, there was full reciprocity here. Naturally, there were things about the USA that could be criticized, in the area of hegemony and expansion, and so on ...

JM: And what about now?

AP: And now without a doubt there are things to be criticized. And they should be analysed and we try to do that in our magazine. Here there is no change. But for real sins, and not just because he's your opponent. Now, the case where they are our opponents, is changing. Politics are becoming more constructive, on a mutual basis, so that apart from everything else there is less and less basis for criticism. But that doesn't mean that everything has changed completely and that you can't now criticize for transgressions.

7. Viktor Filatov

Transcript and translation of taped interview with Major General Viktor Filatov, editor of *Voenno-istoricheskii zhurnal* (*Journal of Military History*), on 25 October 1990 in Moscow.

John Murray: Tell me a little about your magazine.

Viktor Filatov: When I took over two years ago, only two members of the general staff subscribed to the magazine, now we have around 700 subscribers on the general staff. Our readers in the army are conservative, in the good sense of the word. We have no real war historians, all we have is demagogy and opportunists. All our civil press are liars, without talent, our journalism is the worst in the world. They know nothing. They don't understand economics, culture, cinema, theatre, sport. They are dreadful, untalented. Over seventy years all they've learned is to reproduce party slogans and write articles about them. They never think for themselves. And now these jumped-up lackeys have managed to rub their master's face in the muck, they've turned on their masters. That's what our press has become. I detest it, I'm ashamed of it. I'll split up that union of journalists they've got, it's against the people, against the state, anti-army, anti-patriotic. Denigration: all the army is bad, we didn't win the war as we should have, it was won at too great a price. These lackeys are leading people towards civil war, and they'll be the first ones to be hanged, but they can't see this.

JM: What do you think of the recent reassessment in the press of the Soviet army's role in Hungary in 1956 and Prague in 1968?

VF: I have evidence that 1956 was a counter-revolution in Hungary. I have facts and figures to prove that behind the 1956 so-called revolution there were gendarmes, former landlords, spongers, and everybody here keeps quiet about it, although they all know the facts. You see, one of the members of our editorial board, General Lashchenko, was commander of the special unit, the one that went into, what is it called, Budapest, and put the place, so to speak, in order. He was in charge of all those affairs in Budapest. He wrote an article which I published right away, but he's scared. I now have another article which conclusively proves that Gorbachev betrayed all the Socialist countries, that he is guilty of a counter-revolution, that he started the whole thing. I'm not sure whether to publish it.

JM: What do you think of the army's role in Afghanistan?

VF: I was in Afghanistan, three times [as a reporter with the army newspaper, *Krasnaya zvezda*]. I think we were right to have gone in there. It was a huge error to have left. We should send the troops back in there as a matter of urgency. When we left Afghanistan, we immediately got Armenia and Azerbaijan. The conflict began right away. If we hadn't taken the 40th Army, they were an advance post in the Muslim world, we could have captured all the roads, at our back there would have been Iraq. Now the Americans are saying to us, send in your troops to Iraq. I've just returned from America and I told them, fools, why did you pressure us to withdraw. If we were still there, there wouldn't be a problem. The 40th Army was facing Iraq. So, what did I tell them,

I was talking to the Pentagon, the CIA. I told them that, like poor chess players, they play one move in advance, whereas a grand-master thinks ten moves ahead. They should ask us to move back into Afghanistan right away, and then we'd soon put a stop to all the rebellions and uprisings. The Muslims in Central Asia would see that we were standing there as a barrier to Muslim, Arab extremism. With the sort of leaders in the country we have at the moment, there can only be war, nothing else, because their policies are idiotic. And I mean war here, in the Soviet Union in the first place. What can they do about the Persian Gulf now? First of all they spat on the army, insulted it, harried it into a corner, and now they tell us we should be sending in troops to the Persian Gulf. I can assure you, there is not one commander who wants to bring in the army to the Persian Gulf. The swine from the so-called liberal press first of all insulted the army, destroyed morale, and now they want us to go into the Persian Gulf. Ha, ha! No way. Now they can suffer the consequences of their own actions.

... The army listened for a long time, at the beginning it thought that these critics [the liberals] were so intelligent, their suggestions were intelligent. And the army listened to the talkers, but finally, at a certain point, the army understood: they had nothing to offer us, the whole place was falling apart – the economy, the state, the Union. And in my view in the army today there is a very important process taking place. The army is beginning to consolidate. It has finally understood that it can only rely on itself. While all the insults and abuse have been going on, the army has acquired another trait: how to defend itself. You know yourself, when you're continually insulted, then, if you have character, you'll come out stronger at the other end. The more enemies you have, the stronger will be your character in the end. So things are getting better, stronger, the army's getting stronger because it's regrouping itself. That's what's happening in the army today. And in the very near future, you'll see a new army, consolidated and regrouped. And magazines like *Ogonyok*, they haven't realized this yet, and they continue to throw muck at us. I don't understand them myself, I say to them, go on the way you're going, because the more they heap abuse on us, the more the army will draw together and consolidate. I don't want to say that the army's mood is turning nasty, no, but it is consolidating itself. When the country was poor, the army lived poorly, but now you have these co-operative owners, and when these, these scum, get five to ten times more money than an officer, a commander of a regiment, the army will no longer want to defend that sort of Fatherland. It won't defend people like that. It won't defend that sort of Motherland. If they don't solve the social problems within the army after January, then I don't know what will happen, what will happen with the army.

... The army today is not going to mount a coup, but is ... is threatening a coup. The people who want a coup are those who are against the army. Look who is warning people about a coup: Yeltsin, Popov, Sobchak, Stankevich, the whole band of them, the whole pack of mafiosi. But the army won't let them get away with it, it's they who want to carry out a coup, so there won't be an army *coup d'état*.

JM: Do you agree with the assessment of the Brezhnev period of office as the 'era of stagnation'?

VF: I don't include myself, because I work now the same as I worked under Brezhnev. The left radicals are dancing on his grave, that's why nobody's listening to them. You should understand. You're young. You're probably not quite informed about things. Where did Brezhnev come from? We had this awful president, Khrushchev, he was a disaster for our state. Stalin, on the other hand, well at least there was order in the country. People knew where they stood: for doing this you'd be put away, for doing that, you'd be a Hero of the Soviet Union, for that you'd be a Hero of Socialist Labour. People knew: for this you'd get money, for that, you'd get a stretch. When Khrushchev came, that, that congenital fool, idiot – I know, I've studied him – he started to tear the place to pieces. What he said at the 20th Party Congress (the secret speech) was all a lie. We've already found documents to prove that he lied then, he was a liar, his memoirs are all lies. It was bad enough being an idiot, but he began to change everything. He reduced the army by one million ten thousand, he got his hands into everything: into art, oil, agriculture and the theatre – everything. People didn't know whether their job would be there in the morning, or whether he had decided to close them down. People were in a state of shock, because Lenin said: one, two or three reforms and a whole country can collapse. So, under him, everything collapsed at an incredible rate. And people didn't know what to do, because people can't live like that, they need some sort of stability, at the very least relative stability. And that's why he was got rid of: because people wanted stability, and were saying, where is the leader who can stabilize the country, who will let people live in peace, without messing about with any reforms? That's when Brezhnev appeared, who, once he arrived said: that's it; no more reforms. And everybody relaxed and said, thank you Leonid Ilyich, now we can live in peace at least. That idiot Khrushchev got to the people, he managed to get under the skin of the nation. So, people started to work, and for the first five years, things worked fine, but he failed to modernize the socialist economy with technology, that's the reason for the collapse of the economy. Brezhnev came to power, as a counter-weight to Khrushchev, it was only afterwards that things began to collapse. Now I'll tell you how the other gent, Gorbachev, appeared. Everyone had had enough of this stagnation. Then Gorbachev came and said, I want to change everything.

JM: Is he a Khrushchev figure?

VF: Exactly the same as Khrushchev, no difference. But wait for the person who will come and say 'That's it. I promise you no changes. We are going to live as we have lived.' And this person will become the leader of the country. Expect a new Brezhnev, not a new Lenin, or Trotsky who will suggest a revolution. No, the people are now waiting for someone to come and say: that's it. No more. Calm down, let's begin to live peacefully. And this person will become the leader, not the utter fools who are calling for revolutions – no. Expect a new Brezhnev.

7. Russian Journalists Speak

1. Dmitry Ostal'skii
Transcript and translation of taped interview with Dmitry Ostal'skii, news editor of *Nezavisimaya gazeta*, on 28 August 1991 in Moscow.

John Murray: Did the attempt by Leonid Kravchenko in January of this year to rein in the media have any effect on *Nezavisimaya gazeta*?

Dmitry Ostal'skii: No, not really. The television was broadcasting semi-information, but there were alternative sources of information, principally the press, which was free to publish ...

JM: And what about the supreme soviet commission set up after the January incidents in the Baltics to monitor the media?

DO: No practical measures were taken, nothing really came of it, we thought at the beginning that there might be some measures taken, but afterwards the initiative was put on the back burner, so to speak.

JM: And what about the committee?

DO: They issued some meaningless sort of document or something urging balanced coverage and that was the end of it. The whole thing had no practical consequences for us.

JM: How do you assess the reaction of the press to the coup?

DO: Well, what the organizers of the *putsch* failed to take into account was that the fear had left journalists.

JM: They miscalculated the press reaction, you mean?

DO: Yes, in effect, when the whole thing began, when the *GKChP* [State emergency committee, the *putsch* leaders] issued their decrees, they were sabotaged at several levels. As a result there was panic, they started to panic, because they realized that they couldn't rely on support from any quarter, even the army.

JM: So they shut down most newspapers.

DO: No, they closed down the printing works, but we prepared new-

214

sheets: the first day we issued a newssheet, the second day we published a newspaper, by photocopy – we made several thousand copies. People were laughing at the so-called emergency situation when on every column in the metro there were newssheets supporting Yeltsin, there were photocopied newspapers going around.[1]

JM: How come you had such freedom to publish?

DO: Because the militia [police] sabotaged everything. It was quite funny, really. There were only three armoured cars here on Kirov Street: all they did was to stop the traffic. There were army officers, there were militiamen standing beside the armoured cars, people were talking to them, handing out leaflets of support for Yeltsin. Nobody went near them, the militia just stood there, it was all a big show. The coup attempt only really took place in Moscow. People are calling the coup a television coup, because everything took place on the television. If you discount the three unfortunate victims, who were victims of an accident, since if you bring that amount of military hardware into any city there's bound to be an accident, especially when there are people coming out against it. Nobody wanted these victims, the *GKChP* were particularly worried that there would be casualties, though in the final analysis they were responsible for the deaths because they brought in the troops. The soldiers themselves didn't want it to happen, it all happened almost accidentally, though on the other hand it was bound to happen.

JM: What do you make of the removal of Kravchenko [as director of state television] and Spiridonov [as director of *TASS*]?

DO: Well, they're state structures. I think that even Kravchenko behaved quite honourably during the coup. On the first day when we saw *Vremya* [main evening news] everyone was surprised because, in spite of all the *GKChP* decrees, there was a report almost from the White House from Yeltsin's point of view. Given the circumstances, I think he did what he could to give out some sort of information. It's another question entirely whether it would have been better to have refused, to have resigned. But to have

1 See, for example, Murray, 1991b, for interviews with distributors of news-sheets during the coup.

asked that of him is another example of our seventy-year-old custom of demanding of everyone heroic feats. We've got used to demanding heroic deeds of everyone, nothing less, and if someone hasn't committed a heroic feat, then he resigns, at the very least.

JM: I see that *Izvestiya* has declared itself an independent newspaper.

DO: Yes, and it's publishing a lot of very good material.

JM: And why didn't Yeltsin close down *Izvestiya*, since it, like *Pravda*, was one of the papers that came out during the coup?

DO: Because it attempted to give pro-Yeltsin coverage. Anyway, I think it's terrible that Yeltsin has shut down some newspapers, without any legal authority. I have to say that even *Pravda* is a fairly respectable newspaper, it was only natural that they would take the position they did during the coup, it would have been unrealistic to demand of them anything else in the circumstances.

2. Dmitry Ostal'skii

Transcript and translation of taped interview with Dmitry Ostal'skii, news editor of *Nezavisimaya gazeta*, on 4 August 1992 in Moscow.

John Murray: Would you agree that the *glasnost'* era is over and that today's Russian press is free in the Western sense?

Dmitry Ostal'skii: I think the Russian press is once again at a transitional stage. Yes there is some freedom of speech, but we're entering a period of semi-*glasnost'* again, I mean a period of *glasnost'* but not freedom of speech.

JM: How is this manifesting itself?

DO: It's connected with the economic position of the press. It's now not profitable to run a newspaper. This is a result of the enormous cost of paper and of all the printing costs which have made the price of the newspaper so high that the consumer can't afford to buy it.

JM: And what about advertising revenue?

DO: In spite of the fact that all newspapers continue to exist thanks to advertising revenue, the actual revenue it brings in is not enough to finance the expansion of a newspaper. Newspapers with small circulations are still able to exist, somehow, but it is a paradox that the larger a paper's circulation, the more money it loses. This is because of the enormously high price of paper. *Komsomol'skaya pravda* at the moment receives a subsidy of 200 million roubles a month because of their huge circulation.

JM: And who gives the subsidy?

DO: Well, I was coming to that. It is because of the economic difficulties that newspapers are becoming economically dependent on the state. There was a decision made, the only realistic one in the circumstances, that subsidies would be given to, as they put it, socially significant newspapers, in accordance with their circulation. The question of who is to decide which papers are socially significant is being fought out at the moment between the government and parliament. They are deciding who does and who doesn't get a subsidy. ... There's a committee of leading editors who decides who gets a subsidy.

JM: And is *Nezavisimaya gazeta* represented on that committee?

DO: No, but we received our share of the state subsidy, until the middle of the year, after which the conditions under which you can receive a subsidy will change.

JM: Does your paper want to be financially independent?

DO: We want to be, we would like to be but it's not possible at the moment because the economic situation is very, very grave.

JM: Has there been any indication that the government or parliament is trying to interfere in the press?

DO: Without a doubt, though it's too early to talk of obvious efforts, though, how can I put it, in these circumstances newspapers try to find themselves patrons, which I think is dreadful. I think it's terrible that *Izvestiya* is looking to the presidency for a defender from Khasbulatov and the Supreme Soviet; when you look for a defender then you are no longer free to criticize that defender. On the other hand *Rossiiskaya gazeta*, for example, receives a very large subsidy, even though they don't have a very large circulation. They receive the largest subsidy of any paper, because they belong to the Supreme Soviet and even though you might expect all journalists to show solidarity with *Izvestiya*, *Rossiiskaya gazeta* has come out against it.

JM: And does the fact that Moscow city council founded *Nezavisimaya gazeta* affect your editorial freedom in any way?

DO: So far we have had major difficulties with the council. I can say that we try to keep true to our principle of independence. I didn't finish telling you about how papers lose their independence. Some link themselves with the legislature, others with the government executive, and others to commercial structures. In other words, they sell themselves, they enmesh themselves with commercial structures and receive subsidies from banks.

JM: And what's in it for the commercial structures? Do these newspapers print their advertisements?

DO: No, well, ads do play their role, they receive money from banks. But these newspapers follow a particular general political line that is beneficial to them. What happens is that these commercial structures offer financial aid to the papers, and once they've accepted it, well, they can't go against these structures. What I'm saying is that for a few months after August [1991] we had probably the most free press in the world, but since then the process is in reverse. A Greek millionaire, a communist millionaire, bought *Pravda*. Though on the other hand there's a danger that if newspapers receive their subsidies only from the state, if the state becomes the only subsidy-giver, then they'll be in a monopoly position and that would be the end of everything. If some papers are dependent on commercial structures, others on the parliament, others on the government, then perhaps the institution of the press will be able to fulfil its role, the role it must play in providing people with information from various sources.

JM: And where is your own newspaper in this scheme?

DO: We are something of an exception. Whether *Nezavisimaya gazeta* will remain able to follow its independent line will depend on what happens in the very near future. People are now beginning to subscribe for next year, we can only determine our advertising rates based on circulation figures. Here you have to try to find the golden mean. You have to aim to have a circulation that's not too large [because of paper and distribution costs], but not too small either otherwise advertisers won't advertise in the paper.

JM: So how are you faring financially at the moment?

DO: We manage to feed ourselves, but we can't expand. We couldn't dream of setting up our own printing works.

JM: I see you have started your own news agency.

DO: Yes, *NEGA* – it stands for *Nezavisimaya gazeta*. We have a lot of Western subscribers; here in Moscow the radio and television cite the agency very often, if you've noticed.

JM: *Nezavisimaya gazeta*, despite its independence, would be classed as belonging to the 'democratic' camp, the pro-Yeltsin camp.

DO: Well, I don't know about being pro-Yeltsin, but, yes, we are part of the democratic press, the people who work here are supporters of democracy, they consider themselves democrats, but this does not mean that we support everything Yeltsin does. We criticize him ...

JM: And are you criticized for that?

DO: The authorities criticize us, yes, people like Khasbulatov are very wary about us, they don't like papers like us or like *zvestiya*.

JM: And does Yeltsin criticize you?

DO: Yes, though, according to our information he thinks we are ... you see, we are an élite newspaper.

JM: In what sense élite?

DO: Well, *Izvestiya* has a circulation of about one and a half million, it's a more general paper; we sell about 200,000, and the bulk of our readers would belong to the government structures, to the intelligenstia, in that sense it's élite, foreign correspondents, embassies, they are our readers. But to get back to what I was saying, the press is now in a transitional period, and not for the better.

JM: *Glavlit* [the censorship agency] was abolished, so there is now no direct censorship. Is that correct?

DO: Yes, that is correct. In the circumstances each newspaper acts as its own censor to make sure it doesn't harm the interests of its protector, be it the likes of Ruslan Khasbulatov or banks and corporations.

JM: But there still exists an article in the legal code forbidding the telling of state secrets.

DO: Yes, it exists, but there's a funny thing here. There are sanctions imposed on publications that do reveal state secrets, in accordance with the press law, but there is no definition of what exactly constitutes a state secret.

JM: There's no list?

DO: No. There's never yet been a case where a publication was found guilty of revealing a state secret. I don't believe myself that a court would prosecute a newspaper for revealing state secrets, perhaps an individual, but for the moment, while no list of what constitutes a state secret exists, we can be relaxed about publishing occasionally sensational stories and not be afraid that the next day the editor will be arrested. Sooner or later a list will be compiled, but our task is to make sure it won't be so encompassing as to prevent us from writing about anything. From the state's point of view, I suppose it's sensible to have some things kept secret.

JM: Your journalists have begun to write in a manner different to the old style. How did that happen? Where did they draw their inspiration from?

DO: It happened of its own accord. The paper is young, I mean the staff are very young, most of them have worked with different papers, for example a lot of our political reporters have worked as parliamentary correspondents with other papers and have formed their own views on things, each one brought something of their own to the paper and what resulted was *Nezavisimaya gazeta*. You couldn't say that they were trained by anyone in particular. There were some basic principles drawn from what we knew of principles of journalism from around the world, that, for example, information should be a priority, unlike the Soviet press that liked to indulge in moralizing. Each one understood this new journalism – it was new for the former Soviet Union – in their own way.

JM: Has the reader changed also?

DO: I can tell you what I feel myself as a reader. The reader is tired of politics, therefore our newspaper couldn't be said to occupy the most advantageous position at the moment in the market-place. We nevertheless try to remain a serious political paper, even though people are thoroughly fed up with politics, you've seen that yourself, I even find it hard myself to read articles on politics in our own paper, so if someone with a professional interest in politics is fed up, you can imagine how the ordinary reader feels. While the interest in politics may have fallen off, it will come back because everything depends on politics. And we have no intention of changing the profile of the newspaper, of becoming a tabloid newspaper, of joining the yellow press.

JM: And what papers would you class as 'tabloid'?

DO: Well, the clearest example would be *Moskovskii komsomolets*. They have over a million subscribers, they're read by a lot of people.

JM: What about *Komsomol'skaya pravda*?

DO: They're sort of in the middle. There was talk, incidentally, that they might have to close down because of their huge circulation. They had the worst economic problems. They were saved by state subsidies. So that we now have a very interesting situation, a regrouping of the press, with papers with huge circulations losing so many subscribers that they'll retain an absolute minimum number of subscribers. It's difficult to predict, but I think the number of subscribers next year will be practically non-existent. Papers will be sold not by subscription but at newsagents. Of course the problem of distribution and delivery remains, we still haven't found a replacement for *Soyuzpechat'*, who are not only very expensive, but offer an appalling service. Our Saturday issue, for example, is delivered to subscribers on Tuesday, that's in Moscow, and we can do nothing about it.

JM: What do you make of new newspapers, such as *Den'*?

DO: Well, *Den'* is, well, they say it's the organ of the 'spiritual opposition' whereas in reality it's taking more and more a purely fascist position, and I mean fascist, not Russian chauvinist, though they have a fair amount of that element, too. I don't read it very often, but they often say that the Russian nationalist movement and fascism have a lot in common, they have a common enemy in zionism, they say this openly sometimes. Until now the authorities have reacted very weakly to that sort of publication, but they are preparing to take some legal action against them.

JM: In the West the tabloid press has a much larger circulation than the serious press. Do you think the same phenomenon will happen in Russia?

DO: Yes, I do. I think it's a worldwide phenomenon. What's more, I think here especially so, since Russian society has had to put up with so much for so long that people have lost interest in the serious political and financial press, I'm talking about the general public now, who are more interested in stories about brothels and prostitutes. There's nothing you can do about it, you just have to accept it. We'll continue to serve our own type of reader, though.

3. Alexander Pumpyanskii

Transcript and translation of taped interview with Alexander Pumpyanskii, editor of *Novoe vremya* (*New Times*), on 5 August 1992 in Moscow.

John Murray: My first question concerns *glasnost'*. Would you say that the era of *glasnost'* is over and that the Russian press has entered a new phase of press freedom in the Western understanding?

Alexander Pumpyanskii: I think that yes, the era of *glasnost'*, which was an era of enormous significance for society and life in general and for journalists personally, is now over. Over in the sense that it has passed into a new phase which could be called the phase of freedom of speech. Whether it's quite the same freedom as you have in the West, well, the answer is yes and no, because in several areas it is in fact freedom of speech in the fullest sense. But we will later be talking about all the dangers to freedom of speech, all the limitations, but that's a separate topic. Our freedom of speech is unlike the Western variety because our society is so different from yours in so many ways. Our Soviet – I know the Soviet Union no longer exists – but our Soviet phenomena are not comparable with Western ones.

JM: And what are these dangers you were referring to?

AP: If you'll permit me, I'll just say a little bit about how the process has evolved, and then it'll be easier to understand what's happening now and what the new threats and dangers are. There is a certain opinion in currency that before Gorbachev there was not in the slightest degree freedom of speech, that there was no honesty in what journalists wrote, no honest information given. That was plainly not the case. As a general scheme, it's more or less correct. It's true that *Agitprop* existed as a sort of ideological centre, that is, a department of the central committee of the communist party, and that this *Agitprop* solved all problems, personnel questions, which papers should be written in such and such a way, which newspapers should or should not exist. All newspapers and magazines were organs of some body or other, or were connected with some sort of official, bureaucratic structure that would keep control of the publication. However, everything was under the general auspices of *Agitprop*. All editors were nominated by *Agitprop*, Soviet foreign correspondents were nominated and confirmed by them. This was the way things worked, it was a bureaucratic system. The plan for each issue of a newspaper would be sent before publication to *Agitprop*, which didn't mean that it was impossible to bypass this structure. It was possible, and of course there were honest journalists and newspapers that were more liberal and daring than others – *Komsomol'skaya pravda*, where I worked, where it was considered an honour to be able to get something published that would not have been published elsewhere. But this was all within very strictly set down limits and we can remember the times when editors or political commentators were fired for publishing things that by today's standards were laughable. The level of truth was very low, though this didn't mean that the level of courage was low, because even for such a small deviation from the dogma the punishment for both the newspaper and the journalist was very severe.

And then *glasnost'* arrived, which for journalists was an enormous shock to the system because, well, you have to know what was behind the information propaganda system. You see it's interesting to note that in the old language of the communist party, from the time of Stalin right up almost to the pre-Gorbachev days, the word information was not ever mentioned. In the central committee of the CPSU there were departments and sections for everything under the sun, for various sectors of industry, et cetera,

but there was no information department. There was a department
of propaganda, the key word was propaganda, people didn't need
to know what was happening in reality, people needed to receive
the information and picture of the world that was necessary for the
communist party and the ruling circles, so that what you had was a
picture of the world. For example, the history of the party was
Stalin's *Short Course*, there could be modifications, but at any
given time there was a complete and whole history of the world,
and no deviations from that particular history were tolerated.
That's why the whole propaganda system existed, what I call
Agitprop. There were violations of the scheme, but that was the
structure that was in place.

Glasnost' was a violation of this scheme of things. *Glasnost'*
essentially consisted in introducing common sense into this system
which had no common sense, only dogma. So that *glasnost'* was
the opportunity given by the new leadership, by Gorbachev and
[Alexander] Yakovlev in particular, to answer a whole series of
questions, such as 'did 1937 happen?', 'did Katyn happen?', 'how
did the Korean war start?', all these questions had existed in
people's minds but the answers they had been given were totally
idiotic and had absolutely nothing in common with what actually
happened, and it was forbidden to touch upon this area. And then,
under *glasnost'*, all of this was permitted. Above all *glasnost'* was
being realistic about our history. The press itself independently
started looking for the answers to these questions, spontaneously,
as a result of which all our history blew up in our faces. It was the
same in other areas, in relation to contemporary events, but of
course there was no criticism of the incumbent leadership. Of
yesterday's leaders, by all means, of the day before yesterday's, all
the more so, but not, it went without saying, of the current leaders.
And another limitation of *glasnost'* was that the role of socialism
as an idea and of the party as an institution, as an idea, these were
not subjected to criticism and never placed under doubt. All the
crimes, all the dark and terrible things that had happened, it was
all treated as a sort of deviation from the idea, but after every
revelation the idea itself was declared to be honourable and pure.
The figure of Lenin was the embodiment of the idea. This was as

far as Gorbachev wanted *glasnost'* to go. That was *glasnost'*. The genie, however, had been let out of the bottle, or rather lots of genies, because each and every newspaper had its own genie and from each and every one of these bottles, a genie was let free. Naturally this created a storm and it all led to a situation where everything was swept away, very often newspapers such as *Moskovskie novosti* or *Ogonyok*, which had been permitted to publish certain things – these were the children of *glasnost'* – became a problem for the fathers of *glasnost'*. They began to publish material against Gorbachev himself, because they no longer recognized the limits. Although it must be said that, despite certain isolated episodes, Gorbachev and Yakovlev adopted a stoical position, Yakovlev in particular, and Gorbachev with Yakovlev's help, but nevertheless ....

In the previous period, the first to suffer were newspaper editors. Whenever there was a change of the regime's leadership or other changes, the heads of the editors were the first to fly, and a new team of editors was appointed. In that way it was possible for the new leader to gain the personal loyalty of the editors, who would know what to say to the public, what sort of information or pseudo-information should be given to the public. Gorbachev made one timid effort to remove Starkov from *Argumenty i fakty*, but didn't insist on it, fortunately. Everything else he tolerated. Including newspapers that were opposed to him personally, oppositional in the other sense, the orthodox communist sense, like *Sovetskaya Rossiya*. So that, in spite of what he said, at the organizational level he behaved very well towards the press and was respected for it. More importantly, he was respected for giving editors the right to publish freely and openly, and what was no less important, perhaps more important, he introduced organizational changes, censorship was forbidden – and it really was – and he brought in a law on the press a couple of years ago, precisely two years ago, in August 1990. The law was very liberal and meant that any organization or group of people or individuals could set up their own organ of the press, register it and begin publishing. These were unheard of things and this was the legal basis for the freedom of the press.

Then there was one other event, which I now understand from my own personal psychological experience and the experience of the magazine. This was August 1991, which was a test of, so to speak, real *glasnost'*. Up to that time many press organs had registered as independent publications. It was already evident that they could throw down challenges to the authorities, that they could act in a coquettish way in front of them. This much was clear. But it was not clear how much the authorities would put up with before resorting to repressive methods, and not only to closing down newspapers, but worse. This test was taken in August 1991 when a whole series of publications, practically all, rejected the, let us call it, junta, the *GKChP*. And they threw down a challenge, risking all the consequences. That was a test of whether freedom of the press had really reached the country.

JM: Are you talking about during the *putsch*?

AP: Yes. Every newspaper and magazine that rejected the *GKChP* showed that they were free, because, well, it's clear why. That, then, is a success story of how freedom of the press was gained in this country. And now it's time to talk of the defeats or the difficulties encountered by the press, and the threats to press freedom which exist. The threats appeared from that moment in August, which was the pinnacle of freedom. A lot of publications had registered as independent, though now, it should be said, a lot of newspapers call themselves independent – *Pravda* calls itself independent, *Sovetskaya Rossiya* calls itself a popular newspaper, et cetera. If you were to take a photograph of all the newspapers that exist today, then you would see that we have a totally unprecedented level of press freedom.

We have newspapers of absolutely every type, of all political viewpoints. *Sovetskaya Rossiya*, in my view, publishes extraordinary things, extraordinary in their stupidity and offensiveness. Only recently they gave over a whole page[2] to an article which was an extract from a book by – what's his name – Oleinik, a Ukrainian writer, who was unsuccessful as a writer but had a happy bureaucratic fate. He was a member of the CPSU, he was

---

2 Boris Oleinik's article, 'Beware of false believers' (*Beregis' krivoverov*) appeared in *Sovetskaya Rossiya*, 1 August 1992, p.3.

deputy leader of the chamber of nationalities in the Supreme Soviet. He has just been given a whole page where he writes that Gorbachev was begotten by the devil. He said that the devil had placed Gorbachev on the earth and that everything that happened and was now happening was as a result of demonic forces, and that Gorbachev was a disciple of the devil and that it was all in his zodiac sign. All of this was written in this article, it's absolutely extraordinary, and he somehow links the Challenger accident to Gorbachev, how he does it ... it's totally idiotic. Can one publish this sort of thing? Go right ahead. I haven't mentioned pornography. Absolutely anything can be published, regardless of its orientation, you have anti-semitic publications such as *Den'*. Anything can be published. So that there is in this sense full freedom of the press.

How is it different from your freedom of the press? Well, here you can see one difference, since an extreme society is not a balanced society, a country without stability, that finds itself in a crisis, this hysterical state of mind, the critical state of society is reflected in the press. Our freedom of the press has a schizophrenic character. As I've shown you in the examples I gave, the very freedom of the press to publish anything carries in itself a threat to press freedom because a lot of ordinary people already believe that this sort of hysteria and stupidity is a feature of press freedom and therefore, psychologically anyway, they ask themselves why they need freedom of the press if this is what it brings. That's one of the dangers. A second danger, which has appeared unexpectedly, is the economic side of things. The economic basis for freedom of the press is very brittle and precarious. Previously, the press had practically no money worries regardless of whether a paper did or didn't make a profit. Everything, including the prices, was artificially set. *Komsomol'skaya pravda*, for example, was a very profitable newspaper. I know because I worked there. We here at *Novoe vremya* made a small profit of a million or a million and a half roubles, and considered ourselves a very successful publication. In reality the profits were taken from the publications and money was then given back to publications, so that nothing depended on a publication's profitability. If a paper didn't make a profit, they still received money in some form or other, so that in fact the press had no connection with real economics. Now newspapers are faced with questions of survival and continued existence, of whether or not you make a profit or fail to make a profit. And unless a newspaper or magazine is a purely commercial enterprise, it's impossible for them to make money. It's impossible for a normal political newspaper to make a profit.

JM: What do you mean by commercial publications?

AP: I mean, for example, pornographic publications, which you can sell for 100 roubles. Here you can make some sort of profit, that's clear. But for a normal, general political newspaper, it's impossible because the economics of the newspaper and magazine business is completely skewed, there's no real competition between printers, the printers have out-dated technology and there are very few of them. There's no real competition between paper producers, and they are also technologically backward. They have a monopoly, but they themselves are in such a dreadful economic situation that they up their prices as much as they want. The price of paper has risen tenfold and more. It's impossible to put up the price of newspapers because of the practice of subscription. Most people who bought newspapers paid a subscription at the beginning of the year for the whole year, only a few would buy them at retail outlets, but what is a newspaper supposed to do if, after it has received subscriptions, its costs go up by more than ten times, what with inflation. The end result of this is that practically the entire press now finds itself in desperate financial straits. The publication and selling of newspapers does not even minimally cover the costs of the newspaper. And what's more, the more popular the publication the worse the situation they find themselves in. The greater the circulation, the greater the financial losses. As a result, and this is an amazing fact, a free press begged the government for support. Sensible voices from the media are saying that this support should be given in a de-individualized way, by allowing papers not to pay tax, or other ways. For the time being, however, this aid is being handed out in another way. The government, in the form of the ministry for information, has received a certain sum of money from the budget which it hands over directly to newspapers and magazines according to the publication's circulation. For the moment they have been apolitical, in the sense that they give money to, on the one hand, *Komsomol'skaya pravda* and *Izvestiya*, and, on the other, *Pravda*, in accordance with the publication's circulation, on the principle that the greater the circulation, the greater the expenses. But even if they are now acting in a neutral manner, two dangers arise. First, tomorrow they might find themselves with no more money, which would cause great difficulties for newspapers that had got used to living with subsidies, which can only live with this infusion of money. Second, there is a danger that this financial help will be used by politicians as a means of exerting pressure, as a sort of knout. And even if they don't use the subsidy to put pressure on the press, the feeling of dependence clearly exists in one form or another. For the moment the editors of the main newspapers, *Komsomol'skaya pravda*, for example, as far as I know, have been able to see off any political threats. But it's a very dangerous situation.

JM: Does *Novoe vremya* receive a subsidy?

AP: No, we don't. For the moment we can manage without one, but I'm afraid it's possible that we'll soon be forced to apply for help. So, that's how the economic situation is a danger. Another danger is the classical one. The authorities that run the country now, after the August coup, they call themselves democrats because before August, in the political battles that took place before August, that's the name they went under. It was democrats versus communists. Now the democrats are in power, but democrats is simply a name for a sort of party, in the broad sense of the word. That the vast majority of these people are in no sense real democrats in their convictions, their understanding of things, is perfectly plain. They are not people of a liberal cast of mind, they don't have a democratic way of thinking that takes account of certain understanding of democratic norms, such as pluralism or the right of the press to independence. What we now have is a power syndrome.

JM: What is that?

AP: It means that these people believe: 'we are good, and everything that is useful to us is good, and everything that is damaging to us is bad.'

JM: And how is that manifested in the press?

AP: In the press it means that you can't criticize them.

JM: But you have the right to criticize.

AP: That's true, we do have the right to criticize, but at the same time you get endless lamentations, endless complaints from a whole variety of people, especially active in this at the moment is Khasbulatov. Khasbulatov is forever saying that the press is a destructive force, that the press is responsible for stoking up ethnic conflicts, that all the misfortunes of the country can be put down to the press, in the same way as Gorbachev complained, and all the more so all his predecessors. And, accordingly, this self-same Khasbulatov is very direct in both word and deed, he says 'look how much money they are getting, why are they getting this money? Why should the authorities hand over money to a press that is criticizing them? It doesn't make sense.' And according to his logic it doesn't make sense, so he says 'we shall see', which is already a hint. This has been especially apparent in recent days. He would hold the view that the old system of control should be reimposed in the press. An independent press? Why do we need an independent press? We should arrange things so that the press becomes dependent economically first of all, and then organizationally. The current battle between Khasbulatov and *Izvestiya* is a clear example of this. What does Khasbulatov want? He wants *Izvestiya* to be under his control, he wants *Izvestiya* to become again the same as before, an organ of the soviets.

JM: But he says that *Izvestiya*'s declaration of independence was unlawful ...

AP: That's only a trick, that's only a method for trying to regain control of the paper. I'm speaking of the aim. The aim is to regain control. Because if *Izvestiya* went back to being an organ of the Supreme Soviet, then that body, or whatever it might be called, would gain control over the paper. It would be able to appoint or remove an editor, it could interfere in the daily running of the paper and influence the paper's editorial position.

JM: But is not *Rossiiskaya gazeta* not the organ of the Supreme Soviet?

AP: Yes, it is. You see, Khasbulatov made his views very plain at the last sitting of the Supreme Soviet. Poltoranin [minister for information] was speaking, maybe you heard him, it was a poor speech, but his position was in support of *Izvestiya*; but it was a bad speech. 'Yes', he said, 'papers have often behaved irresponsibly'. He was trying to compromise, he was trying to speak in a language that the parliament understood. He mentioned *Den'* and *Sovetskaya Rossiya*, and they were good examples; but then he was interrupted by Khasbulatov who said 'why stop there?' He then mentioned *Komsomol'skaya pravda, Izvestiya* – in other words he completely distorted what Poltoranin was saying, 'all newspapers apart from our own *Rossiiskaya gazeta*': those were his words – 'all newspapers, apart from our own *Rossiiskaya gazeta*'. That was his ideal scheme of things, that there was only one good newspaper, because it was his newspaper, and indeed it does what it's told, it does criticize in an unbridled way everyone except Khasbulatov and those whom Khasbulatov needs. There you have once again that absolutist way of thinking, the only difference being that before it came from the *Agitprop* of Brezhnev, Suslov or whoever, now it's *Agitprop* in the name of Khasbulatov. All this is an attempt to return things to their former state. To a time when the press was obedient and loyal to the leadership, when it saw everything through the eyes of the authorities, when it spoke from their mouth. It's quite another thing that none of this will succeed. I don't think Khasbulatov will succeed in his current legal battle against *Izvestiya*.

JM: And who brought whom to court?

AP: It was three deputies, Shakhrai and two others, who demanded – as is their right – that the issue be determined by the constitutional court. Their action was carried out with the aim of defending *Izvestiya* and was done with the paper's agreement. But I was saying that Khasbulatov's efforts will come to nothing for various reasons, because what we see here is no more than Khasbulatov and parliament playing a political game against the president and the government, the ministry of information, et cetera. So that this is rivalry between the different authorities.

JM: Surely not the whole parliament?

AP: No, not the entire parliament, but if we are speaking about numbers, then the overwhelming majority. Over half voted for Khasbulatov's resolution [against *Izvestiya*] and played into his hands, so that it would be a mistake to hold any illusions on that score. It won't succeed because the level of press freedom already achieved by the press is quite high and the press will oppose any attempts at reimposing control. And I believe it will receive support from abroad and the political consequences of such a violation of press freedom for the government, for the president, would be very serious. The second reason it will fail is because, as I said, the whole thing has become a political battle and the government, and to some extent the president, are on the side of the press, not because they're great democrats or anything, or great defenders of press freedom, even though they declaim these slogans, but because that's the way the battle-lines are drawn. In another situation they could constitute a threat to press freedom.

JM: Why are the government and the president now on the side of *Izvestiya*?

AP: That's obvious. Because they don't want the paper to fall into Khasbulatov's hands because that would make Khasbulatov too strong a figure. That's why they support the press at the moment. Though I repeat, it is only on the surface that they come out declaiming slogans supporting freedom of the press, independence and so forth. So, these are the dangers for the press at the moment.

JM: In the area of international politics you told me two years ago that the Russian reader was interested in foreign news only if it had a bearing on home affairs. Has the situation changed since then?

AP: No, it's more or less the same. What's more, it has in some sense got worse because a whole series of problems that were purely internal, Soviet problems, have now become international problems. The relations between Russia and Ukraine, for example. Is that an internal problem or an international one? Now, in theory, it's an international problem, though it's treated as if, well, it's the 'near abroad' [countries that used to be Soviet republics]:

there's a contradiction here. Or what about the war in Karabakh? Is it an internal or an international problem?

JM: And how does your magazine treat the problem of Karabakh?

AP: Well, it's a contradiction, because on the one hand it's an international conflict between two sovereign states, but it's also our problem, it's our problem as well. I wouldn't go along with the idea, and neither does our magazine, that it's an international problem and that therefore we can isolate ourselves from it. This temptation to isolate oneself from new international problems such as this, ones that are within the limits of the old Soviet Union, this attempt to isolate ourselves from them, is very dangerous.

JM: What precisely is the danger?

AP: That we say that Karabakh, for example, is between the Armenians and the Azerbaijanis, so let them just fight it out between themselves, it's got nothing to do with us. That's a dangerous and incorrect point of view, because it still is our problem because, for one, it was created by this country, albeit in another form, in its earlier form, but nevertheless by this country, but also because emotionally, physically or whatever way you like, it's still our problem.

JM: What in your view are the most important questions of international politics for Russia at the present?

AP: Strange as it may appear, the most important question of international, or any other for that matter, politics for Russia at the moment is the search for a new identity and what sort of relations the country will have with countries from the so-called 'near abroad'. That's the most important question, because it's the most urgent and dangerous question because we have a concept of a patriotic [literally, Fatherland] war, which is what the war with Napoleon was called and what the war from 1941 to 1945 with Hitler was called. Now we have a lot of small patriotic wars going on and their possibilities are absolutely without limit, they're very dangerous indeed. Solutions and formulas that prevent these wars from getting out of hand must be found. Because the civilized world has reached a stage of, well, I don't know what, but at least they don't have wars. In Europe the absence of war is guaranteed: there could be all sorts of other problems, but not war because nobody would fight. Here you have wars breaking out, streams of refugees, and so forth. That complex of problems is the most important and urgent one for us at the moment.

Another area is the search in this country for a new relationship with the world. Under Gorbachev it was said that we wanted to become a part of civilization. But what does that actually mean? How do we reform the economy and how do we become part of the wider world? Nobody knows the answers to these questions. That's the second important question. At a concrete level things are changing. For example, Yeltsin very quickly signed a nuclear arms reduction treaty which was very important and which went against a lot of old principles. Since the very basis of things has changed, we are no longer enemies, we can cut our heavy rockets which were once the holy of holies. Or in the field of nuclear testing, on the other hand, the Americans always insisted that it was going to continue, now a decision has been made that it will cease for a number of years. So that in specifics, changes are taking place. But in general terms, not in the field of diplomacy or in negotiations. First of all it's necessary to carry out the type of economic reform in the country which we seem unable to carry out, though it's not at all certain what type of reforms these should be, but that the economy should be open to world capital and become a part of the world market. But how, how quickly and when should all this be done, and how should one deal with all the accusations that arise from the process, including charges of treachery, that the motherland is being sold off, and so on?

JM: I notice that the portrait of Lenin you had hanging on the wall is gone.

AP: Yes. There's the nail it hung from. That was actually a very interesting incident. In every office Lenin's portrait hung, the first trace of liberalism in this office was when there appeared an unofficial portrait of Lenin, and not one of the usual photographs, but a portrait done by a real artist, Khachatrian. He drew it a few years ago and it appeared on the cover of the magazine on the occasion of some Lenin jubilee. And my predecessor decided to hang the portrait of Lenin because he liked Khachatrian and his work – he's a friend of the magazine. So, it was a sort of liberal brush stroke. I didn't take it down out of respect for Khachatrian, not for Lenin, but for Khachatrian because it was above all a work of art, and out of respect to my predecessor to whom the portrait belonged. But on 19 August, exactly a year ago, when we held a kind of permanent editorial meeting, somebody got up and took it from the wall and walked away with it. Where it was taken, why it was removed, I don't know, it was a purely revolutionary action! [laughs loudly] It wasn't a command, somebody just couldn't take it any more. So you could say it was the action of the revolutionary democratic masses carried out in an office.

4. Vladimir Buslaev

Transcript and translation of taped interview with Vladimir Buslaev, commercial director of *Moskovskii komsomolets*, on 12 August 1992 in Moscow.

John Murray: So, things are difficult for newspapers?

Vladimir Buslaev: There are a lot of problems in society at the moment and nobody quite manages to get around to worrying about the press.

JM: Is there a shortage of paper?

VB: There's no shortage of paper. The problem is not availability, but the price, which is growing all the time. Taxes are increasing, the cost of raw material, of pulp, like everything else, is going up. It starts with the wages of the lumberjacks going up and continues all along the line until it reaches us. Then on top, we have to pay a 28 per cent value added tax for God knows what reason.

JM: By how much has the price risen in the course of the year?

VN: There's been a fivefold increase. I can give you figures. Last year [1991] we bought paper for 2,000 roubles, 2,500 roubles a tonne by the end of the year. In the new year we paid 4,000 to

4,500 roubles, and now, according to this telegram that I've just received, it will cost 28,000 roubles a tonne, including tax. We use between 40,000 to 45,000 tonnes for one issue of our newspaper, we come out 22 times a month, so you can work out how much we pay.

JM: So you then raise the cost of your newspaper to meet your rising costs?

VB: We can't raise the price because we have subscribers, 99 per cent of our readers are subscribers who paid their subscriptions last year at a cost of eight copecks per issue.

JM: Do they mostly subscribe for a whole year?

VB: Mostly. You can take out a subscription for a month or less, or whatever, but mostly for the year.

JM: So you'll have to put up the subscription rates for next year.

VB: For next year, yes. Subscriptions for the following year start in August.

JM: By how much will you increase the price?

VB: Very difficult to say, but I wouldn't be wrong if I said by fifteen times, or rather twenty times.

JM: So you can expect to lose subscribers, then.

VB: Well, people are getting used to the prices, too. The first reaction is one of shock, but then readers gets used to it, their salaries are also going up, but the rise in people's living standards always lags behind the rise in our costs, so you're right, we will lose readers because to pay anything from 400 to 1,000 roubles to take out a subscription is a very hard thing for people to do. The price of paper is just one of our problems, the other problem is the postal service, which is really putting on the pressure. They've increased the cost of delivery very considerably. At the beginning of this year they charged us four copecks for every paper they delivered to a subscriber. From the beginning of July they raised the charge to 36 copecks. We didn't of course pay them that amount, we wrote to them and said we couldn't understand why they had raised the cost since we had agreed delivery costs for the whole year at the beginning of the year. They wrote back to us saying that what they were doing was not breaking any agreement, et cetera, et cetera, that – look, here's the letter –

'owing to the increase in the cost of fuel oil', 36 copecks, if you please. That means we have to find an extra 14 million roubles to cover that increase. But where do you get 14 million roubles?

JM: So the paper has a financial crisis.

VB: For us it's a crisis. We wrote back to them that whatever they had said we were not going to pay them any more money.

JM: And how did they respond to your letter?

VB: Well, we haven't got a reply from them yet. It's a crisis for all newspapers, not only for us.

JM: So, do you make most of your profit from advertising?

VB: Yes, from ads.

JM: And who would place ads in your newspaper?

VB: All sorts. I don't know, Sony put ads in, our own companies.

JM: And would there be more native ads than foreign ones?

VB: Without a doubt, of course.

JM: Who owns *Moskovskii komsomolets*?

VB: We do.

JM: And how did that happen? You used to be an organ of the *Komsomol*.

VB: We used to be an organ, then there was a meeting at which we decided who would be the founder of the newspaper, and now the staff is the paper's founder.

JM: So all the profits go to the staff?

VB: Except that we only have losses at the moment.

JM: But you have a huge circulation.

VB: But this is the paradox. We have a huge circulation, at last year's subscription rate of eight copecks an issue. The cost of producing one issue of the paper is now about 60 copecks. How could we expect to make a profit on what we earn from subscriptions?

JM: What are your predictions for the newspaper world for next year?

VB: It's very difficult to say, I wouldn't like to make any predictions.

JM: I suppose the newspapers with a larger circulation find it easier to survive.

VB: I don't think so. They have to buy bigger quantities of paper, they spend more money in distribution costs. When things are stable, then, yes, papers with a large circulation fare better. When the law works. But now you have one law that works for a week and is superseded by a new law the following week. Things will improve when a more sensible tax system is in place.

JM: What sort of changes will take place in the paper itself?

VB: Well, I can only answer you as commercial director. I think we will have more advertisements.

JM: And more pages?

VB: Unfortunately not. Our printers couldn't cope with printing more pages. They barely manage to print the amount we have now, we have a very large circulation, and they have to print a whole series of other papers.

JM: Is there any foreign interest in *Moskovskii komsomolets*?

VB: We have had several offers, and have never hidden the fact, and at the moment we are talking to a French group, *Socpresse*. I'm expecting their representatives in twenty minutes.

JM: And what are they proposing?

VB: To publish our paper jointly with them.

JM: And how would that be beneficial for you?

VB: Well, we would be able to improve the production quality of the paper with their participation, with the help of computers, we would become a modern paper.

JM: And what is their interest in the deal? Advertising?

VB: I don't know. It's hard for me to say. At the moment it's only at the negotiation stage. When it comes to the time for agreements to be signed, then it'll become clearer what everyone's interests are. They are saying at the moment that the deal would be beneficial to them. They're a very big publishing company, they publish 32 newspapers, including *Le Figaro*, their director is a Mr [Robert] Hersant.

5. Mikhail Shcherbachenko

Transcript and translation of taped interview with Mikhail Shcherbachenko, editor of *Coliseum* (*International*) (formerly of *Trud*), on
25 and 26 March 1993 in Dublin.

John Murray: Could you give me a brief outline of your journalistic
   career to date?

Mikhail Shcherbachenko: I started work as a journalist in *Stroitel'naya
   gazeta* [Construction Newspaper] in 1976. It was an interesting
   year in that *Stroitel'naya gazeta* had until that time been a
   specifically trade newspaper, not very well known, its only readers
   were people in the building industry itself, and not by any means
   all of them. It had a very small circulation, it was a departmental
   paper in the very worst sense of the word. I started work there
   precisely at the time when the paper began to be modernized,
   when it changed from being an insignificant little newspaper into a
   decent newspaper with good journalists on the staff. In this sense I
   was fortunate to begin my career working with good people. I
   worked there for a very long time and it was there that, you could
   say, I learned the profession of journalism. I worked there as a
   correspondent, in an editorial capacity, as head of a department,
   that's where I learned about architecture, which I like. Then I
   moved to *Trud* where I worked as a special correspondent working
   directly with the editorial department (not the news section, with
   which reporters work). You probably know that that job was, and
   still is, considered an élite position in a newspaper. You're more
   or less a free agent, you're your own boss, you don't have to turn
   up to work every day. You have to write on important topics,
   that's why you work directly with the editorial department, you're
   not dealing with the everyday news.

JM: And were you free to write about what interested you yourself?

MShch: Yes, well, on the one hand you were more or less free, you
   were on the look-out yourself for topics to write about, you were
   allowed to write long articles, and that was what was expected of a
   newspaper's special correspondent. They gave the newspaper its
   particular identity, so to speak. I wouldn't dream of comparing
   myself with these people, but I'm talking about people like Agra-

novskii, Tat'yana Tess, that is, the cream of journalism at that period. So, I worked as a commentator for some years. But the newspaper was, how could I put it, well, the special correspondent, who should feel like an artist of sorts ... there were a lot of things forced on you, you found yourself in the very rigid discipline of the paper, so the job lost its appeal, though it served as an excellent school, but it became very tiresome.

JM: What did you write about in *Trud*?

MShch: The economy, though apart from my special area, I wrote on theatre, cinema, I myself wrote some plays, I worked in television.

JM: And did you choose your own topics?

MShch: Unfortunately, usually not. That was the unfortunate thing about that position, because the special correspondent is someone who should be given time to think, to ponder things, to store up information, to investigate one story in depth. That's how Agranovskii worked, for example. He was never seen in the office, then there'd be murmurs in the office that he'd disappeared, that he wasn't writing anything, not producing anything. Then he would arrive, hand in his article – which would be published – and then everyone would shut up because what he'd produce would be superb, and it was immediately obvious who Agranovskii was and who the rest were. That was the ideal model of what a special correspondent was. But *Trud* was a very silly sort of newspaper, it got lots of requests which meant I was always travelling around the country doing stories that were not at all what interested me. On the other hand I wrote a lot of articles that came from my own ideas and managed to get published. And then something interesting happened. *Stroitel'naya gazeta*, which had always been the organ of the ministry for construction – it was at this time that Yeltsin came to Moscow. Before he became first secretary of the Moscow party committee, he was the central committee secretary for construction. He was the first central committee secretary solely concerned with questions of construction. He's a construction engineer by profession. And Yeltsin wanted his own newspaper. It was then that they made *Stroitel'naya gazeta* an organ of the central committee. So its rank grew accordingly. It came in second place behind *Pravda, Sotsial-isticheskaya industriya* [Socialist industry], *Sel'skaya zhizn'* [Village life], and *Sovetskaya Kul'tura* [Soviet Culture]. So, what the paper was allowed to do was radically changed, so that it became a paper that could really do things.

JM: When did this happen?

MShch: In 1987. So, the editor, Sharov, whom I had worked under before, and whom I admired a lot, asked me to join the paper again as a member of the editorial staff, with the brief to write about social issues. It was a large department and it was a genuinely interesting assignment. The possibilities of the paper were extensive. We managed to get a lot of material printed that otherwise wouldn't have appeared if we had remained a departmental paper belonging to the ministry. But three years later the central committee decision on the status of the newspaper was revoked. Together with *Sotsialisticheskaya industriya*, we were abolished. It was thought that, well, the party altered its tactics, it was thought that it shouldn't interfere in the economy. It was thought that that was the business of the ministry, but we, the party, don't need a newspaper, we have an ideology, the party line was that it had an ideology. That's why they kept *Sovetskaya kul'tura*. And *Sel'skaya zhizn'* they kept because, well, it always had been traditionally theirs. So, they closed down these two newspapers and opened instead *Rabochaya tribuna* [Workers' Tribune], which to this day exists. So, when they closed down *Stroitel'naya gazeta* I left and joined *Megapolis* of which I was an editor and still am. We have a lot of magazines, one of which is *Coliseum*. It's not *Megapolis ekspress*, a weekly which is independent. We were its founders, but they sail under their own flag, and it's not a bad newspaper. *Coliseum* is an architectural magazine. It comes out in colour, it looks at the world's cities and town-planning. It was the idea of the Moscow city council to have a magazine that would gather information on capitals and large cities and on how to run them. So, that was my main career. Along the way I worked in television, I presented a series of music programmes, programmes on construction.

JM: How would you rate Chikin and Kravchenko as journalists?[3]

MShch: If you speak to people who worked with Kravchenko, he, unfortunately, is someone who quickly changes his views along with the political situation. I encountered him on *Stroitel'naya gazeta*, in *Trud* and on television, I came across him a lot. Maybe circumstances forced him to change, maybe he himself didn't resist, maybe he's been blamed for too much now that he's fallen. He can be judged in different ways as a person or as a politician, but nobody who has ever worked with him will deny that he was a true professional.

JM: You mean he was easy to work with?

MShch: It was very easy to work with him. As a professional, he was a very talented journalist. Nobody would dare, or if they did, they'd be lying, he was without doubt a true professional. A good newspaper editor, a good organizer in television. That can't be taken away from him.

JM: And what about Chikin?

MShch: Well, I never worked with Chikin, maybe it's just as well because ...

JM: Was he a good editor?

MShch: He was unquestionably a talented editor. During the heyday of *Sovetskaya Rossiya* at the end of the seventies, when it really was the best newspaper in the country, the avant-garde of Soviet journalism, Chikin was first deputy editor of *Sovetskaya Rossiya*, Nenashev was editor. Nenashev was a very gifted organizer, but he was never a journalist, and you need a professional to get a newspaper out, and Chikin was the one who got the paper out. And *Sovetskaya Rossiya* at that time was an excellent newspaper, for the time it was an extremely left-radical newspaper, it was for the time a fantastically daring newspaper.

JM: What was considered radical at that time?

MShch: Well, first of all they sort of distorted the party line, in so far as they were able to do so. Which meant that the strict instructions they were given, well, under different pretexts they distorted them, adapted them to the situation. Nenashev was a brave editor and a real leader. He was not one to be easily controlled. He

3 Both prominent conservative figures in the later *glasnost'* years. See above, pp.186–7.

wasn't the type of editor who responded to the telephone call from the special line telling him off or telling him to do this or that. He was a genuine editor. That's the sort of editor he was, a genuine politician. Chikin, on the other hand, as the journalist, made sure that all the articles were up to standard, that they had taken everything into account. It was a very daring paper for the time. You couldn't say it was objective, because that was just impossible at that time. But there is no question but that *Sovetskaya Rossiya* was ahead of all the rest in terms of content.

JM: Within certain constraints, you mean.

MShch: Yes. It's like a man sitting in a cage. As Yury Lyubimov,[4] a good friend of mine, put it when he was made artistic director of the Old Theatre on the Taganka, it was just four walls, it used to be a cinema. But, he said, when you start out with nothing, that's when the imagination begins to work. It was exactly the same with *Sovetskaya Rossiya*. They were always working within difficult constraints, but they found ways of working through them. They were very original in terms of the lay-out. They personified the newspaper. Their articles weren't by-lined by faceless names, they introduced their special correspondents to the readers. They'd say this is so and so and this is his view. That's why you find articles by-lined not P. Ivanov, but Pyotr Ivanov, for example. They personified the paper, they showed the reader their journalists. Then they had a column called the 'The Commentator's platform'. What I'm saying is that they were innovative in form. And very successful in this. They had articles on things that had never been written about before, absolutely original, anything from the existence of paid applauders at the Bolshoi theatre, to articles dealing with very serious political and economic questions. It was a newspaper for ... it wasn't written for the working class, it wasn't like *Trud*.

JM: And what was *Trud* like as a paper? Who was it aimed at?

MShch: Trud had a very definite readership in mind: the working class. It always had, still has and always will aim for that readership.

---

4 Artistic director of the Taganka Theatre, the most radical and daring theatre during the latter years of the Brezhnev era.

JM: And was that evident in the type of language in which it was written?

MShch: Very noticeably. The language was simplified to the limit, as were the ideas expressed in it. In one way that's not a bad thing for the journalist, when you reduce all your thoughts to one simple formulation, it's a form of training the brain. But in *Trud* you have to do that all the time. It's one thing when you have a complex and profound idea or thought which you express in simple terms, but quite another when you start out with a simple thought which you express in simple language, such as 'It is dangerous to bathe in cold water', then it's not as stimulating. So, *Trud* has its own specific audience. The paper is changing because of economic pressures. Its circulation is dropping, it had a fantastic circulation of ten million, now it's down to six, I think, but the readership is the same as before. It's the working class, and exclusively the working class, who continue to read *Trud*.

JM: Why has there been a drop in newspaper sales in general?

MShch: When the reins were slackened, when the paper producers, printers and distributors, that is, the ministry for communications, were made independent, they immediately took advantage of their freedom. Prices literally rocketed. All newspapers were shaken to their foundations. All newspapers, even papers that take a lot of advertising, take *Izvestiya* for example – they carry an enormous amount of advertising, including whole blocks from Germany – but the ads are a long long way from covering the cost of producing the paper. Even *Komsomol'skaya pravda*, a newspaper with a huge circulation, their advertising income doesn't cover the cost of printing and distributing so many copies. It's a paradox, because the higher the newspaper's circulation, the more popular it is, the closer it is to economic ruin.

JM: And is there an optimal circulation?

MShch. Yes, I suppose there is. I couldn't say what it is exactly. It's one thing for a city newspaper, another for an all-Union paper, because the city paper has much lower distribution costs, while an all-Union newspaper has to be dragged around the whole country, their situations are different.

JM: So that it would be easier for *Moskovskii komsomolets* [a city paper] to survive economically than, say, *Komsomol'skaya pravda* [a national paper].

MShch: Yes, much easier. *Moskovskii komsomolets* usually get a bunch of kids to sell their newspaper around the city, and those kids are very effective in selling the papers on every corner. That's an alternative form of distribution because it's very difficult to work with the ministry of communications, and that's why a lot of papers bypass them, or at least partially bypass them, especially the city newspapers. Though for all-Union newspapers it's impossible to organize the distribution of a newspaper without them because the entire system is operated by the ministry alone. When they hike up the price for delivery, all the newspapers quake, all the commercial directors are screaming because advertising doesn't cover the paper's costs, though advertising rates have also risen steeply. But as regards an optimum circulation, for a city newspaper I'd say somewhere around 150,000, or 100,000. From 100,000 to 200,000. Any higher than that and you have difficulties; 100,000, 120,000, 150,000 – anywhere around there would be fine, but *Moskovskii komsomolets* has a circulation of about two million, maybe even more. It's a very popular newspaper.

JM: Which is the most left-wing and which the most right-wing newspaper at the moment?

MShch: It's difficult to talk about the most left-wing or right-wing newspaper because there are so many newspapers at the moment. But I suppose you could say that the most extreme right-wing newspaper is *Den'*. But having said that there are lots more idiotic newspapers on sale representing this or that patriotic group, and which are much more right-wing than *Den'*. Papers that have for a long time been shouting for all and sundry to be executed. But these papers don't count, if you're talking about papers that are more or less generally well-known, then the most right-wing newspaper would be *Den'*. As for left-wing newspapers, it's very difficult to say.

JM: What about objective newspapers, ones that don't follow any political line?

MShch: You mean papers that give information without comment?
I don't think such papers exist. I doubt whether there could ever
be papers like that. If the staff at a newspaper are a unit, then
whether they intend to or not, they will have some sort of political line. I don't think you would find such a huge difference in
viewpoint between extreme left and right in Ireland, or elsewhere in Europe, for that matter, as we have in Russia. Or if you
look at America, someone who wasn't educated in American
politics wouldn't be able to distinguish between a Republican and
Democrat. In Russia the difference between left and right is
colossal so that in the first place it's impossible to take a middle,
purely objective line, and secondly, if you did try to take an
objective line then you'd be attacked from the right and the left
and you'd become an insignificance. That's what happened with
Gorbachev, at least in his statements, he tried unsuccessfully to
steer a middle line. It's not working for Yeltsin either. The gale on
that ocean is too violent at the moment for objectivity.

JM: Do you think the new journalism has lost anything from the Soviet
school of journalism?

MShch: Yes, I think so. An awful lot has been lost. You have to
take into account that I haven't worked on a newspaper for three
years, I have friends in newspapers. I follow events. I have a
pretty good idea of what's going on in the newspaper business. It's
clear that they've moved away from the old forms and in some
ways have moved towards a Western approach, to a neutral form
of imparting information. I'd like to get back to the question of
taking a central, middle position. It's what the first [CIS] television channel tried, or is still trying, to do. After all the battles
between different [former] union republics about the future of the
old national Soviet television station, they all came to the
conclusion – it was Yegor Yakovlev[5] who negotiated this – that
they would keep the first channel, on condition that it held a
strictly neutral line. That it give out information and nothing more.
So that if, for example, there was a report on the war in Nagorny
Karabakh, you'd hear reports from the Armenian government

---

5   Former editor of *Moscow News* appointed head of Russian television after the August
1991 coup, removed by President Yeltsin in November 1992.

information agency and the Azerbaijani one, and on the question of who was right or wrong, of who was guilty in the conflict – that shouldn't be even hinted at, even as a subtext. The idea was that here we are giving you the information, assess it as you will. But I'm absolutely convinced that neither a newspaper nor a television channel is capable of that sort of objectivity. And I'll give you an example of this: the removal of Yegor Yakovlev for, in the words of Yeltsin, broadcasting incorrect information on the events in Northern Ossetia. It all depends on how you interpret things. If on one day you do a story that gives the point of view of Northern Ossetia, and do not give the Georgian position, then you are already being tendentious, or so it appears. So, there's a lot of specious reasoning in the objectivity argument. It's another question altogether whether or not Yakovlev was correct, but total objectivity is impossible.

A journalist is a living person. If he files a report from a place strewn with dead bodies stabbed with bayonets, where children or old people are dying, he can't just report it without any emotion, he wouldn't be a journalist. Just take a look at the work of Western journalists, educated to give facts and only facts, or so it appears. I see mainly *BBC* reports from Bosnia and I see that they also give an assessment of what they see, either through their intonation ... or simply by the camera showing the horrors of what's going on, the viewer's perspective is being shaped, so that there cannot be full objectivity. That was in answer to your earlier question. As regards the journalistic skills of today's journalists, the shift to an information-based approach has been, I would say, quite successful, journalists have learned how to change their way of thinking, they've put themselves into the minds of the readers who may well not be in the least interested in hearing my idiotic thoughts. The reader wants facts, give him facts, he's busy. The last thing he needs is some journalist he's never heard of pontificating about this or that. That sort of thing can be done over a bottle of vodka. The reader wants the facts and the facts to be explained and we must have learned something because that's what the best papers do now.

JM: Where did they learn how to do this?

MShch: Evidently from the Western press. That's my own view, because Soviet newspapers were very different from Western newpapers. I'm no expert on the Western press, but even at a glance the Western influence is clear, even in headlines. Before, you had a headline often with a subhead underneath and then the article. Now you have one long headline, 'Parliament demands such and such ... ', a headline five lines long. Before you would never have had headlines as long as that, it would never have occurred to anyone. The limit was five words. But now if you look at headlines in *Izvestiya* you see they carry the essence of the story. That, I think, has also come from Western practice. But that said, there continues to be a mix of the new Western style and the old style and there could be found here some sort of symbiosis, if the new style was used to improve what was good in Soviet journalism. This was *publitsistika*,[6] this form of writing was held in great esteem in journalism. The *publitsist* was treated as royalty of sorts. Even take our best reporters, they could take a simple event, a fire, an accident on a submarine, or whatever, and transform it so that it filled an entire page by looking at the event through the prism of their own ideas, by pondering it and examining it themselves.

JM: And how are the thick journals faring now?

MShch: I don't really know, but there is no doubt that their popularity has fallen drastically. During the heyday of *glasnost'* and *perestroika* we literally devoured journals and magazines, because they published things we knew nothing about, all our émigré literature and what had never been published here. All of this appeared in the journals and people simply read everything they could lay their hands on. You collected the journals to re-read them. Then, I suppose, a process of saturation set in, on the one hand, and, on the other, all the best things that could be shown to the public had been published, for example Grossman, Nabokov – I'm just naming a few at random – nearly all of Solzhenitsyn, Vladimov. Many more writers were published that I just can't recall at the moment.

JM: Could you say a few words about the Union of Journalists?

6 Long discursive essays commenting on public affairs.

MShch: This is just my own opinion.

JM: I understand.

MShch: For me personally the Union of Journalists is, how can I put it, unnecessary. The House of the Journalist[7] is necessary. I like it, it serves as a club for us. It's where we meet, where you meet old friends who are glad to see you, where you can have a drink and a chat with friends, it's all very pleasant.

JM: And what about before, under Brezhnev. What was the union like then?

MShch: The union was of course, well, in the first place it organized courses for improving journalists' qualifications. For example as a young journalist I took part in meetings twice a year between young journalists, young talented journalists from all parts of the Soviet Union. There were seminars, we studied the classics in journalism, wrote things, exchanged views and so forth. The union did have a function as a creative centre, a creative trade union. And maybe it still is and I'm just not aware of it, they always have some sorts of posters hanging there, though I think that if something interesting was going on I'd have heard about it from someone or through someone. The economic situation of the union is also not the best. They have problems in dividing up the property of the union: what belongs to the Moscow branch, what to the Russian organization, or to the Soviet organization. That all happened when the union split up. They have a new Journalist's Day, 5 May. It commemorates the publication of the first Russian newspaper, not *Iskra* or *Pravda*, but the first in Russian history.

JM: And what do you think of the Law on the Press? Was it considered a good law when it was passed in 1990?

MShch: Yes, it was considered a good law. That, at least, was the view among journalists, if only it was applied. The important thing is to be able to apply the law.

JM: It abolished the official censorship agency.

MShch: That's true. *Glavlit* does not interfere with newspapers. It really has ceased to exist. Before, when we were putting out a paper, we had to drag every page to the *Glavlit* room in the

---

7 *Dom zhurnalista*, the headquarters of the union.

building and they came back with indications that this and that and the other could not be printed. But *Glavlit* had grown weaker itself over the years. At the beginning it was concerned with, I think, purely political censorship. Subsequently they interfered less and less, they looked out for military secrets, but in this sense *Glavlit* was a help to editors in some ways. How could they know whether to name such and such a factory a reporter might have mentioned? *Glavlit*'s job was to make sure things didn't slip through. The censor was supposed not to interfere with the editor, only to guard secrets. Now I think they've even stopped guarding secrets. I don't know whether there are many secrets eft.

JM: Do newspapers have the same fear as in Ireland of losing large amounts of money in the courts in libel and slander cases?

MShch: There is I think, I don't really know the law well, but there is an article dealing with liability for libelling someone. But in the first place I don't know what is considered libellous in our legislation and I have no recollection of any newspaper, or anyone at all, ever being brought to court for libel. But if someone punches you in the face on the street, for that you can still prosecute, then you can bring someone to court if you catch them, if they come. But as regards libel, well, all I'm aware of are protests, threats that 'I'll bring you to court for libel', but I have no recollection of a case ever having been successfully prosecuted in court.

JM: And what about the article in the law that obliges civil servants to answer journalists' enquiries?

MShch: John, I'm afraid of being inaccurate here.

JM: I'm just interested in your perception.

MShch: I'm not sure how this is expressed in the law, but what I can say, and this is no secret, there were a whole series of stories on the subject of how government officials demanded payment in hard currency for giving out information.

JM: Was it only of Western journalists that they demanded hard currency?

MShch: Well, if they asked us for hard currency, well, I know the Russian language quite well, I think I'd find the appropriate words to respond to the person who asked me for hard currency. But the situation before was like this. If I did an interview, then I would get the fee for the interview. That's our system, a small salary and a small fee for articles published, here you only have a salary, but a good salary. But before I would always share the fee with the person I interviewed. If that person gave me a good, honest and frank interview, I would give that person half the fee, since he gave up his time to me and told me lots of things I didn't know about before. This was done a lot and I think it was a sign of good manners. The person never demanded money, you just went to the person with the money. They were grateful for the money and thought, yes, this journalist has acted in a gentlemanly fashion. Now it's different. Those being interviewed say 'Yes, I'll give you an interview. How much will you give me for it?' Maybe that's the way it should be done, I wouldn't want to judge. Lyubimov told me a story once. A journalist wanted to interview him. Lyubimov said 'fine, how much?'. The journalist said 'well, you understand, we don't have much money, we're a poor paper.' Lyubimov said 'that's fine, that's your problem, I won't be giving you an interview then.' Maybe he was making it up, I don't know. But you know, John, I really don't know what's right in these situations. Maybe it's right to ask for money, it's a way of giving value to your labour. As for government officials asking for hard currency from Western journalists for giving interviews – well ...

JM: I think the Japanese had the largest budgets and got the biggest stories.

MShch: Yes, they spent a lot. The prosecutor general, [Valentin] Stepankov, was accused of demanding money, but I don't know all the details, whether he was asking for money for himself, or whether he was going to share it with his staff. These are two different things. Maybe if he revealed some secret or other he's entitled to get something.

JM: The whole thing was a little shocking in the West because here government officials as a rule do not receive money for giving interviews.

MShch: I understand but, you see, you have to see the other side of the argument as well. I don't really think that Stepankov would have risked his reputation by asking for money the way it was reported in the West. I think there must have been something else happening. I think some journalist must have twisted the story to make a sensation out of it. That's also a possibility, you'll agree. It's unthinkable that the prosecutor general – whose every move is being scrutinized by every pair of binoculars in the country in connection with the 1991 coup – it's just not possible that he'd do something that would risk his position. But I don't really know whether the Law on the Press deals with situations such as this.

JM: I was just interested in your views on the law.

MShch: Well, you know as well as I do that journalism is a profession based a lot on gossip so that it's not always possible to believe what a journlist says.

I'd like to return to what we talked about yesterday, about how Russian journalism has abandoned its traditions and moved in the direction of Western journalism. Well, I would say that it has reached a middle point. A lot of what was good in the *publitsistika* tradition has been lost, while it has not yet reached what would be considered the level of the best Western journalism, in the classical sense of the word. At this juncture there is a very clear problem emerging, that of journalists' professional standards. That's because a lot of journalists from the 1960s and the 1970s, experienced and talented journalists, are now leaving the scene for reasons of age or other reasons. But when they leave a newspaper it's very obvious how much more professional they were and how they were better journalists than those who are taking their place.

JM: But are their traditions not being handed on to the younger journalists?

MShch: It is possible to pass on a tradition, but the thing is that these people who are leaving the profession were not only talented writers themselves, but they were the bearers of a school. They had received solid professional training, in spite of all the pressures put on journalists, in spite of all the complications they came up against in questions of politics, or when the regime became more repressive, or without freedom of speech. In spite of all this when pressure was exerted upon them they fought back.

In the process they became good professional journalists. They were real journalists. They knew how to write an article, they could look at an article and point out precisely what was needed here, here and here, put questions in the margins, make the reporter rewrite the piece. Sometimes when he'd have had enough of correcting an article, he'd rewrite the piece himself. So that these people, and there weren't that many of them, were very good journalists. This was the generation of the 1960s, the time of Khrushchev's thaw. At that time there appeared a circle of very talented commentators [*publitsisty*] and these are the people who are now leaving journalism and their replacements are quite clearly far less gifted writers. And those who come after their replacements are even poorer journalists. That's why the papers are having problems with editors, not reporters, but editors, that is the editor, the deputy editor, the news editor [*otvetsvenny sekretar'*], the members of the editorial board, heads of departments. This is by far the most vulnerable place of today's press. Because those now occupying these positions are not up to the demands of the job in the same way as their predecessors.

JM: What exactly is a news editor [*otvetsvenny sekretar'*] in the Russian sense?

MShch: Well, it's a good example of a position that shows how standards have gone down. Because a genuine news editor is in essence the paper's editor. In essence he is the number two in the newspaper. You have the editor who was traditionally concerned with, well he did contribute in a small way to putting out the paper, but his real job was to make sure everything was in order with the political leadership. It was he who set out the general guidelines of how the staff conducted themselves. But it was the news editor who actually got the paper out. He worked with the reporters, compositors, decided what was going into the paper a week or a month ahead. He was the paper's strategist and tactician at the same time. He was the mainstay of the whole paper. And that was precisely what that job was understood to be. The news editor checked all stories. We had the following system. I was a special correspondent. I had my own direct department head. I give my piece to him, he may make some corrections or hand it back to me or throw it in the wastepaper bin, he signs the piece and sends it on to the news editor's department [*sekretariat*], the – since the language was militarized – the headquarters. There all the stories would be gathered. People would go to the news editor with ideas for stories. Newspaper campaigns or special topics would be initiated from the news editor's department. But your story would eventually end up on the desk of the news editor or his deputy and his decision to publish or not would be final. He could make corrections, edit it down or throw it into the bin or say it was unsuitable, go back and rewrite it, go back and finish it off properly, whatever. So that the real productive power in the newspaper was in the hands of the news editor. The creative side of the newspaper, and not only that. It was the news editor's department that took care of the production side, that is the composition and layout of the paper, the link with the printers. In other words everything that went into getting a paper ready before printing was the job of the news editor's department. And it was always considered that the news editor should be someone who only second of all should understand the production and technical side of the paper, but should primarily be a thinker, a journalist that the paper trusts, because he had the right to reject a piece. And as well as obeying the news editor as a matter of duty, I [the journalist] should understand that this person was more qualified than me, and that if he handed me back a piece and explained what was wrong with it, then I should agree with his opinion. Because I recognize his authority. His professional authority.

Now, that generation of news editors who were capable of doing all that is leaving journalism. And in their place are coming people who [only] understand the production end of the paper: how to lay out the page, how to shorten or lengthen a piece, how to switch articles from page one to page five, how to make headlines and so on. It's at this level that news editors now work. They no longer participate in the politics of the paper, they are no longer strategists or thinkers. They are basically technicians. So that the essence of the job has changed. And this change says a lot. There are very good newspaper technicians, so to speak, but nevertheless this is a different understanding of the profession. Those lucky enough to come into contact with the good journalists from the old school ... I was fortunate to have worked with somebody like this for a year, if I know anything about journalism, then it's thanks to him. I worked with him when I began with *Stroitel'naya gazeta*. He had worked in *Novy mir* under Tvardovskii, he was a real old hardened journalist who'd been through the wars. He'd received admonishments from the party, he'd been fired for political mistakes. I worked with him for a year and what he managed to impart to me is what I live by to this day. Those who managed to come into contact with people like him have picked up something. The next generation will get less, the next, less again. I don't know and I may well be mistaken, but I suspect that the present generation of young journalists are worse off, because their teachers were less able than, say, my teachers. But I was also unlucky, because the generation that came before me was more fortunate than I was. And my impression is that the standard is dropping.

And another thing, the old journalism – for all its being stagnant – respected a certain hierarchy in journalism. It was clear that maybe an editor could be a fool, because the editors were appointed by, well you know by whom. The editors could make mistakes, they could be totally unsuited to the profession, and more often than not they were people who had no relation to journalism whatsoever, in the same way as our culture was administered by chemists and agricultural specialists. In the same way people who were completely untrained for the job were appointed editors to newspapers. If you got a good editor, like Nenashev, you thanked your lucky stars. He's not a journalist, but a very creative and intelligent person, a good organizer and true to his political convictions. Nenashev, he used to be editor of *Sovetskaya Rossiya*, he never compromised his views, and to this day he's held in esteem, in spite of his having been in charge of the television – he was there before Kravchenko – he was lambasted by the deputies in parliament, but he remains an absolutely uncompromised figure. He's untainted and respected, and even the left-wing *Ogonyok* can publish an interview with him as a figure worthy of respect. You can agree or disagree with him, but he never tainted himself, we respect him. But if you had the wrong sort of editor, then the deputy editor, the news editor had to be a professional.

JM: And how did you work under the pressures that existed? If, for example, in *Trud*, you wanted to cover a strike, I suppose that was not allowed.

MShch: That depends on what period you're talking about. If you're talking about the pre-Gorbachev years, then, to begin with, there were no strikes. Secondly, if somewhere there were attempts at going out on strike, then these attempts were usually stamped out there and then, where they occurred.

JM: So you would never have got to hear about it?

MShch: That's right. For that, there were strong provincial party committees, with their own methods of work, and they ... but I'm not actually aware that there were ever any attempts at going on strike, because everyone was perfectly aware that if one person rocked the boat, means would be found to calm him down. They'd use the stick or the carrot, their methods were well known. Maybe there were strikes, it's just that I never heard of any. And even if there had been a strike people would never have learned about it through the press.

JM: Was the provincial press always weaker than the national press?

MShch: That's hard to say, there were some very good regional newspapers.

JM: I mean were they more vulnerable to local pressures than the national press?

MShch: The principle here was, the smaller the area, the more the papers suffered from local pressure from the authorities. The papers that suffered most were probably those that were in some small provincial town where some petty tyrant ruled, the chairman of the town executive committee or the party first secretary. He could do with the newspapers whatever he wanted. Journalists who tried to do something different were simply crushed, they had no prospects at all.

JM: And the national press was in this respect stronger.

MShch: Yes, they were stronger. If pressure was applied to them, then it wasn't in the same direct, blunt way as could be done in some little town somewhere in the provinces. Here, too, there always were people whose job it was to monitor the press, to apply pressure on editors. Editors were fired, they were beaten up, but they would never do what they did to journalists in the small country papers. There, they made very short shrift of them, they chopped their heads off and that was that. And you can understand the position of the journalist sitting in the offices of a small town paper. Thrown out of work tomorrow, he'd have no chance of finding another job. In Moscow it was different. If you were fired, or given a party reprimand, then some newspaper or editor would give you a job. And when Kravchenko was modernizing *Stroitel'naya gazeta*, he needed a team of good journalists. The staff there were not very good, they knew about construction, but they weren't good journalists. He needed journalists, because he wanted to transform a departmental news-sheet into a national newspaper. But who would want to work with *Stroitel'naya gazeta*? The paper didn't have much of a reputation. That was why he relied on two categories of journalist. Either on young journalists, just starting out – I was in this category at the time – or on journalists who had suffered in some way, who had received party reprimands. He employed them and they worked wonderfully. So, he joined up young journalists with older, experienced journalists who had got into trouble with the authorities and who had been fired from other papers, and who needed a place to work for a couple of years, and for a few years we had a very good set of writers. Kravchenko made the right decisions for the time. Later on the journalists who had been sacked left the paper and joined the bigger papers, and the younger ones did the same. That's when the paper began to decline and it proved impossible to halt its decline.

I'm telling you all of this by way of explaining to you that if before the editorial staff of a newspaper – if not necessarily the editor – had to be professionals, now, well, what with the huge number of newspapers that have appeared, and taking into account my total confusion as a reader ... I don't know, but every day I see new papers appearing. I don't buy them, I'm not really interested in them, especially when 90 per cent of them give exactly the same information. I don't even know how they manage to find so many people to write these papers. They say journalists are threatened with unemployment: I don't think they are at all. They said there was no paper in the country. There may be no paper but there are literally hordes of newspapers appearing all the time. Plus a pile of absolutely idiotic publications – all printed on newsprint – anything from patriotic papers to pornographic magazines to magazines on eastern mysticism, so that there's enough of everything. The danger, you see, is that, before, journalists were afraid of losing their job, because there were only about ten or so big newspapers, everyone knew one another, so that if you did something ... that made you look bad, then everyone would know about it very quickly. Now you have a situation where someone unable to write a news brief is an editor. It should be obvious what sort of paper he's editor of and what sort of editor he is. Though, on the other hand, the paper exists, comes out regularly; people are paid a salary, they sell papers, they sell advertising space.

You may think that this is all sounding like nostalgia, but in fact there is a lot of good in the current state of affairs, because now, having plunged into this absolute freedom, the newspapers have to do everything from scratch. Now the newspapers have to earn money. You have to in order to have a newspaper. Anyone has the right to go to the ministry of the press and register and found their own newspaper. If you're capable of running a newspaper, go right ahead, there's nobody stopping you. Write what you want, find your reader, there's nothing stopping you. If the intelligent young journalists that are around at the moment – the likes of Ostal'skii or Sokolov[8] – if they succeed – even in the situation of saturation we have at the moment – in setting up a new paper, you see they intend to set up a good paper which people are going to read. They are professionals. When *Kuranty* [Chimes], *Megapolis ekspress*, *Nezavisimaya gazeta* were set up, that was a different time. When my friend the editor of *Megapolis ekspress* set up the

---

8 Dmitry Ostal'skii, formerly news editor of *Nezavisimaya gazeta*, and Maksim Sokolov, formerly political commentator of *Kommersant*. Both joined *Segodnya (Today)*, founded in 1993, Ostal'skii as editor.

paper three years ago, I remember asking him what the point was. He agreed but said he'd have a go anyway, even though we both agreed that the niches were occupied. If I'd known then that there was going to be such a vast number of new publications! There are no niche markets: people enter the marketplace when and where they please. There is a positive side to all of this: journalists are becoming organizers. Maybe you're a terrible journalist but a good organizer. If so, then go ahead and call yourself an editor, go and employ a good, professional deputy editor, pay him good money and he'll give you a good paper. You can sit there and watch the money coming in. I'm sad about this, maybe because of old age, maybe because at one time journalism seemed to me an attractive profession, and it doesn't any longer. And it's now next to impossible to make a name for yourself as a journalist. Precisely because of the superfluity of newspapers, you won't be noticed. If before everything was level and five heads stood out, now everything is so hazy and unclear. Well, I think I've talked enough nonsense to you.

Appendix: Circulation of the press

The following table gives the circulation in millions of the main national newspapers for 1987, 1988 and 1989 as reported in *The USSR Yearbook '88* (1988, p.263), *'89* (1989, p.270) and *'90* (1990, p.201):

	1987	*1988*	*1989*
Trud	18.2	19.6	19.8
Komsomol'skaya pravda	17.0	17.6	17.6
Izvestiya	8.0	10.0	10.1
Pravda	11.3	9.7	9.7
Sel'skaya zhizn'	8.7	8.6	6.6
Sovetskaya Rossiya	4.4	5.3	4.2
Literaturnaya gazeta	3.1	6.2	6.3

The reliability of these figures, however, is questionable. The figures given in each yearbook for the circulation of newspapers for the preceding years show large discrepancies. For instance, the 1990 yearbook gives the following figures for the circulations of the same newspapers listed above:

	1987	*1988*
Trud	18.2	19.0
Komsomol'skaya pravda	17.0	17.6
Izvestiya	8.0	10.4
Pravda	11.1	10.7
Sel'skaya zhizn'	8.8	7.5
Sovetskaya Rossiya	4.6	5.2
Literaturnaya gazeta	3.1	3.8

Circulation figures for 1991 compared to 1990 are given in *Newspaper Focus* (Simpson, 1991, p. 11):

	Circulation early 1991	Change since 1990 (per cent)
Trud	18,600,000	−7.6
Komsomol'skaya pravda	16,850,000	−20.5
Sel'skaya zhizn'	5,772,000	−12.5
Sovetskii sport	5,500,000	+19.6
Izvestiya	4,700,000	−50.5
Pravda	3,000,000	−53.8
Moskovskii komsomolets	1,556,000	NA
Krasnaya zvezda	1,000,000	−54.5
Moskovskaya pravda	700,000	NA

The first four titles in this table were the four top-selling daily (hence the omission of the weekly *Argumenty i fakty*) newspapers in Europe, according to Simpson's list of Europe's top 200 newspapers.

Compare the following table of subscriptions for daily and weekly publications with that published in *Kommersant*, 1991:

	Subscriptions for 1991	Subscriptions for 1992
Argumenty i fakty	23,840,000	22,599,000
Trud	18,292,000	12,320,000
Izvestiya	3,873,000	2,781,000
Megapolis Ekspress	93,000	1,600,000
Ogonyok	1,723,000	1,492,000
Moskovskii komsomolets	1,538,000	1,338,000
Pravda	2,221,000	874,000
Sovetskaya Rossiya	1,321,000	780,000
Ekonomika i zhizn'	515,000	585,000
Rossiiskaya gazeta	252,000	577,000
Moskovskie novosti	1,297,000	337,000
Kommersant	113,000	220,000
Nedelya	76,000	70,000
Nezavisimaya gazeta	no subscriptions taken	64,000

The following table of circulation figures in millions for 1992–93 is made up of statistics from *L'Express*, 25 February 1993 (E), and Radio Free Europe/Radio Liberty Research Report, 28 February 1992, p.55. The *L'Express* figures are the number of issues sold by subscription, as are the RL/RFE figures. There is a discrepancy between the RL/RFE and *L'Express* figures for *Izvestiya*. See also McKay, 1992, p.14, who says that 80 per cent of the 3.8m. figure went to subscribers, giving a figure of 3,040,000 subscriptions.

	1992	1993
Pravda	1.4 (RL)	0.47 (E)
Izvestiya	3.0 (E); 3.8 (RL)	0.8 (E)
Trud	4.3 (RL)	2.0 (E)
Komsomol'skaya pravda	12.0 (E)	1.8 (E)
Sovetskii sport	NA	0.49 (E)
Argumenty i fakty	25.0 (E)	8.9 (E)
Spid-Info	NA	2.7 (E)

The following table is composed of sections of the above data. Because of the different ways in which the figures were arrived at, the table should be seen as a more or less accurate general illustration of the rise and decline in circulation figures (in millions) of four of the country's leading mass circulation newspapers since 1987.

	1987	1988	1989	1990	1991	1992	1993
Pravda	11.3	9.7	9.7	4.6	3.0	1.4	0.47
Izvestiya	8.0	10.0	10.1	7.0	4.7	3.8	0.8
Trud	18.2	19.6	19.8	20.0	18.6	4.3	2.0
Koms. pravda	17.0	17.6	17.6	20.0	16.8	12.0	1.8

References

Adzhubei, Alexei (1988), 'Te desyat' let (Vospominaniya)' (Those ten years (Reminiscences)), *Znamya*, N° 6, pp.81–123 and N° 7, pp.80–133.

Afanas'ev, Viktor G. (1977), 'O rabote Soyuza zhurnalistov i zadachakh sovetskoi zhurnalistiki v svete reshenii XXV s"ezda KPSS (IV s"ezd Soyuza zhurnalistov SSSR)' (On the work and tasks of the Union of journalists in light of the decisions of the XXV congress of the CPSU (IV congress of the Union of journalists of the USSR), *Zhurnalist*, N° 4, pp.4–12.

— (1986), 'Segodnyashnii nomer gazety' (Today's issue of the newspaper), *Zhurnalist*, N° 5, pp.2–4.

Afanas'ev, Yurii (1988), 'Perestroika i istoricheskoe znanie' (*Perestroika* and historical knowledge), in Yu. Afanas'ev (ed.), *Inogo ne dano* (No other choice), Progress, Moscow, pp.491–506.

Agishev, Nina (1987), '"Poteryannoe" pokolenie' (The 'lost' generation), *Moskovskie novosti*, 6 September, p.3.

Aksyutin, Yu. (1989), 'Khrushchev against Stalin', *Nikita Khrushchev, Life and Destiny*, Novosti, Moscow, pp.14–18.

Amlinskii, Vladimir (1988), 'Ten"' (Shadow), *Literaturnaya gazeta*, 7 August, p.12.

Anan'ev, A.A. (1987), 'A chto u vas?' (And what about you?), *Literaturnaya gazeta*, 16 September, p.7.

Andreeva, Nina (1988), 'Ne mogu postupat'sya printsipami' (I cannot forgo my principles), *Sovetskaya Rossiya*, 13 March, p.3.

Andrew, Christopher and Oleg Gordievsky (1990), *KGB. The inside story of its foreign operations from Lenin to Gorbachev*, Hodder & Stoughton, London.

Barsht, Konstantin (1990), 'Ot glasnosti k svobode slova' (From *glasnost'* to freedom of speech), *Ogonyok*, N° 10, pp.23–5.

Bestuzhev-Lada, Igor' (1988), 'Pravdu i tol'ko pravdu' (The truth and nothing but the truth), *Nedelya*, N° 5, pp.14–15.

Bivon, Roy (1971), '*Element Order: Studies in the Modern Russian Language*', N° 7, Cambridge University Press, Cambridge.

Boulton, Leyla (1991), 'Soviet journalists fight off attacks without weapons', *Financial Times*, 31 January, p.3.

Bovin, Alexander (1987), 'Net nichego trudnee etogo' (There's nothing more difficult than this), Alexander Bovin, Valentin Zorin and Yegor Yakovlev interviewed by Galina Nikulina, *Ogonyok*, N° 34, pp.4–5.

— (1989), 'Glasnost' – vozdukh perestroiki' (*Glasnost'* – the air of *perestroika*), *Moskovskie novosti*, 5 March, p.12.

Brown, Kathryn (1992), 'The Russian Media Defend Their Independence', *RFE/RL Research Report*, Vol. 1, N° 35, 4 September, pp.45–51.

Burlatskii, Fedor (1989a), 'Khrushchev: Strokes on a Political Portrait', in *Soviet Historians and Perestroika: The First Phase*, edited by Donald J. Raleigh, Sharpe, Armonk, NY, pp.228–40.

— (1989b), 'Brezhnev and the End of the Thaw', in *Leonid Brezhnev: The Period of Stagnation*, pp.34–46, Novosti, Moscow.

— (1991), *Khrushchev and the First Russian Spring*, translated by Daphne Skillen, Weidenfeld & Nicolson, London.

Burtin, Yury (1987), 'Vam iz drugogo pokoleniya' (To you from another generation), *Oktyabr'*, N° 8, pp.191–202.

Chegodaeva, Mariya (1989), 'Neissyakaemy istochnik vdokhnoveniya. Po stranitsam odnogo zhurnala (Iskusstvo, 1950)' (Inexhaustible well of inspiration: From the pages of a journal (*Isskustvo*, 1950)), *Moskovskie novosti*, 26 February.

Chikin, V. (1988), 'Otvetstvennost' i kompetentnost' zhurnalista (doklad v sokrashchenii)' (Responsibility and journalistic competence (summary of speech), *Zhurnalistskie novosti*, N° 1, p.2.

Chudakov, Grigory (1988), 'Dialog o problemnom reportazhe' (Dialogue on problematic photoreportage), *Sovetskoe foto*, N° 1, pp.16–19.

Churchward, L.G. (1975), *Contemporary Soviet Government*, Routledge & Kegan Paul, London.

Cohen, Stephen and Katrina vanden Heuval (1989), *Voices of Glasnost: Interviews with Gorbachev's Reformers*, Norton, New York and London.

Comrie, Bernard and Gerald Stone (1978), *Russian Language since the Revolution*, Oxford University Press, Oxford.

Conquest, Robert (1965), *Russia after Khrushchev*, Pall Mall Press, London.

Cornwell, Rupert (1990a), 'Slow shift of power in the Politburo', *The Independent*, 7 February, p.11.

— (1990b), 'Capitalism can be as unkind as the censor', *The Independent*, 17 August, p.9.

Daly, Conor (1988), '*Glasnost* warms Soviet view of US elections', *The Daily Californian*, 4 April, p.4.

Djilas, Milovan (1963), *Conversations with Stalin*, Penguin, London.

Dobbs, Michael (1990), 'Soviet censors go, but advice is for hire', *International Herald Tribune*, 2 August, p.1.

Dogovor (1991), 'Dogovor ob obrazovanii soyuza zhurnalistov na konfederativnoi osnove' (Agreement on the formation of the Union of journalists on a confederative basis), *Zhurnalist*, N° 4, pp.2–3.

Dovlatov, Sergei (1983), *Compromise*, translated by Anne Frydman, Hogarth Press, London.

D'yachenko, Viktor (1987), 'Okromya yavlenii schast'ya...' (Apart from happy events...), *Zhurnalist*, N° 12, pp.7–9.

Dzhirkvelov, Ilya (1987), *Secret Servant*, Collins, London.

Economist (1988a), 'It's war', 30 April, pp.23–4.

— (1988b), 'Man of Letters', 7 May, p.24.

— (1988c), 'A guide to glasnost', 6 July, pp.18–19.

— (1989), 'The party loses its grip', 5 August, pp.19–20.

Fedotov, Mikhail (1991), 'Tsenzura nikogda ne izchezala' (Censorship never disappeared), *Moskovskie novosti*, 10 February, p.8.

Financial Times (1992), 'FT and Izvestia in joint publishing deal', 28 July, p.4.

Gambrell, Jamey (1992), 'Moscow: The Front Page', *The New York Review of Books*, 8 October, pp.56–62.

Ginzburg, Yevgeniya (1988), 'Krutoi marshrut. Khronika vremyon kul'ta lichnosti' (Reap the whirlwind: Chronicle from the times of the personality cult), extract published in *Yunost'*, N° 9, pp.35–67.

Golovskoy, Valery S. (1985), *Is there censorship in the Soviet Union? Methodological problems of studying Soviet censorship*, Keenan Institute for Advanced Russian Studies, Occasional paper N° 201, Smithsonian Institution Building, Washington DC.

Gorbachev, M.S. (1988a), 'Speech to 19th Party Conference', quoted in *Time*, 11 July, p.8.

— (1988b), 'Speech to commemorate 70th anniversary of October 1917 revolution', printed in all national dailies, 4 November.

— (1991), *The August Coup*, Harper–Collins, London.

Goryaeva, T.M. (1990), 'Zhurnalistika i tsenzura' (Journalism and censorship), *Istoriya SSSR*, N° 4, pp.112–23.

Gostyushin, Anatoly (1989), 'Vniz po kanalu imeni Stalina' (Down the Stalin canal), *Moskovskie novosti*, 5 March, p.16.

Groys, Boris (1983), 'Schweigen ist Gold. Zur Sprache der *Prawda*' (Silence is golden: On the language of *Pravda*), *Süddeutsche Zeitung*, 15 January, p.112.

Guardian (1991), 'Bugging equipment found above Yeltsin's office', 8 February, p.9.

Guardian Weekly (1988), 'A clean sweep by Mr Gorbachev', week ending 9 October, p.1.

Guetta, Bernard (1988), 'Gorbachev plans press freedom – with strings', *Guardian Weekly*, week ending 13 November, p.13.

Gutionov, Pavel (1991), 'Khronika "obyavlennoi smerti"? Kak i pochemu razvivalsya konflikt v redaktsii Izvestii' (Chronicle of 'declared death'? How and why the conflict in *Izvestiya* developed), *Zhurnalist*, N° 9, pp.11–14.

Henry, Peter and Katya Young (1983), *Gazeta/Gazeta: Clippings from the Soviet Press*, Collets, Wellingborough.

Hill, Ronald J. (1985), *The Soviet Union: Politics, Economics and Society from Lenin to Gorbachev*, Pinter, London.

— (1989), *'Glasnost'* and Soviet politics', *Coexistence*, N° 26, pp.317–31.

— and Peter Frank (1986), *The Soviet Communist Party* (third edition), Allen & Unwin, London.

Hollander, Gayle Durham (1972), *Soviet Political Indoctrination*, Praeger, New York.

Hosking, Geoffrey (1992), *A History of the Soviet Union* (third and final edition), Fontana Press, London.

Hyland, William and Richard Wallace Shryock (1970), *The Fall of Khrushchev*, Pitman, London.

Ignatenko, V. (1992), 'Ne menyayu litso pod obstoyatel'stva' (I don't change faces according to circumstances), *Argumenty i fakty*, N° 29–30, p.2.

Irish Times (1988a), 'Newspapers reflecting information revolution', 18 July, p.7.

— (1988b), 'Gorbachev puts his stamp on streamlined new administration', 3 October p.10.

— (1988c), 'Soviet bureaucracy blamed for hindering rescue work', 20 December, p.9.

— (1989), 'Gorbachev Prepares Major Purge, Politburo member, Mr Yegor Ligachev,
called for more curbs on the media', 22 July, p.1.

— (1991), 'Gorbachev fails to win support for curbs on the press', 17 January, p.9.

Ivanov, Vyacheslav Vsevolodovich (1988), 'Natsiya. Yazyk. Literatura' (Nation. Language.
Literature), as member of round-table discussion-group, *Druzhba narodov*, N° 6,
pp.245–62.

Jacobssen, Goeran (1969), 'The Use of Gerunds and Active Participles in Modern Russian
newspapers', *Slavica Gothoburgensia*, N° 3, University of Gothenburg.

Johnstone, Monty (1987), 'Gorbachev's Thousand Days', *Australian Left Review*, Vol. 102,
pp.22–9.

Kabakov, Alexander (1988), 'Spetskhrana net. Chto est'?' (No restricted access section.
What is there?), *Moskovskie novosti*, 11 December, p.14.

— (1990), 'Journalisme affranchi ṛ ais impuissant' (Journalism liberated but powerless),
Les Nouvelles de Moscou, N° 32, p.3.

Kaiser Robert G. (1976), *Russia: The People and the Power*, Atheneum, New York.

Kapanadze, L. A. (1983), 'Leksiko-semanticheskie osobennosti razgovornoi rechi' (Lexico-
semantic peculiarities of conversational speech), in *Russkaya razgovornaya rech'*
(Russian conversational speech), edited by E.A. Zemskaya, pp.142–72, Nauka,
Moscow.

Karacs, Imre (1990), 'Gorbachev's glasnost cuts censors out of Soviet picture', *The Independent*, 2 August, p.8.

Karpenko, Igor' (1987), Personal communication, 15 October, Moscow.

Keller, Bill (1988), 'Kremlin Urges Market Reforms', *International Herald Tribune*,
6 October, p.1.

Khrushchev, Sergei (1991), *Pensioner soyuznogo znacheniya* (Pensioner of Union status),
Novosti, Moscow.

Knight, Andrew (1991), 'Gorbachev at bay: the grim view from his Kremlin cage', *The
Sunday Times*, 12 May, p.2.

Kommersant (1991), 'Podpiska na budushchii god: zachitaetsya' (Next year's subscriptions:
people becoming immersed in reading), N° 46, 25 November– 2 December, p.2.

Kondrashov, Stanislav (1989), 'Iz mraka neizvestnosti. Probleski glasnosti v tsarstve voen-
nykh tain' (From the murk of obscurity. Gleams of *glasnost'* in the kingdom of military
secrets), *Novy mir*, N° 8, pp.178–206.

Korneshov, L. (1987), '"Izvestiya" vchera, segodnya, zavtra' ("Izvestiya" yesterday, today,
tomorrow), *Rasprostranitel' pechati*, 3 March, pp.4–7.

Kozhemyako, Viktor (1986), 'Tak li govoryat nashi geroi?' (Do our heroes really speak like
that?), *Zhurnalist*, N° 1, pp.14–15.

Krivopalov, Alexander (1988), Personal communication, 12 July, Dublin.

Krylova, O. and S. Khavronina (1988), *Word Order in Russian*, Russkii Yazyk, Moscow.

Kryuchkov, Mikhail (1991), 'Gazetchiki po sovmestitel'stvu' (Journalists as well), *Moskovskie novosti*, 29 September, p.12.

Kuzichkin, Vladimir (1990), *Inside the KGB, Myth and Reality*, translated by Thomas Beattie, Andre Deutsch, London.

Lakshin, Vladimir (1987), 'Sovremennost' mysli. Tragedii i puti literaturnoi kritiki' (Contemporariness of thought: Tragedies and paths of literary criticism), *Moskovskie novosti*, 16 August, p.11.

Laptev, Ivan (1987), 'Gotovyas' k slavnomu yubileyu. Doklad' (In preparation for a glorious jubilee: Speech), *Zhurnalist*, N° 7, pp.1–4.

Lenin, Vladimir Ilyich (1972), *Lenin about the Press* (Quoted in McNair, 1991), International Organisation of Journalists, Prague.

Leonhard, Wolfgang (1962), *'The Kremlin since Stalin'*, translated from German by Elizabeth Wiskemann and Marian Jackson, Praeger, Oxford.

Levada, Yu. and O. Sheinis (1988), 'Pogruzhenie v tryasinu. Akt pervy: 1964–1968' (Sinking in the quagmire: Act one: 1964–1968), *Moskovskie novosti*, N° 46, pp.8–9.

Lutyi, Alexander (1992), 'The Truth is not out yet', *The Guardian*, 17 March, p.23.

Martin, Seamus (1993a), 'Intervention by patriarch may help end Russian confrontation', *Irish Times*, 1 October, p.7.

— (1993b), 'Yeltsin bails out of meeting EC leaders', *Irish Times*, 15 October, p.10.

McCauley, Martin (1991), *Nikita Khrushchev*, Cardinal, London.

McKay, Betsy (1992). 'It's a Mad, Mad Media', *Moscow Magazine*, April/May, pp.13–15.

McNair, Brian (1991), *Glasnost, Perestroika and the Soviet Media*, Routledge, London and New York.

McReynolds, Louise (1991), *The News under Russia's Old Regime*, Princeton University Press, Princeton, NJ.

Medvedev, Roy (1975), *On Socialist Democracy*, Norton, London.

— (1980), *'Nikolai Bukharin. The Last Years'*, Norton, New York and London.

— (1988), 'Preimushchestvo posredstvennogo, Leonid Brezhnev. Ocherk k politicheskomu portretu' (The primacy of the mediocre, Leonid Brezhnev: Sketch for a political portrait), *Moskovskie novosti*, 11 September, pp.8–9.

Mickiewicz, Ellen (1984), 'The Functions of Communications Officials in the USSR: A Biographical Study', *Slavic Review*, Vol. 43, N° 1, pp.641–56.

— (1985), 'Political Communication and the Soviet Mass Media', in *Soviet Politics, Russia after Brezhnev*, edited by J.L. Nogee, Praeger, New York and London, pp.34–65.

Miller, John (1993), *Mikhail Gorbachev and the End of Soviet Power*, St. Martin's Press, New York.

Miloslavsky, I. G. (1987), *Kratkaya prakticheskaya grammatika russkogo yazyka* (Short practical grammar of Russian), Russkii yazyk, Moscow.

Mochalova, Inara (1991a), '... k vsem grazhdanam rossiiskoi respubliki' (... to all citizens of the Russian republic), *Ogonyok*, N° 21, pp.10–13.

— (1991b), 'Svobodnoe slovo ne mozhet byt' strashno dlya demokratii' (Freedom of speech can not be frightening for democracy), *Druzhba narodov*, N° 10, pp.211–40.

Moskovskie novosti (1988), Public meeting with members of the newspaper's editorial board, Moscow, 11 August.

— (1991a), Special issue with extensive coverage of, and commentary on, the Soviet army's actions in Vilnius, 16 January.

— (1991b), 'Kak dogovorilis' Anatolii Ivanovich s Nikolaem Ivanovichem' (How Anatolii Ivanovich and Nikolai Ivanovich came to an agreement), 10 February, pp.9–10.

— (1992), 'Izyat' vsyakie upominaniya; Uroki tsenzury' (Remove all mention: Lessons of censorship), 9 August, p.20.

Mostovshchikov, Alexander and Viktor Loshak (1987), 'Svoim golosom' (In one's own voice), *Moskovskie novosti*, 9 August, p.14.

Murray, John (1988a), 'Glasnost and the Press', *Alumnus 1988*, Trinity College Dublin, pp.27–9.

— (1988b), 'Perestroika: Can Gorbachev pull it off?', *Magill*, Dublin, December, pp.26–9.

— (1989), 'Truth, shock, horror', *Times Higher Educational Supplement*, 10 November, p.14.

— (1991a), 'Glasnost' 1990', *Irish Communications Review*, Vol. 1, pp.13–17.

— (1991b), 'Moscow newspapers during the coup', *Sunday Tribune*, 25 August, p.16.

— (1993), 'Yeltsin makes enemies by curbing press', *Sunday Tribune*, 10 October, p.14

Narkiewicz, Olga A. (1986), *Soviet Leaders from the Cult of Personality to Collective Rule*, Wheatsheaf, Brighton.

Navstrechu 70-iyu letiyu Velikogo Oktyabrya (Meeting the 70th anniversary of Great October) (1987), *Pravda*, 2 February.

Nemirovskii, E.L. and V.I. Kharlamova (eds) (1983), '*Istoriya knigi v SSSR, 1917–1921*' (History of the Soviet book), Vol. 1, Kniga, Moscow.

Nenashev, Mikhail (1986), '*Gazeta, chitatel', vremya*' (The newspaper, the reader, the time') Mysl', Moscow.

— (1987), 'Koordinaty glasnosti' (Coordinates of *glasnost'*), *Zhurnalist*, N° 11, pp.10–14.

Nikol'ski, B.N. (1987), 'A chto u vas?' (And what about you?), *Literaturnaya gazeta*, 2 September, p.7.

Ni-Li, Gennady (1987), 'Pochemu nam nuzhna demokratiya' (Why we need democracy), *Izvestiya*, 31 October, p.1.

Nove, Alec (1975), *Stalinism and After*, Allen & Unwin, London.

Oberg, James (1989), *Uncovering Soviet Disasters: Exploring the Limits of Glasnost*, St Edmundsbury Press, Bury St Edmunds.

Observer (1988), 'Soviet PM Blasts Quake Rescue', 18 December.

O'Clery, Conor (1988a), 'Gorbachev puts his stamp on streamlined new administration', *Irish Times*, 3 October, p.10.

— (1988b), 'Soviet censors open files on Trotsky', *Irish Times*, 12 November, p.7.

— (1988c), 'Armenian quake brings foreign policy triumph to Gorbachev', *Irish Times*, 17 December, p.6.

— (1990), 'A mouthpiece for the president, gags for the press', *Irish Times*, 7 April, p.5.

— (1991), 'TV series marks end of Kremlin wall of silence', *Irish Times*, 27 May, p.9.

Ogonyok (1990), Statistics on circulation and the number of letters received, N° 1, p.4.

Ostrogorskii, V. (1988), 'Bol'she ne glushim' (We don't jam any more), *Moskovskie novosti*, N° 51, p.5.

Ozhegov, S.I. (1977), *Slovar' russkogo yazyka* (Dictionary of the Russian Language), Russkii yazyk, Moscow.

Parkhomovskii, E. (1988), 'Bol'she demokratii – men'she tain. Otkrovenny razgovor s nachal'nikom Glavlitom SSSR' (More democracy – fewer secrets: A frank conversation with the head of the USSR censorship agency), *Izvestiya*, 3 November, p.3.

Pechat' SSSR v 1986 godu (The Soviet press in 1986) (1987), Finansy i statistika, Moscow.

Pel't, V.D. (1985), *Zametka kak gazetny zhanr* (The *zametka* as a newspaper genre), Moscow University Press, Moscow.

Perestroika (1988), 'Perestroika v zerkale pressy i pressa – v zerkale perestroiki' (*Perestroika* in the mirror of the press – and the press in the mirror of *perestroika*), Round table discussion with Alexander Bovin (*Izvestiya*), Viktor Kozhemyako (*Literaturnaya gazeta*), Alexander Levikov (*Novosti*), Mikhail Poltoranin (*Voprosy ekonomiki*), Gavriil Popov (economist and occasional columnist) and Dmitri Kazutin (*Moskovskie novosti*). The contributers held these jobs at the time of the discussion, *Moskovskie novosti*, 24 April, pp.8–9.

Pethybridge, Roger W. (1966), *A History of Postwar Russia*, Minerva Series of Students' Handbooks, N° 14, London.

Petrovskaya, Irina (1991), 'Vozvrashchanets: avtorskoe televidenie Leonida Kravchenko' (The returnee: authorial television of Leonid Kravchenko), *Ogonyok*, N° 6, pp.3–4.

Pipes, Richard (1990), *The Russian Revolution 1899–1919*, Collins Harvill, London.

Plenary session (1988), 'Plenum pravleniya Soyuza zhurnalistov SSSR. Iz stenogrammy' (Plenary session of the directorate of the Union of journalists of the USSR: From the stenogramme), *Zhurnalistskie novosti*, N° 1, p.3.

Pravda (1987), 'Otchyot o rabote VTsSPS i zadachi professional'nykh soyuzov v svete reshenii XXVII s"ezda KPSS' (Report on the work of the Trade Union [*Profsoyuz*] organization and the tasks of trade unions in light of the decisions of the XXVII congress of the CPSU', 25 April, pp.2–6.

Proekt (1989), 'Proekt 'Zakona SSSR o pechati i drugikh sredstvakh massovoi informatisii' (Law on the press and other mass media), *Izvestiya*, 4 December, p.3.

Radov, Alexander (1989), 'Ironiya gruboi vlasti' (The irony of crude power), *Ogonyok*, N° 10, pp.4–7.

Remington, Thomas (1985), 'Politics and Professionalism in Soviet Journalism', *Slavic Review*, Vol. 44, N° 3, pp.489–503.

Remnick, David (1992), 'Letter from Moscow', *The New Yorker*, 23 March, pp.65–87.

Resolution (1987), 'Rezolyutsii VI s"ezda Soyuza zhurnalistov SSSR' (Resolutions of the VI congress of the Union of journalists), *Izvestiya*, 17 March, p.3.

Romanov, Andrei (1987), 'Terpimost'. Raznye mneniya na stranitsakh gazety' (Tolerance: Different opinions on the pages of the newspaper), *Moskovskie novosti*, 6 Sept. p.13.

Roxburgh, Angus (1987), *Pravda: Inside the Russian news machine*, Gollancz, London.

Rules of CPSU (1987), *Ustav Kommunisticheskoi partii Sovetskogo Soyuza* (Rules of the CPSU), Politizdat, Moscow.

Salykova, Ol'ga (1991), 'Zapret na fakt' (Veto on a fact), *Ogonyok*, N° 5, p.4.

Schapiro, Leonard (1977), *The Origin of the Communist Autocracy*, Macmillan, London.

Schillinger, Elizabeth and Catherine Porter (1991), 'Glasnost and the Transformation of *Moscow News*', in Marsha Siefert (ed.), *Mass Culture and Perestroika in the Soviet Union*, Oxford University Press, New York.

Selyunin, Vasily (1988), 'Istoki' (Sources), *Novy mir*, N° 5, pp.162–89.

S"ezd (1987), 'Iz stenogrammy VI s"ezda Soyuza zhurnalistov' (From the stenogramme of the VI congress of Union of journalists), *Zhurnalist*, N° 4, pp.21–4.

Shmelyov, D.N. (1977), '*Sovremenny russkii yazyk*' (Modern Russian), Prosveshchenie, Moscow.

Simonov, Vladimir (1987), 'Idyot v nogu s perestroikoi' (In stride with *perestroika*), *Moskovskie novosti*, 2 August, p.13.

Simpson, Paul (1991), 'East is Eden', *Newspaper Focus*, Vol. 1, N° 6, pp.11–41.

Solganik, Grigory Yakovlevich (1976), *Sistemny analiz gazetnoi leksiki i istochniki eyo formirovaniya* (Systemic analysis of newspaper lexis and the sources of its formation), synopsis of doctoral dissertation, Moscow University Press, Moscow.

— (1980), 'Leksika sovremennoi gazety' (Lexis of the contemporary newspaper), in '*Yazyk i stil' massovoi informatsii i propagandy (pechat', radio, televidenie, dokumental'noe kino)*, (Language and style of mass information and propaganda (press, radio, television, documentary cinema)), edited by D.E. Rozental', Moscow University Press, Moscow, pp.23–35.

— (1981), 'Yazyk i stil' peredovoi stat'i' (Language and style of the editorial), in '*Stilistika gazetnykh zhanrov*' (Stylistics of newspaper genres), edited by D.E. Rozental', Moscow University Press, Moscow, pp.3–28.

— (1987), Personal communication, 14 December, Moscow.

Soloveichik, Simon (1990), 'Inside the potato plot', *New Times*, 16–22 October, pp.4–7.

Solzhenitsyn, Alexander (1968), *Rakovy korpus* (Cancer ward), YMCA–Presse, Paris.

Sovetskoe foto (1988) 'God spustya – chto izmenilos'?' (One year one – what has changed?), N° 1, pp.8–9.

Steele, Jonathan (1988), 'Lessons learnt from disaster', *The Guardian Weekly*, week ending 8 December, p.6.

— (1989), 'Open season on the press', *The Guardian*, 23 October, p.27.

Suslov, Ilya (1989), 'Censoring the Journalist', in Marianna Tax Choldin and Maurice Friedberg (eds), *The Red Pencil, Artists, Scholars, and Censors in the USSR*', Unwin-Hyman, London, pp.145–54.

Tatu, Michel (1969), *Power in the Kremlin: From Khrushchev's decline to collective leadership*, Collins, London.

Temushkin, Oleg (1988), 'Golos vremeni – golos istiny' (Voice of time, voice of truth), *Nedelya*, N° 7, pp.16–17.

Tolz, Vera (1990), 'The Impact of the New Press Law: A Preliminary Assessment', *RFE/RL Report on the USSR*, 9 November.

— (1991a), 'Recent Developments in the Soviet and Baltic Media', *RFE/RL Report on the USSR*, 7 June.

— (1991b), 'Recent Developments in the Soviet and Baltic Media', *RFE/RL Report on the USSR*, 12 July.

— (1991c), 'How the Journalists Responded', *RFE/RL Report on the USSR*, 6 September.

— (1992), 'The Soviet Media', *RFE/RL Research Report*, 3 January.

Trapeznikov, Valdeslav (1991), 'Shake-up in the Soviet Union', *Journalist*, Vol. 75, N° 2, April, p.8.

Traynor, Ian (1988), 'Truth about Stakhanov', *The Guardian Weekly*, 11 September, p.11.

Trotsky, Leon (1968), *Stalin: Volume One: Rise of a Revolutionary*, Panther, London (first published in 1941).

Trud (1992), '"We are going through a burning forest", interview with Mikhail Poltoranin' (14 January), re-printed in *Current Digest of the Post-Soviet Press*, Vol. XLIV, N° 4, pp.14–15.

Tucker, Robert (1987), *Political Culture and Leadership in Soviet Russia from Lenin to Gorbachev*, Wheatsheaf, Brighton.

USSR Yearbook '88 (1988), Novosti, Moscow.

USSR Yearbook '89 (1989), Novosti, Moscow.

USSR Yearbook '90 (1990), Novosti, Moscow.

van den Bercken, W.P. (1980), *Het beeld van het Westen in de Sovjet pers* (The image of the West in the Soviet press), Walter-Noordhoff, Groningen.

Vasilyeva, A.N. (no date given), *Particles in Colloquial Russian*, Progress, Moscow.

Vevers, Simon (1991a), 'New president's job to defend glasnost', *Journalist*, Vol. 75, N° 2, April, p.8.

— (1991b), 'Soviet Union papers in dispute', *Journalist*, Vol. 75, N° 4, June, p.9.

Vladimirov, Leonid (1989), 'Soviet Censorship: A View from the Inside', in Marianna Tax Choldin and Maurice Friedberg (eds), *The Red Pencil, Artists, Scholars, and Censors in the USSR*, Unwin–Hyman, London, pp.15–20.

Volkogonov, Dmitri (1991), *Stalin. Triumph and Tragedy*, Weidenfeld & Nicolson, London.

Vomperskii, V.P. (1970), *Stilisticheskoe uchenie M.V. Lomonosova i teoriya 3-kh stilei* (The stylistic teaching of M.V. Lomonosov and the theory of the three styles), Moscow University Press, Moscow.

Vstrecha (1988), 'Demokratizatsiya – sut' perestroiki. Vstrecha v tsentral'nom Komitete KPSS' (Democratization – the essence of *perestroika*. Meeting in the central Committee of the CPSU), *Rabochaya gazeta* (and all national newspapers), 14 January, pp.1–3.

Vyatkin, N. (1988), 'Tema razgovora – perestroika' (Conversation topic – *perestroika*), *Sovetskoe foto*, N° 2, p.16.

Walker, Martin (1987), 'Truth is not what it used to be', *The Guardian*, 12 January, p.11.

Weasel, The (1990), 'Up and down the city road', *The Independent Magazine*, London, 26 May, pp.10–11.

Wedgwood Benn, David (1987), *'Glasnost'* in the Soviet Media: Liberalization or

Public Relations', *The Journal of Communist Studies*, Vol. 3, September, Nº 3, pp.266–76.

Werth, Alexander (1971), *Russia: the Post-War Years*, Hale, London.

Wheeler, Marcus (1978), *The Oxford Russian–English Dictionary*, Clarendon Press, Oxford.

Whelan, Martin (1992), *A comparison of Soviet and Western coverage of the Chernobyl accident*, unpublished study, Trinity College, Dublin.

White, Michael (1993), 'Hurd turns on "destructive" media and politicians', *The Guardian*, 13 March, p.5.

White, Stephen (1992), *Gorbachev and After*, Cambridge University Press, Cambridge.

Whitney, T.P. (1963), (ed.) *Khrushchev Speaks*, University of Michigan Press, Ann Arbor, MI.

Wishnevsky, Julia (1990), 'A Rare Insight into Soviet Censorship', *RFE/RL Report on the USSR*, 7 September.

— (1993), 'Media Still Far from Free', *RFE/RL Research Report*, 14 May.

Womack, Helen (1991), 'Soviet editors fear clampdown', *The Independent*, 2 March, p.10.

Yakovlev, Yegor Vladimirovich (1987), Round-table discussion in *Ogonyok*, Nº 34.

— (1989), 'Redaktor s kotorym khotelos' by rabotat'' (An editor with whom one would like to work), *Moskovskie novosti*, 23 July, p.3.

Yeltsin, Boris (1990), *Against the Grain: An Autobiography*, Cape, London.

Yevtushenko, Yevgeny (1963), *A Precocious Autobiography*, Collins and Harvill Press, London.

— (1991), 'Plach po tsenzure' (Mourning for censorship), *Ogonyok*, Nº 7, pp.22–5.

Zagal'skii, L (1987), '*Tvorcheskaya vstrecha s nauchnym otdelom i otdelom sotsial'nykh problem Literaturnaoi gazety*' (Public meeting with scientific and social problems departments of *Literaturnaya gazeta*), at Moscow University, 17 September.

Zakhar'ko, V. (1989), 'V Turtsii est' vsyo' (Everything is available in Turkey), *Izvestiya*, 25 August, p.5.

Zasurskii, Ya. N. (ed.) (1987), *Zhurnalistika i politika* (Journalism and politics), Moscow University, Moscow.

Zemskaya, E.A. (1987), *Russkaya razgovornaya rech': lingvisticheskii analiz i problemy obucheniya* (Russian conversational speech: linguistic analysis and problems of teaching), Russkii yazyk, Moscow.

Index

accidents, catastrophes 10, 28–9, 32, 97–
  100, 149
  Armenian earthquake 98–9
  Chernobyl 97–8
  Ukraine famine 15–16
administrative reforms 24–5, 28, 30, 33
advertising 200, 216, 218
  decree 3, 4, 5
  Izvestiya 11–12, 175–6, 200
  liberalization 11–12
  Moskovskii komsomolets 237
  Westernization 145
Adzhubei, Aleksei 18
  Izvestiya 26–7, 30, 42
  Komsomol'skaya pravda 26–7
  news suppression 28, 29
  Stalin 20, 21
  TASS 27, 62
Afanas'ev, Viktor 102
Afghanistan
  army's role 210–11
  news suppression 112–14
Agitprop 223, 224
  see also Propaganda Department
Agranovskii, Anatoly 240
agriculture 28
  collectivization 13, 13–14, 126
  fotoreportazh 125–6, 128–9
Akhmatova, Anna 96
Alekseev, P. 112
All-Russian Committee for the Relief of the
  Starving 11
Andreeva, Nina 105–6
anti-Nazism 22
APN (Novosti) 51, 196–7, 199, 202
Argumenty i fakty 205, 225, 261, 262
Armenian earthquake 98–9
army 209–12
Associated Press 157–8, 159
August 1991 coup 226
  'enemy voiced' 95
  Izvestiya 150
  photocopied newspapers 214–15

Baburin, Sergei 71
banned literature 28, 96, 179, 248
Baranov, Alexander 63, 80
Bavykin, A. 81
BBC 95, 247
Becker, Boris 96
Beria, Lavrenti 23–4
black economy 188
Boldyrev, Vladimir 58–60, 63
bolsheviks 1–12, 87–9
Bovin, Alexander 110–11, 111
Bragin, Vyacheslav 67, 72, 73
'breaking' news 92–3, 93–4
Brezhnev, Leonid Ilyich 98
  censorship 59–62
  Filatov's opinion of 212–13
  fondness of official titles 38, 125
  language, speeches 31, 135
  personality cult around 37–8
  press under 31–8
  rehabilitation of Stalin 36–7
BTA 153
Bukharin, Nikolai 17
Bulgaria 111–12
Buryatiya 149
Buslaev, Vladimir 235–8

catastrophes *see* accidents
censorship
  before and after *glasnost'* 57–73
  journalists' view 189–90, 196–8, 219–
    20, 249–50
  see also Glavlit
Cherkezishvili, N. 79
Chernobyl disaster 97–8, 191–2
Chikin, Valentin 61, 103–4, 104, 187
  talented editor 242–3
  Union of Journalists speech 79
child prostitution 163–4
China 109
Chubais, A. 69–70
CIA 158

circulation
  before and after *glasnost'* 48–57
  figures 260–62
  optimal 244–5
  size and losses 216–17, 228–9
  see also under individual publications
CIS heads of state meeting 151–2
cliché, use of 123–4
cliché substitution 160–62
closure of newspapers 70–71
Coliseum 241
collectivization of agriculture 13, 13–14, 126
colloquial language 122, 136
commercial publications 228
commercial structures 218
Communist Party *see* party
correspondence, readers' 105–7, 113, 173–4, 176–7
costs *see* distribution; paper prices
council of ministers 185, 187
criticism
  Izvestiya 75, 175
  journalists' views 175, 178, 230
  Khrushchev administration 27
  Nezavisimaya gazeta 219
  party policy 61–2
  pre-*glasnost'* 89_90
  within party 105

Daniel, Yuli 35
decree against denigrating the president's name 198
Decree on the Press (1917) 1–3, 4
decree against vandalizing monuments connected with the revolution 198–9
delivery *see* distribution
Den' (Day) 3, 165, 166, 167, 221, 245
Derevenskaya bednota (Rural poverty) 3
distribution (economic problems) 191
distribution and delivery of press 53, 221, 245
  crippling costs 54, 236–7
Djilas, Milovan 20
domestic language 126–9
Druzhba narodov (Friendship of Peoples) 48
D'yachenko, Viktor 47, 115–16, 117, 119
Dzhirkvelov, Ilya 109–10

earthquakes 97, 98–9

economic jargon 161–2
economic reporting 14–15, 89, 116–17, 119–20
editorials 93
  language 130–40
  readers' letters as proxy 106, 107
editors
  innovative 62–3
  party control of appointments 40–42, 225
  role 253, 255–6
educative role of press 87–9
Ehrenburg, Ilya 28
Ekho planety (Echo of the Planet) 194
Ekonomika i zhizn' (Economics and Life) 261
elections, foreign 110
elevated language 124, 134
emergency, state of (1993) 70–71, 73
Emergency Committee (*GKChP*) 95, 150, 214, 215, 226
'enemy voices' 94–5
Estonian Popular Front 99
euphemism 32–3

families 121, 125–9
famines 10–11, 15–16, 97
Federal Information Centre 73
Fedotov, Mikhail 52, 76
Figaro, Le 161
Filatov, Major-General Viktor 49, 209–13
Financial Times 160–61
Fokin, V. 152
foreign news coverage 107–14, 144–5
  journalists' opinions 207–7, 232–3
  language 135–6, 157–62
foreign radio 94–5
foreign reports, translated 163–4
fotoreportazh 120–30
France Presse 157–8
'fraternal' socialist countries 108–9, 111–12, 193, 206

Gaidar, Yegor 55, 156, 166–7
general secretary (use of title) 37–8
genre-borrowing 146, 162–5
  see also Westernization
Ginzburg, Yevgeniya 18, 20
GKChP (State Committee for the State of Emergency) 95, 150, 214, 215, 226

glasnost' 39–86
 censorship 57–73
 circulation 48–57
 journalists' opinions 171–2, 204–6, 216, 222–5
 Law on the Press 73–8
 phases 90–91, 204–6
 polarization 100–105
 retrospective 96, 104, 177, 224–5
 state control 39–48
 Union of Journalists 78–86
Glasnost' 169–72, 180–81
Glavlit 23
 abolished 57, 74, 91
 before and after *glasnost'* 57–64
 journalists' opinions 189–90, 249–50
 see also censorship
'gold fever' 108, 159–60
Golembiovskii, Igor' 66–7, 67, 70
Golos demokrata (Democrat's Voice) 52
Gomulka, Wladyslaw 26
Gonzalez, Eduard 154–6
Gorbachev, Mikhail 31, 100
 criticism of 95
 glasnost' 204, 224, 225
 as political weapon 90
 journalists' opinions 213, 246
 Law on the Press 65–6
 proposed suspension 65–6
 Leningrad visit 62, 174
 Nobel prize 207
 objectivity 66
 press language under 115
 state control of press under 42–8
Goskomimushchestvo 69
Goskompechat' 50
Gospriyomka 117
government officials, and payment for information 250–52
Grazhdanskii mir (Civic World) 52
Grigoryants, Sergei 169–72, 180–81
Grossman, Vasily 179
GRU 109
GUOT 57, 196

heroification of workers 120, 123–5, 133–4
history *see* retrospective *glasnost'*
home news coverage 89–91
 Westernization of language 146–57
Hungary 27, 33, 210

ideological intervention 59, 197
Ideology, Department of 40
Ignatev, Kirill 72
Independent 199, 201–2
independent publications 85, 100, 226
 economic pressure 51, 52
 Law on the Press 76–7
 need for support within country 180–82
 industry 13–14, 34
 information-based approach 246–8
intelligentsia, creative 28, 35–6
internal censor 60–61, 190
International Monetary Fund (*MVF*) 162, 166
international politics 233–4
ITAR–TASS see TASS
Izvestiya
 accidents, catastrophes 97, 99
 advertising 11–12, 175–6, 200
 Adzhubei, 26–7, 30, 42
 changes in language in 1979 and 1987 115–43
 circulation 48, 172–3, 219, 260–62
 closure of *Nash golos* 5–6
 creative intelligentsia 35
 criticism 75, 175
 deification of Stalin 19
 'enemies of the people' 17–18
 fewer editorials 93
 foreign coverage 109, 112, 112–13, 114, 157–9
 Gorbachev's Leningrad visit 62
 home news 89, 146–57
 'hurrah industry' 14, 15
 interview with Karpenko 172–6
 journalists' opinions 205, 216, 217, 230–32
 Khrushchev's ousting 30
 Kronstadt rebellion 10
 NEP 9
 'Notes of the Commentator on Public Affairs' 131–2, 140–43
 'On the Theme of the Day' 131–2, 142
 polarization 105
 and *Pravda* 26–7, 33–4, 34–5
 prodnalog 8
 readership 44
 registration 74
 re-registration battle 68–70, 74, 230–32
 staff 199

state control 40, 41, 42, 43, 53, 194
and *TASS* 62, 64m 66–7, 174
Volga famine 10–11
war communism 7
Westernization of language 144, 146–56,
   157–9, 163, 165, 248
Second World War 22

Japan 160
Journalists, Union of 78–86, 248–9
journalists
   interviews with Russian 214–59
   interviews with Soviet 169–213
   right to refuse to do work 188–9

Karabakh 233
Karpenko, Igor' 62, 172–6
Karyakin, Yuri 66
KGB 58, 109–10
Khasbulatov, Ruslan 67–70, 155–6, 230–
   32
Khrushchev, Nikita 23–31, 42, 45, 177
   de-Stalinization 25, 27–8, 37
   Filatov's opinion 212–13
   ousted 30, 32–3
   'secret speech' (1956) 19, 24–6, 212
   style of speeches 29–30, 31
Kiev CIS heads of states meeting 151–2
Kommersant 75, 76, 144, 161–2, 261
Komsomol 40, 52
Komsomol'skaya pravda 227
   circulation 260–62
   economic problems 54–5, 221, 244
   journalists' opinions 194–5, 205, 221
   official news 26–7
   Stalin 21
   subsidies 217, 229
   Westernization 144, 160–61, 162
Kondrashov, Stanislav 112–14
Korneshov, L. 102
Korotich, Vitaly 63, 101, 104, 107, 176–82
Kozhemyako, Viktor 103
Krasnaya zvezda (Red Star) 261
Kravchenko, Leonid 51, 72, 80, 83, 215
   journalists' opinions 185–6, 242, 257
   media crackdown (1991) 64, 214
   Moscow Association of Journalists 83
Krivopalov, Alexander 62
Kronstadt sailors' rebellion 3, 9–10
kulaks 13

Kuranty (Chimes) 195, 258
Kurile Islands 160
Kuzichkin, Vladimir 109

Langfank, Yevgeny 50, 63
language 115–43
   editorial 130–40
   fotoreportazh 120–30
   militarization of 6–7
   political abuse 16–18
   Westernization 144–68
   zametka 115–20
   zametki publtsista 140–43
Laptev, Ivan 42, 102
Lashchenko, General 210
Law on the Press 73–8, 91, 225
   journalists' opinions 187–9, 196, 249–52
   proposed suspension 65–6
Lazarev, G. 82
lead news stories 149–56
Lenin, Vladimir Ilyich
   journalists' views 180, 190–91, 207–8
   Khachatrian portrait 207–8, 234–5
   press under 1–12, 13
Leshchinskii 60–61
Levikov, Alexander 106
libel 250
   see also slander
Ligachev, Yegor 45, 47, 101, 186, 204
Literaturnaya Armeniya 201
Literaturnaya gazeta 21, 44, 48, 260
Lithuania 64–7
loans, state 55
Losev, Sergei 186
Lukyanov, Anatoly 84–5
Lyubimov, Yury 243, 251

Maksim Gor'ky steamship 83
Malashenko, Igor' 72–3
Malenkov, Georgi 24
market economy 191
Maslennikov, A. 108, 159
Matveev, V. 79–80
May Day parade 1990 183–4, 185
Medvedev, Roy 20, 36, 38
Medvedev, Vadim 45–6, 186
Megapolis ekspress 241, 258–9, 261
Merezhkovskii, Dmitry 6–7
Minkin, A.E. 5
mnogotirazhki (in-house newspapers) 82–3

monuments connected with the revolution, decree against vandalizing 198–9
Moscow 192–3
Moscow Association of Journalists 83–4, 84
Moscow city council (*Mossovet*) 195–6, 201, 217–18
Moskovskaya pravda (Moscow Truth) 104, 107, 187, 195, 261
Moskovskie novosti (Moscow News) 46, 75, 204–5
  advertising 176
  Armenian earthquake 99–100
  circulation 261
  criticism 225
  fotoreportazh 122
  limited circulation 50
  Lithuania 1990 coverage 64–5
  Mathias Rust 94
  Yakovlev, Yegor 42–3, 71–2, 94, 101
Moskovskii komsomolets 200
  access to printing presses 52, 53
  Buslaev interview 235–8
  circulation 221, 237, 261
  commentaries 203
  journalists' opinions 194–5, 203
  paper-boys 53–4, 245

Nash golos (Our Voice) 5–6
nationalist language 165–8
Nedelya (The Week) 96, 163–4, 165, 176, 261
NEGA 219
Nenashev, Mikhail 64, 107, 255–6
  criticism 105
  Goskomizdat 101
  innovative editor 61, 242–3
  language 102–3, 131
New Economic Policy (*NEP*) 8–9
New York Times 161
news editor, role of 253–6
newsprint prices 49, 50, 52, 53
Newsweek 163
Nezavisimaya gazeta 51–2, 76, 258
  censorship 70
  circulation 201, 219, 261
  interview with Zakharov 194–203
  interviews with Ostal'skii 214–22
  printed in *Izvestiya* plant 53
  Westernization 144

nomenklatura appointments system 40–42, 51, 75
Northern Ireland 206–7
'Notes of the Commentator on Public Affairs' 131–2, 140–43
Novaya rech' (New Speech) 6
Novoe vremya (New Times) 3
  interviews with Pumpyanskii 204–9, 222–35
Novosti (*APN*) 51, 196–7, 199, 202
Novy mir 35–6, 48, 112, 200
nuclear arms 234

objectivity 66, 67, 246–7
  Western 145–6
Obshchaya gazeta (General Newspaper) 68
'October Plenum,' 32–3
official bodies, ties with 51–2
official language 135–6
official news 43, 174–5
official reports 149–50, 202–5
Ogonyok 46, 255–6
  circulation 48, 176, 261
  criticism 93–4, 178, 225
  fotoreportazh 122
  interview with Korotich 176–82
  journalists' opinions 204–5
  readers' letters 107, 176–7
oil 152–3
Oleinik, Boris 226–7
'On the Theme of the Day' 131–2, 142
opinion polls 107, 174
Ostal'skii, Dmitry 258
  interview 1991 214–16
  interview 1992 216–22
Ostankino protest 71
'oversight council' 68, 71

Palashin, Vladimir 165–6
Panorama novostei (News Panorama) 118
paper prices
  problem for press 54, 200–201, 216–17, 228, 235–6
  Yeltsin decree 54, 55
paper production, state monopoly on 75–6
parliament, suspension of 70–71, 154–6
particles 141–2
party
  censorship 28
  current role 178

death of ideological function 50–51
income from publishing 76
Law on the Press 75
manoeuvring after Stalin's death 23–4
newspapers' propaganda role 87–8
polarization 101
press disagreement over role 33–4
promotion of unity 9, 12, 23
protest against leadership 183–5
state control of press 29–48, 145–6
Union of Journalists 80–82
payment for information, from government
    officials 250–52
perestroika 47, 103
    language 115–43
    rhetoric 138–40
Persian Gulf 211
personality cult
    Brezhnev 37–8
    Stalin 19–21, 27–8
photographs, articles with 120–30
Pikul', Valentin 179
plan targets 14–15
Poland, 26–7, 33
polarization 100–107
Poleshchuk, Andrei 53
political abuse 16
political news 144, 154–7, 220–21
Poltoranin, Mikhail, 55, 68, 71, 73, 82
    Law on the Press 76
    paper producers 54
    re-registration of *Izvestiya* 69, 231
    Yeltsin's battle with parliament 72
Polyarnaya pravda (Polar Truth) 81
Ponomaryov, Lev 203
Poptsov, Oleg 71
power syndrome 229–32
Pravda 98, 173
    advertising 175–6
    Armenian earthquake 99
    authoritativeness 46–7; loss of 50–51
    circulation 260–62
    foreign news 159–60
    and *glasnost'* 49
    government aid 55–6, 56
    Izvestiya and 26–7, 33–4, 34–5
    Khrushchev ousted 32
    nationalism with xenophobia 166, 167–8
    purchased by Yannikos 55, 218
    readership 44–5

rehabilitation of Stalin 36–7
re-registration 70
sensationalism 165
Stalin and editorial staff 21
state control 39, 41, 43
Union of Journalists 78, 85
preliminary censorship 59–60, 63–4, 70, 77
president's name, decree against
    denigrating 198
Press Tribunal 5
prices
    general rise 160–61
    newsprint 49, 50, 52, 53
    paper *see* paper prices
printing presses
    seizure of 3
    state control of access 52–3
prodnalog 8
production, productivity 14–15, 116,
    119–20
Prokhanov, Alexander 71
professional standards 252–5
profitability 227–8
propaganda 87–9, 147
Propaganda Department 40, 58, 224
provincial press 80–82, 256–7
public opinion polls 107, 174
publitsistika 248
Pumpyanskii, Alexander
    interview 1990 204–9
    interview 1992 222–35

quality 117
question-and-answer construction 137–8

Rabochaya tribuna (Workers' Tribune) 241
radio 99–100
    foreign 94–5
Radio Free Europe 94, 99
Radio Kiev 98
Radio Moscow 98
railway company 173–4
readers' correspondence 105–7, 113, 173–
    4, 176–7
Rech' (Speech) 3
regional press 80–82, 256–7
registration 74, 76
    re-registration of *Izvestiya* 68–70, 74,
    230–32
repression 16–17, 22–3

retrospective *glasnost'* 96, 104, 177, 224–5
Reuters 153, 157–8
Rossiiskaya gazeta 55, 56, 217, 231, 261
Rumyantsev, Oleg 34–5
Russian journalists, interviews 214–59
Rust, Mathias 94
Rutskoi, Alexander 156
Ryabov, Nikolai 67, 71
Rybakov, Anatoly 96

Sagalaev, Eduard 83–4, 86
samizdat 36
Satyukov, Pavel 30
'secret speech' *see* Khrushchev
Segodnya (Today) 70
self-censorship 60–61, 190
self-immolation story 162
Sel'skaya zhizn' (Village Life) 241, 260–61
Selyunin, Vasily 14, 15, 179–80
sensationalism 48, 91–7
  language 162–8
Serbia 152–3
sex 163–4
Shcherbachenko, Mikhail 239–59
Shestakov, Boris 46, 105, 182–94
Shin, Vladimir 122
show trials 16–17
signed leading articles 132, 142
Simonov, Konstantin 21
Sinyavskii, Andrei 35
slander 178
  see also libel
socialist countries 108–9, 111–12, 193, 206
Socpresse 238
Sokolov, Maksim 258
Soldatskaya pravda (Soldier's Truth) 3
Solganik, Grigory 88, 131
Solyanka 173–4
Solzhenitsyn, Alexander 28, 182
Somalia 159
Sotsialisticheskaya industriya (Socialist Industry) 241
Sovetskaya kul'tura (Soviet Culture) 241
Sovetskaya Rossiya 56, 81, 160, 184
  Andreeva letter 105–6
  circulation 260–61
  innovativeness 61, 242–3
  journalists' opinions 186–7, 226–7
  re-registration 70

sensationalism and nationalism 165–6
TASS and 79, 186–7
Sovetskii sport 261, 262
Soviet journalists, interviews 169–213
Soyuzpechat' 53, 221
Spid-Info 262
Stakhanovite movement 14
Stalin, Joseph
  cult of personality 19–21, 27–8
  journalists' views 177, 180, 190, 212
  nationalist press 166
  press under 12–23, 97
  rehabilitation of 36–7
  Russian language 29
  standards, professional 252–5
Starkov, Vladislav 205, 225
State Committee for the State of Emergency (*GKChP*) 95, 150, 214, 215, 226
state control of press 39–48, 145–6
state of emergency (1993) 70–71, 73
state loans 55
state secrets 59, 64, 250
  no definition 219–20
  operation of censorship 197
  preliminary censorship 60
  reduction 63
stengazeta (wall newspapers) 41
Stepankov, Vladimir 35
strikes 256
Stroitel'naya gazeta (Construction Gazette) 239, 240–41, 257
Sturua, Melor 163
subscription system 54, 228, 236
subsidies 55, 56, 217, 228–9
superfluity of newspapers 257–9
suppression of bad news 13
  see also accidents
Supreme Soviet committee on the mass media 67–8
Suslov, Mikhail 28, 30
suspension of parliament 70–71, 154–6

tabloid press 221–2
Tadzhikistan earthquake 97
TASS 51, 99
  Adzhubei 27, 62
  interview with Shestakov 79–80, 182–94
  Izvestiya and 62, 64, 66–7, 174
  KGB and GRU 109, 110
  state of emergency (1993) 73

television 57, 246–7
  crackdown (1991) 64
  protest (1992) 71
  Yeltsin 71–3
Temushkin, Oleg 17
'Thaw, the' 28, 30–31, 35–6
Third World 206–7
Time 163
Tito, Josip Broz 22
translation of foreign reports 163–4
Trotsky, Leon 29
Trud 43–4, 53, 173
  circulation 244, 260–62
  readership 44, 243
  Shcherbachenko 239–40, 243–4
Turkey 112
Tyutyugina, A. 80–81

Ukraine 157, 232–3
  famine (1932–34) 15–16, 97
  oil to Serbia 152–3
Union of Journalists 78–86, 248–9
Union of Soviet Socialist Republics
  (USSR), refusal to accept end of 166
United States of America (USA) 158, 159,
  208–9
unofficial publications *see* independent
  publications; *samizdat*
US News and World Report 167–8

Vechernyaya Moskva (Evening Moscow)
  195
vilification, personal 16–19
vocabulary 92
Voenno-istoricheskii zhurnal (Military-
  historical magazine) 49, 209–13
Volga famine (1921) 10–11
Vremya (Time) 98, 215
Vybor (Choice) 52

wall newspapers (*stengazeta*) 41
war 233–4
  Second World War 22
war communism 7–8
West, portrayal of 107–8, 110
Westernization 91, 114, 144–68, 246–8

foreign news 157–62
home news 146–57
objectivity 145–6
sensationalism 96–7, 162–8
workers, heroification of 120, 123–5,
  133–4

xenophobia 166–8

Yakovlev, Alexander 59, 167
  glasnost' 46, 100, 204, 222, 225
Yakovlev, Yegor 67, 167
  Lithuania 65
  Moskovskis novosti 42–3, 71–2, 94, 101
  precedent 63
  sensationalism 100
  television 71–2, 246–7
  Union of Journalists 85
Yannikos, Yannis 55, 218
Yefimov, Nikolai 42, 67
Yeltsin, Boris 215, 219
  battle over *Izvestgiya* 68–70
  earnings disclosed in press 163
  journalistgs' opinions 191, 216, 234, 246
  Medvedev 45–6
  nationalist press 166–7
  Ogonyok 63
  Poltoranin 82
  state of emergency and closure of
    newspapers 70–71
  suspension of parliament 154–5
  television 71–2
Yevtushenko, Yevgeny 28
Yugoslavia 153
Yunost' (Youth) 35–6

Zagal'skii, L. 63
Zakharov, Igor' 64, 194–203
Zalygin, Sergei 101
zametka 115–20, 129–30
zametki publitsista see 'Notes of the
  Commentator on Public Affairs'
Zamyatin, Leonid 51, 109–10
Zhelev, Zhelyu 208
Zhivkov, Todor 111, 112
Zhurnalist 47, 85, 103